NAHUM
HABAKKUK
ZEPHANIAH
HAGGAI
ZECHARIAH
MALACHI

ABINGDON OLD TESTAMENT COMMENTARIES

NAHUM
HABAKKUK
ZEPHANIAH
HAGGAI
ZECHARIAH
MALACHI

JULIA M. O'BRIEN

Abingdon Press
Nashville

ABINGDON OLD TESTAMENT COMMENTARIES
NAHUM, HABAKKUK, ZEPHANIAH, HAGGAI, ZECHARIAH, MALACHI

Copyright © 2004 by Abingdon Press

Library of Congress Cataloging-in-Publication Data

O'Brien, Julia M.
    Nahum, Habakkuk, Zephaniah, Haggai, Zechariah, Malachi / Julia M. O'Brien.
        p. cm.—(Abingdon Old Testament commentaries)
    Includes bibliographical references.
    ISBN 0-687-34031-4 (binding: pbk. : alk. paper)
    1. Bible. O.T. Minor Prophets—Commentaries. I. Title. II. Series.

BS1560.027 2004
224'.907—dc22

2004009332

All scripture quotations unless noted otherwise are taken from the *New Revised Standard Version of the Bible*, copyright 1989, by the Division of Christian Education of the National Council of the Churches of Christ in the United States of America. Used by permission. All rights reserved.

Scripture quotations noted ASV are from the American Standard Version of the Bible.

Scripture quotations noted AT are the author's translation.

Scripture quotations noted JPS are from The Holy Scriptures According to the Masoretic Text. Copyright © 1917, 1955 by The Jewish Publication Society of America. All rights reserved.

Scripture quotations noted KJV are from the King James or Authorized Version of the Bible.

Scripture quotations noted NASB are from the NEW AMERICAN STANDARD BIBLE®, © Copyright The Lockman Foundation 1960, 1962, 1963, 1968, 1971, 1972, 1973, 1975, 1977. Used by permission.

Scripture quotations noted NIV are from the HOLY BIBLE: NEW INTERNATIONAL VERSION®. Copyright © 1973, 1978, 1984 by the International Bible Society. Used by permission of Zondervan Publishing House. All rights reserved.

Scripture quotations noted NAB are from the New American Bible, copyright © 1986 by the Confraternity of Christian Doctrine. All rights reserved.

Scripture quotations noted NJB are from THE NEW JERUSALEM BIBLE, copyright © 1985 by Darton, Longman & Todd, Ltd. and Doubleday, a division of Random House, Inc. Reprinted by permission.

Scripture quotations noted NKJV are from the New King James Version. Copyright © 1982 by Thomas Nelson, Inc. Used by permission. All rights reserved.

Scripture quotations noted RSV are from the *Revised Standard Version of the Bible*, copyright 1976, 1952, 1971 by the Division of Christian Education of the National Council of the Churches of Christ in the United States of America. Used by permission. All rights reserved.

Scripture quotations noted *TANAKH* are from *The Tanakh: The New JPS Translation According to the Traditional Hebrew Text.* Copyright 1985 by the Jewish Publication Society. Used by permission.

04 05 06 07 08 09 10 11 12 13—10 9 8 7 6 5 4 3 2 1

MANUFACTURED IN THE UNITED STATES OF AMERICA

CONTENTS

FOREWORD

The *Abingdon Old Testament Commentaries* are offered to the reader in hopes that they will aid in the study of Scripture and provoke a deeper understanding of the Bible in all its many facets. The texts of the Old Testament come out of a time, a language, and socio-historical and religious circumstances far different from the present. Yet Jewish and Christian communities have held to them as a sacred canon, significant for faith and life in each new time. Only as one engages these books in depth and with all the critical and intellectual faculties available to us, can the contemporary communities of faith and other interested readers continue to find them meaningful and instructive.

These volumes are designed and written to provide compact, critical commentaries on the books of the Old Testament for the use of theological students and pastors. It is hoped that they may be of service also to upper-level college or university students and to those responsible for teaching in congregational settings. In addition to providing basic information and insights into the Old Testament writings, these commentaries exemplify the tasks and procedures of careful interpretation.

The writers of the commentaries in this series come from a broad range of ecclesiastical affiliations, confessional stances, and educational backgrounds. They have experience as teachers and, in some instances, as pastors and preachers. In most cases, the authors are persons who have done significant research on the book that is their assignment. They take full account of the most important current scholarship and secondary literature, while not attempting to summarize that literature or to engage in technical academic debate. The fundamental concern of each volume is analysis and discussion of the literary, socio-historical, theological, and ethical dimensions of the biblical texts themselves.

The New Revised Standard Version of the Bible is the principal translation of reference for the series, though authors may draw upon other interpretations in their discussion. Each writer is attentive to the original Hebrew text in preparing the commentary. But the authors do not presuppose any knowledge of the biblical languages on the part of the reader. When some awareness of a grammatical, syntactical, or philological issue is necessary for an adequate understanding of a particular text, the issue is explained simply and concisely.

Each volume consists of four parts. An *introduction* looks at the book as a whole to identify *key issues* in the book, its *literary genre* and *structure*, the *occasion and situational context* of the book (including both social and historical contexts), and the *theological and ethical* significance of the book.

The *commentary* proper organizes the text by literary units and, insofar as is possible, divides the comment into three parts. The *literary analysis* serves to introduce the passage with particular attention to identification of the genre of speech or literature and the structure or outline of the literary unit under discussion. Here also, the author takes up significant stylistic features to help the reader understand the mode of communication and its impact on comprehension and reception of the text. The largest part of the comment is usually found in the *exegetical analysis*, which considers the leading concepts of the unit, the language of expression, and problematical words, phrases, and ideas in order to get at the aim or intent of the literary unit, as far as that can be uncovered.

Attention is given here to particular historical and social situations of the writer(s) and reader(s) where that is discernible and relevant as well as to wider cultural (including religious) contexts. The analysis does not proceed phrase by phrase or verse by verse but deals with the various particulars in a way that keeps in view the overall structure and central focus of the passage and its relationship to the general line of thought or rhetorical argument of the book as a whole. The final section, *theological and ethical analysis* seeks to identify and clarify the theological and ethical matters with which the unit deals or to which it points. Though not aimed primarily at contemporary issues of faith and life, this section should provide readers a basis for reflection on them.

Each volume also contains a select bibliography of works cited in the commentary as well as major commentaries and other important works available in English.

The fundamental aim of this series will have been attained if readers are assisted not only to understand more about the origins, character, and meaning of the Old Testament writings, but also to enter into their own informed and critical engagement with the texts themselves.

Patrick D. Miller
General Editor

LIST OF ABBREVIATIONS

AT   author's translation
BHK   *Biblia Hebraica*, ed. R. Kittel
BHS   *Biblia Hebraica Stuttgartensia*
BZAW   Beihefte zur Zeitschrift für die alttestamentliche
         Wissenschaft
JSOTSup Journal for the Study of the Old Testament:
         Supplement Seriess
LXX   Septuagint
MT   Masoretic Text
ZAW   Zeitschrift für die alttestamentliche Wissenschaft

INTRODUCTION

PROPHETS AND PROPHETIC BOOKS

Over the centuries, the Old Testament prophets have been understood in a wide variety of ways. In different times and places, prophets have been seen as predicting the future, as recording mystical experiences of the divine, as championing individual piety over religious ritual, as transmitting and enlivening religious tradition, and as crying for social justice. In contemporary scholarship, prophets are often portrayed as having interpreted the significance of world events for their own time—as inspired individuals who discerned for their religious communities the implications of current behavior for the present and for the future.

These various understandings, however, have something important in common: their reconstructions of the biblical prophets rely heavily (and, for some, exclusively) on the interpretation of the books that bear their names. That is, the phenomenon of ancient Hebrew prophecy, however immediate and interpersonal it may have been, is mediated to contemporary persons through the documents now preserved and labeled as books of the prophets.

Just how closely the current shape of the prophetic books corresponds to the ancient prophets themselves is a matter of great debate. Most scholars agree that the final forms of all of the prophetic books likely derive from periods much later than those described in their superscriptions—those informational openings that provide various types of information, including the prophet's name, background, and historical context. Within individual books, vocabulary and style shift, and different geographical and chronological settings are presupposed.

The superscriptions themselves bear clues that they were written at a time later than that described within the books themselves. For example, Amos 1:1 explains that Amos spoke "two years before the earthquake," reflecting a postearthquake perspective, and all of the prophetic superscriptions presuppose that the prophetic activity they document has ended. Because the superscriptions contain date formulae and descriptions of political history that parallel closely the schema presented in the Deuteronomistic History (the books of Joshua, Judges, Samuel, and Kings), many scholars attribute them to a Deuteronomistic editor or, given their variety, to a series of like-minded editors. Although the Deuteronomistic origin of the superscriptions cannot be decisively defended, in their *effect* the superscriptions do forge a solid link between the Former Prophets and the Latter Prophets within the Jewish canon, setting prophets from different times and places into grand national history.

Some redaction critics—scholars who study the process by which biblical books were edited—believe that the application of particular critical tools can unravel the stitching by which the prophetic books were woven together, separating the later additions from the original words of the prophet. This approach was especially prominent in the early- to mid-twentieth century, when some argued that redaction criticism could burn off the dross of the editor and leave behind the pure utterance of the man of God:

> Instead of viewing it [redaction criticism] as laying a rough hand on sacred and inviolable books, one should rather regard it as a reverent effort to give to us of this day the authentic messages of these inspired men just as they fell from their lips. (Calkins 1947, 7)

Current trends in prophetic scholarship, however, have challenged redaction criticism's confidence that it can isolate the kernel of the book and especially its assumption that the "original" kernel preserves the oral speeches of a historical, individual prophet. Increasingly in prophetic studies, even those who remain open to the historical reality of prophets refuse to privilege the "original" layer of the book. Instead, they argue that editors and not prophets should be considered the authors of prophetic books. Editors may have used some traditional materials, but it was they who created books about prophets, addressing the needs of their own communities by crafting books for the sake of readers, not for the sake of historical accuracy.

Given the distance between the "real" prophets and the final form of their books, then, the sense of immediacy that the prophetic books evoke—the feeling that one is hearing the words of inspired speakers—may derive more from their highly crafted poetic style than from their preservation of the original words of the prophets. That is, prophetic books have been constructed by their writers and editors to *sound like* the words of ancient prophets.

Various literary techniques help the authors of the prophetic books achieve such effects. The labeling of the books as "words of God to the prophet" in the superscriptions, as well as the books' repeated use of "messenger speech" (in which the speaker reports the voice of God and the quotations often end with, "thus says Yahweh"), invites the reader to accept the materials contained as transcripts of conversations between God and the prophet. As Floyd (2000, 171) notes, the prophetic books also address a reader directly, as a prophet would have addressed a hearer.

THE PROPHETIC GENRE

Prophetic books might properly be said to constitute a genre of material: a distinctive category of composition. Each opens with a superscription, the function of which is manifold.

Superscriptions link the material to follow with a concrete individual by giving the name of the prophet and sometimes also that of the prophet's father or extended family. Most superscriptions also set the prophet within a particular historical context in the life of Israel or Judah by giving the names of native kings or foreign rulers. The superscriptions also grant the book to follow divine authority by identifying it as the "word" that came from Yahweh, as an "oracle" or as a "vision."

The main body of prophetic books is devoted to speeches (with occasional narratives) that (1) announce punishment on Israel or Judah, (2) announce punishment on other nations, and/or (3) announce salvation to Israel or Judah. Many of the books end with an announcement of salvation.

Stylistically, speeches within the prophetic books are often marked with a formula known as messenger speech. Just as messengers of ancient Near Eastern kings transmitted the wishes of their masters with "thus says King X," so too the prophetic words are marked with "thus says Yahweh." Together with the superscription, messenger speech instructs the reader to treat the words of the prophet as an accurate report of Yahweh's words in a particular time and place. Because a given book can contain material referring to time periods different from the one described in the superscription, a prophetic book often takes on a predictive tone as well; although the prophets are located in time and space, the divine perspective that the book records transcends the limits of temporality.

Prophetic books are primarily in poetic form. Unlike the stories about prophets in the Deuteronomistic History, the prophetic books use a nonnarrative, evocative style. As in the Psalms and books such as Job, this poetry is characterized by parallelism, bold imagery, frequent metaphors, terseness of style, and nonstandard syntax. The prophetic materials use more hyperbole and shocking metaphors than other biblical poetry, however. The language is often crass—as when Jeremiah (ch. 2) compares Judah to a camel in heat and when Ezekiel describes in great detail the sexual appetites of Samaria and Jerusalem (Ezek 16, 23).

THE TWELVE OR JUST TWELVE?

The particular prophetic books treated in this commentary are the final half of a collection called the Minor Prophets by Christians and the Book of the Twelve by Jews. Both labels reflect the fact that the books Hosea through Malachi are short—the longest containing only fourteen chapters (Hosea and Zechariah), as compared to Isaiah's sixty-six.

In Judaism, the Twelve are written on a single scroll; and in ancient descriptions of the canon, they were counted as a single book. Although these small books may have been so clustered because of their brevity and to economize on scroll production, some scholars have suggested that the individual prophetic materials were intentionally edited to be read as a single book. James Nogalski has most extensively explored the traces of redactional activity in the Minor Prophets that was undertaken to unify the Book of the Twelve (1993a; 1993b), though numerous other interpreters have argued that the Twelve presents a grand theological perspective.

The arguments for the unity of the Twelve are not finally convincing. The superscriptions, for example, suggest that the final redactors of the books intended them to be read as separate compositions, as discrete words of God in unique times and places. That is not to imply, however, that the books are unrelated. Clearly, the prophetic books are highly similar in theme, style, and vocabulary; and books such as Zephaniah appear generically "prophetic." These similarities may derive from a common editor, but they may also indicate that the prophetic books were written, and circulated, within a small scribal circle.

THE PROPHETS AND ETHICS

In the late-eighteenth and early nineteenth centuries, many Protestant interpreters identified the prophets as spokespersons for ethical monotheism. Against the background of a pantheistic ancient Near East and a syncretistic Israel, the prophets called their people to worship Yahweh alone and to treat one another with justice. Amos's rousing cry for justice to run down like waters (5:24) was seen by turn-of-the-twentieth-century Protestant interpreters as the voice of a moral revolutionary. Similarly, liberationist readings of the prophets in the mid- to late-twentieth century found in the prophets champions of the poor and politically disenfranchised.

By the late-twentieth century, however, many interpreters described the prophets as ethically problematic. Feminist criticism, for example, highlighted that although the prophets may champion some of the oppressed, they also consistently use metaphors and other speech that denigrate women. As Judith Sanderson points out,

> Amos specifically condemned wealthy women for oppressing the poor (4:1) but failed specifically to champion the women among the poor. . . . As Amos singled out wealthy women—a small group—for special condemnation, a balanced analysis would also have singled out poor women—a much larger group—for special defense and a show of that solidarity of which he was so clearly capable. (1992, 206)

Twentieth-century experiences of war and of the Holocaust also drew greater attention to the violence of the prophetic books and to their ideologically dualistic world. Nahum, for example, not only revels in the image of Nineveh's destruction, but also portrays the world as in a struggle between "us" and "them." In this way, it resonates with the physical and ideological battles between Israelis and Palestinians, Hutus and Tutsis, Serbs and Croats, "terrorists" and "the West"—battles that are overly familiar in the modern world.

The books addressed here have fared especially poorly in the estimation of interpreters over the ages. Apart from isolated quotes taken out of context (for example, Habakkuk on "faith"), these six books have been either ignored or denigrated: Nahum has been demeaned for its violence, Zephaniah for its vision of a vengeful God, Haggai and Zechariah for their support of the establishment, and Second Zechariah for its apocalypticism. The goal of this commentary is not to "rehabilitate" these prophets or to argue for their worth. Rather, it seeks to engage their language, their assumptions, and their possible background so that a reader might engage the books in an attitude of respect—remaining open to the possibility that these books might critique us as much as we critique them.

FINDING MEANING IN ANCIENT PROPHECY

In their attempts to find contemporary meaning in prophetic books, many interpreters treat the words of the prophets as timeless advice to the people of God. The names of contemporary communities and individuals are simply substituted for the prophets' descriptions of "Israel," "Judah," and "Jerusalem." In this understanding, the prophetic announcements apply directly to the contemporary synagogue or church, or even to a contemporary nation. Habakkuk's promises to those who remain faithful (2:4), Haggai's linking of religious obligation with material success (1:7-11), and Malachi's insistence on the paying of tithes (3:8-12) are understood as God's word to all people in all times and places.

This way of reading, for all of its apparent appeal, fails to take seriously the material's compositional history. As suggested above, the prophetic books are largely retrospective, as writers or editors presented what God had done and said in the past as a means to communicate with their own people.

Moreover, the universalization of the prophetic message ignores the self-presentation of the prophetic books. These books present themselves as historically contextual works. All have superscriptions that ground the book in time and place, and most are peppered with "historical" references and narratives. The superscriptions appear to be reading instructions. The prophetic message is to be interpreted within a concrete historical context. Readers are instructed to consider that God spoke through a prophet to a specific community in the past. Perhaps, as for original readers, the task is then to discern what significance the ancient message has for the contemporary scene.

The historicized nature of the prophetic books invites a contextualized theology as well. By stressing the importance of the time period in which the prophets delivered the divine message, they suggest that God does not speak the same word in all times and places. In that way, they work against any theology that would define God's nature in static terms.

These six books, set in the Assyrian, Babylonian, and Persian periods, depict God in various ways—as angry, as powerful, as jealous, as hurt, as caring, as tender. This exploration of their message and their style will attempt to hear the distinctive voice of each.

INTRODUCTION: NAHUM

N ahum is a single-minded book, exclusively devoted to a diatribe against Nineveh, the capital of the Assyrian Empire. Its only parallel in the Old Testament is the book of Obadiah, itself a book-long tirade against Edom. Calls for vengeance against foreign nations appear within other prophetic books, however. Often called Oracles against the Nations (OAN), these materials focus God's wrath against those who stand in opposition to Yahweh (see, for example, Isa 13–23, Jer 46–51, Ezek 25–32, and Amos 1:3–2:3).

Like the OAN, Nahum envisions the fate of the enemy in violent and graphic terms. The destruction of Nineveh is portrayed with realistic images of death ("piles of dead, heaps of corpses, dead bodies without end!" 3:3) and in bold metaphor (especially the public sexual humiliation of Woman Nineveh in 3:5-7). It is not a book for the fainthearted.

Although for much of the nineteenth and twentieth centuries Nahum was denigrated for its violence, especially by Christian interpreters who considered it morally inferior to the New Testament, recent approaches have attempted to reevaluate Nahum in light of its historical context. Feminist interpreters, however, have raised additional concerns about the book's disturbing images of violence against women.

LITERARY ANALYSIS

Even those who treat Nahum as ethically problematic recognize the literary artistry of the book. It is rich in literary features:

assonance, alliteration, repetition, and a wide range of metaphors abound. Particularly in chapters 2 and 3, Nahum arrests its readers with the vivid immediacy of battle, as chariots race through the public streets, whips crack, and horsemen charge. Even the personification of Nineveh as a whore in chapter 3, for all of the ethical problems it raises, dramatically and powerfully demonizes Judah's foe.

The delineation of Nahum's units is contested by interpreters. Roberts (1991) and Sweeney (1992), for example, find a four-part scheme, while Smith (1911) discerns eleven distinct units. My own outline of Nahum is as follows:

1:1	Superscription
1:2-10	A God of power and might
1:11-14	Yahweh's response to evil
1:15–2:13 (Heb. 2:1-14)*	The assault of Nineveh
3:1-19	An oracle against Nineveh

After a short though fairly standard superscription, the book turns to a description of Yahweh, in the form of a theophanic hymn that describes Yahweh as the Divine Warrior. Some interpreters have seen in the hymn a partial alphabetic acrostic that may derive from an earlier cultic liturgy. In the current form of the book, however, 1:9-10 follows directly from and belongs with the theophany: because of God's might, those who plot against God are doomed to failure.

Marked by a shift in pronouns, a short unit begins at 1:11 and continues through 1:14. Here, God's intention toward a specific enemy is outlined. The enemy is not plainly identified, however, described only with pronouns without clear antecedents.

Nahum 1:15 (Heb. 2:1) announces good news to Judah: Judah is called to celebrate because Nineveh is about to be devastated.

---

*Hebrew and English Bibles differ in the break of the first chapter. Nahum 2:1 in Hebrew is found as 1:15 in English, and hence in chapter 2 the Hebrew numberings of verses are one higher than their English counterparts.

The remainder of chapter 2 paints the scene of Nineveh's destruction: the armies of Yahweh, the Divine Warrior, rage through the city, and all opposition melts before their might.

Nahum 3 begins with "woe" (NRSV: "Ah!") often an indicator of a new unit. It provides a second and more graphic image of Nineveh's fall. Here, Nineveh is personified as a prostitute. Yahweh publicly humiliates her by pulling her skirts over her face, and the chapter ends with a taunt against the king of Assyria. The last verse is a rhetorical question, the only biblical book other than Jonah to end in this way. It implies that the fate of Assyria is deserved, given its cruelty.

All three chapters employ numerous pronouns, many of which have unclear antecedents, and hence the party being addressed or described at any given time is open to interpretation. The book may best be understood to describe four primary characters: Judah and Nineveh, portrayed as feminine; and Yahweh and the king of Assyria, characterized as male. Throughout Nahum, these characters stand in tension with one another. Judah's fate is the obverse of Nineveh's, and Yahweh's power overrides that of the Assyrian king. In the analogy of the lion's den in 2:11-12 (Heb. 2:12-13), the Assyrian king (unlike Yahweh) is the one who cannot protect his female.

SOCIAL AND HISTORICAL ANALYSIS

Primarily because of its concern with Nineveh, the capital of the neo-Assyrian empire, the book of Nahum is usually dated within the seventh century B.C.E. The earliest date usually suggested for the book is 663, when the city of Thebes fell to the Assyrians, given that 3:8-10 refers to the destruction of Thebes as a past event. The book is usually understood to have been written before 612, when Nineveh itself fell. Such a dating is supported by the argument that the powerful emotions of the book and the use of Assyrian imagery (lions, for example) reflect a date of composition close to the events described.

If Nahum were indeed written during the Assyrian period, its animosity toward Nineveh would be understandable. Assyria was a major military power in the ancient Near East during the eighth and seventh centuries. Assyrian royal inscriptions attest not only to the army's facility with iron weapons and siege technology, but also to its systematic brutal treatment of captives: the slaughter of tens of thousands; the deportation of large population groups (some to slave labor camps); and the selective blinding, flaying, and impalement of enemies—both alive and dead. In 721, Assyrian armies besieged Samaria and ended the political autonomy of the northern kingdom, perhaps alluded to in the claim of Nah 2:3 that the destruction of Nineveh will restore the pride of Jacob/Israel. In 701, Sennacherib occupied all of Judah except Jerusalem, such that the southern kingdom of Judah served as a vassal state of Assyria for much of the seventh century.

An argument based on Nahum's Assyrian theme, however, does not necessarily account for the dating of the final form of the book. The presence of the superscription, which refers to Nahum's activity in the past, suggests that the current book of Nahum bears material from later than the Assyrian period: the superscription describes Nahum as a figure from the past. James Nogalski has further argued that the opening theophanic hymn was a later addition to Nahum by the redactors of the Book of the Twelve, an addition intended to universalize Nahum's message by focusing on the character of Yahweh (Nogalski 1993, 127-28).

Nahum, then, may have been edited, or even composed, at a time later than the Assyrian period. Since readers in a later time would have known that Nineveh had indeed fallen, the book would be interpreting the events of history as a paradigm of how God treats all opposition. Coggins suggests that Nahum is an example of an Oracle against the Nations moving from specific to more general applications:

> The foreign nations oracles came increasingly to be used as a vehicle for asserting the sovereignty of Yahweh. . . . Nahum marks an important point in the development in this direction. The foreign enemy against whom he inveighs is recognizably Assyria, an all too real empirical threat to Judah's peace of

mind at the time of the prophet's ministry. Yet the real center of gravity is not in Nineveh; . . . Nineveh symbolizes all that might stand in opposition to that power. (Coggins 1985, 13)

Whatever the book's compositional history, the superscription invites the reader of Nahum to read the book within the context of the Assyrian period, to believe that the evil of Assyria is a real and present danger. That is, Nineveh is the book's *literary* foe if not the author's own *historical* foe.

THEOLOGICAL ANALYSIS

For most of the nineteenth and twentieth centuries, commentators lambasted Nahum for its violence. Nahum does not merely *describe* war in its bloody detail; it *revels* in imagining the destruction of the Assyrian foe, apparently finding glee in the panic and death of others.

In 1903, the British interpreter G. A. Smith expressed the conviction that the sentiments of the prophet Nahum were far less ethical than those of Smith's own culture:

For he [Nahum] represents no single movement of his fickle people's progress, but the passion of the whole epoch then drawing to a close. . . . Such is the sheer religion of the Proem to the Book of Nahum—thoroughly Oriental in its sense of God's method and resources of destruction; very Jewish, and very natural to that age of Jewish history, in the bursting of its long pent hopes of revenge. We of the West might express these hopes differently. We should not attribute so much personal passion to the Avenger. With our keener sense of law, we should emphasize the slowness of the process. (G. A. Smith, 1903, 91-92)

In a similar vein, J. M. P. Smith, in 1911, argued that Nahum was morally inferior not only to Smith's own society, but also to the other prophetic books. Unlike Jeremiah, who wept over the fate of the Judeans whose punishment he was called to announce, Nahum expressed no concern for the dying Ninevites (1991, 281).

From a twenty-first-century perspective, such evaluations of Nahum appear culturally and religiously arrogant. G. A. Smith's marking of all vengeful feelings as "oriental" and "Jewish" not only ignores the long legacy of violence perpetrated by "the West" and by Christians, but also reflects (and perpetuates) a clear anti-Jewish bias. Similarly, J. M. P. Smith's negative comparison of Nahum to Jeremiah relies on a selective reading of both books, failing to take into account the vehemence that Jer 46–51 expresses against the foreign nations.

Although some contemporary interpreters continue to denigrate Nahum, others since the 1950s have understood Nahum in a more positive light. One such effort has been to explain the fervor of the book as the understandable and appropriate response to cultural and military oppression. The most clear articulation of this position had been that of Wilhelm Wessels (1998), who draws parallels between the poetry of Nahum and anti-apartheid literature from South Africa. Both Nahum and South African resistance poets, Wessels claims, employed the power of the aesthetic to challenge the hegemony of those in power. By imagining a world in which the oppressor falls, resistance literature serves the political and psychological function of bolstering alternative understandings of reality.

In a related argument, Peter Craigie compares the Assyrians against whom Nahum railed with the synonym of evil in the twentieth century: "Just as Nazi Germany still evokes the images of terror in the minds of those Jewish people who survived the Holocaust, so too in Nahum's world Assyria was the embodiment of human evil and terror" (1985, 58). By correlating Assyrian rule with the Holocaust, Craigie reminds contemporary readers of the brutality of Assyrian oppression: if a contemporary reader believes that resistance to evil is justified, then Nahum is a heroic, not a jingoistic, book.

Elizabeth Achtemeier and others find value in Nahum in yet a different way, maintaining that, especially in its final form, Nahum is about not human revenge, but the power and sovereignty of God:

Nahum is not primarily a book about human beings, however—not about human vengeance and hatred and military
conquest—but a book about God. And it has been our failure
to let Nahum be a book about God that has distorted the value
of this prophecy in our eyes. (1986, 5-6)

Nahum's attestation to the sovereignty of God and God's passion
for justice renders it, for Achtemeier, an important and theologically sound affirmation.

These responses helpfully remind modern readers that Nahum
speaks, even if only literarily, out of a particular historical context. The enemy against which the book's anger is directed is not
a small, similarly harassed state, but an empire under whose
oppression much of the ancient Near East groaned.

The attempts to paint Nahum in a positive light, however,
tend to downplay—or outright ignore—the type of punishment
Nahum envisions and the glee with which that punishment is nar-
rated. Particularly, these attempts fail to acknowledge the thoroughgoing violence against women embedded in the book's use of
metaphor and personification. Judith Sanderson (1992) well
explains how dangerous the description of Woman Nineveh's
punishment in Nah 3 is in our own day: not only does the book
condone rape as punishment, but also, even more problematically,
Yahweh is portrayed as the rapist. Sanderson agrees that modern
readers should understand the cultural context out of which Nah
3 grew (such as the ancient assumptions about men's rights to
women's sexuality), but she claims that such misogynist images of
God have no place in contemporary discourse.

As important as Sanderson's remarks are, they do not go far
enough in recognizing how pervasive gender codes are in the
book of Nahum. In addition to portraying the assault of Woman
Nineveh, the book also portrays Judah as a female in need of
protection by Yahweh and manifests a pervasive concern with
male honor. Even the humiliation of Woman Nineveh is part of a
larger gender message of the book. The end of Nahum makes
clear that the assault of Nineveh is primarily a means of shaming

the king of Assyria. Like the lion in the allegory of Nah 2, the Assyrian king cannot not protect the female under his protection.

Such observations suggest that the assumptions and ideologies that undergird the book of Nahum cannot be easily separated from the "real" message of the book, but instead are integral to its rhetoric. That is, even if Achtemeier is right that the book is about God, nonetheless the characterization of God in Nahum depends on assumptions about masculinity and femininity, shame and punishment that many in our own day recognize as dangerous. The "problem" of Nahum goes beyond its overt violence to the very assumptions on which the book rests.

How, then, does a contemporary reader *both* appreciate the book's powerful stance against oppression *and* acknowledge its problematic ideologies? One approach is to read Nahum in parallel with contemporary culture, seeing in both the way in which liberation movements often demonize their enemies and the way in which the rhetoric of demonization feeds a cycle of violence, as the oppressed becomes the oppressor. Seeing the complications of resistance in Nahum may allow us to discern the same in our own world. And that discernment may spur us to find new ways of responding to violence, which do not perpetuate the mentalities on which violence depends.

COMMENTARY: NAHUM

SUPERSCRIPTION (1:1)

The superscription to the book of Nahum does not mention the prophet's time period or his place of current residency. Instead, it gives (1) three nouns describing the content of the book *(maśśā᾽, sēper,* and *ḥāzôn)*; (2) the target of the message; and (3) the name and the geographical origin of the prophet. Together, this material establishes for the reader the divine origin and historical context of the material to follow.

Literary Analysis

Nahum's designation as a *maśśā᾽,* "an oracle," connects it with a network of other texts. The same term introduces collections that begin at Zech 9:1, 12:1; Mal 1:1; and, more important, the extended diatribes against foreign nations in Isa 13–23. The Isaiah texts are Oracles against the Nations (OAN), a common prophetic genre in which the prophet announces God's intentions toward nations other than Israel and Judah. The term *maśśā᾽* does not by itself reveal that Nahum fits the OAN genre, since not all OAN texts begin with *maśśā᾽* and not all prophecies marked as *maśśā᾽* are OANs. In being directed against Nineveh, however, Nahum reveals that it is both a *maśśā᾽* and an OAN, the only collection outside of Isa 13–23 that fits both categories.

All *maśśā᾽* texts are characterized by a strong dichotomy between "us" and "them": the wicked stand opposed to the righteous (Hab 1:4; Mal 3:18), and the nations stand opposed to

Jerusalem (Zech 9, 12). The label *maśśāʾ*, then, invokes a literary world in which punishment for the wicked is necessary for the salvation of the righteous, and it clues its reader to expect harsh words for "them" and promises of salvation for "us."

Exegetical Analysis

The best translation of the term *maśśāʾ* is debated, as reflected in the difference between the NRSV "oracle" and the KJV "burden." A noun form of the verbal root *nśʾ*, to "lift up," *maśśāʾ* is variously understood (a) to assume "the voice" as its object, thus signifying a technical term for prophecy (best rendered as "oracle"); or (b) to refer to anything that is lifted up ("burden"). Vigorous discussion about the "proper" meaning of the term can be found throughout commentaries, but Jer 23:33-40 suggests that ancient hearers were aware of the connections between the two terms; thus, even if *maśśāʾ* were a technical term for a prophetic utterance, its aural association with "heaviness, burden" would have been common for ancient hearers and readers.

In addition to being described as an "oracle," Nahum is also designated as a *sēper*. The English term "book," by which it is translated, implies one particular technology of collecting writing materials: a bound collection of loose pages, properly termed a "codex." The Hebrew term *sēper* does not carry the same set of associations. In the Bible, it refers to any written document, including a letter; the codex form does not appear until a much later period. Although other prophetic materials are linked with writing (Jer 36:2; Hab 2:2; Ezek 3), no other prophetic superscription identifies the material to follow as a *sēper*. Such an identification not only demonstrates that, as R. Smith suggests, "Nahum is self-consciously a piece of literature" (Smith 1984, 71), but also sets reading boundaries. Authority resides not in the vision itself, not in the experience of a prophet named Nahum, but in the words and letters bounded by the beginning and ending of these particular words.

More precisely, Nahum is called the book of a "vision" (*ḥāzôn*). On first reading, it appears ironic that the only prophetic material called a book also is described as the result of a vision—a seeming contradiction of media—yet much of the prophetic literature portrays itself as a written version of what a prophet has perceived by the eye or the ear. The frequent use of prophetic messenger speech, "thus says Yahweh," reinforces that perception, as does the frequent use of the term "vision" to characterize what the prophets proclaim.

The word *ḥāzôn* appears only in the prophetic books, in which it is used almost exclusively for prophecy; its only other referent is to a "night vision" (Isa 29:7). Isaiah and Obadiah are also labeled visions in their superscriptions, and 2 Chr 32:32 calls the book of Isaiah the "vision of the prophet Isaiah." The superscriptions of Amos, Micah, and Habbakuk (which, like Nahum, is also called a *maśśā*) refer to what the prophet "saw," using the related verbal form *ḥāzāh*. The word *ḥāzôn* refers not simply to data registered by the eyes, but rather to truth made known by God, as Jer 23:16 makes clear: "They [false prophets] speak visions of their own minds, not from the mouth of the LORD." In apocalyptic contexts, where it is especially prevalent (*ḥāzôn* appears eleven times in the book of Daniel), it implies an ecstatic vision of the future.

Described both as an "oracle" and as "a book of the vision," Nahum thus opens with two independent phrases describing its contents. Scholars often view a composite introduction as an indication that two independent collections of prophetic materials have been brought together. Amos 1:1, for example, heaps up clauses of introduction, raising the possibility of preliminary collections of (a) the words of Amos, preserved in chapters 1–6; and (b) the visions that he saw concerning Israel, preserved in chapters 7–9. Nahum's dual superscription may suggest that two collections have been merged, or perhaps that multiple headings were given to the book over time. Nogalski suggests that the first *(maśśā)* was the original title of the book and that the second *(sēper ḥāzôn)* was added later (Nogalski 1993, 100).

The superscription bears not only these labels but also an indication of the target of the prophet's message. The identification of Nineveh here is important, since Nineveh is not mentioned again until 2:8 (Heb. 2:9). As discussed in the introduction to

Nahum, Nineveh was the capital of the powerful neo-Assyrian empire, known throughout the ancient world for its military prowess and fierce warfare practices. Its art and literature affected a "calculated frightfulness" (Grayson 1992, 748). Clarifying that the prophet's words were against this evil empire prepares the reader for the harsh words ahead.

The name Nahum, which follows, may be either a noun meaning "comfort" or a shortened form of Nehemiah, "Yahweh has given comfort." Other names taken from the same Hebrew root appear in the Bible and in related ancient Near Eastern cultures. While most commentators draw no connection between the name and the message of the book, it is indeed appropriate—if at first glance ironic—that a message of such devastation is spoken by one who brings comfort. In the literary world of the OAN and of the *maśśāʾ*, harsh words directed against "them" are intended as comfort for "us," striving to convince the reader that an unjust world is soon to be rectified.

Nahum is described as the "Elkoshi," that is, one from the town of Elkosh; Micah's superscription gives a similar kind of designation by identifying Micah as a Moreshite (Mic 1:1). Some scholars have attempted to locate the city in Galilee or in southwestern Judah or even near Nineveh, though the only evidence for its location is derived from the book of Nahum itself. Literally, "Elkoshi" means "the God who makes hard," utilizing the same verb used throughout Exodus to describe the "hardening" of Pharaoh's heart—certainly an evocative etymology in such a "hard," "burdensome" book.

Theological Analysis

Nahum's superscription sets the tone of the book, inviting the reader to interpret what follows as divine will communicated in a particular time and place and to hear its harshness against Nineveh as a word of comfort to Israel. That Nineveh, the ultimate powerhouse of the ancient Near East, is its addressee also suggests that whatever anger God will direct its way will be deserved.

In dealing with the violence of the book of Nahum, some interpreters have drawn comfort in the fact that Nahum's portrait of Nineveh's destruction is labeled not a "word of Yahweh," but rather a vision, which could imply that it is less a concrete battle plan to be waged against the Assyrians than an orienting perspective or fantasy of the fate that awaits all who stand in opposition to God. Such an interpretation might be bolstered by the fact that the only other stand-alone Oracle against the Nations—the book of Obadiah—is also described as a vision.

However, the violence of these books is not so easily controlled by their description as a vision. In Obadiah, for example, the book's description as a "vision" is followed by "thus says Yahweh." Moreover, as we have seen, ḥāzôn is nearly synonymous with prophecy, much of which is very concrete and immediate in its focus (for example, Isa 1:1; 1 Chr 17:15).

Nahum's opening, therefore, introduces its reader into an ethically dualistic world. It encourages its reader to understand the book as divine response to the problem of evil.

A GOD OF POWER AND MIGHT (1:2-10)

In Nah 1:2-10, the might and power of Yahweh are described in a classic theophany: God marches as a Divine Warrior to crush enemies and rescue friends. Nineveh, mentioned in the superscription, is the most obvious target of Yahweh's anger, but the literary style of the unit suggests that all do well to align themselves with God.

Literary Analysis

This second unit of the book of Nahum is a complex one. Its ending point is debated, variously defined as 1:8, 1:10, and 1:14.

The case for ending the unit at 1:8 has been made by various scholars since the 1850s who argue that Nah 1:2-8 is a partial alphabetic acrostic, its lines successively beginning with the first eleven letters of the Hebrew alphabet, aleph through kaph. This theory has formed so great a consensus that the most popular modern Hebrew Bible, the BHS, prints the alphabetic sequence in the margin of the text.

Floyd (1994), however, has pointed to the difficulties with understanding Nah 1 in this way. To discern even an incomplete acrostic, scholars must emend the text in ways that are not otherwise necessary or desirable—for example, in 1:4, changing a word beginning with *aleph* to a word beginning with *dalet*. Floyd suggests that the apparent acrostic is more coincidental than a deliberate compositional strategy.

Floyd also argues the structural coherence of the larger unit of 1:2-10, demonstrating how both 1:6 and 1:9 follow general descriptions with rhetorical questions and how 1:11 signals a new unit by a change in addressee. Nahum 1:9-10 follows the portrait of the divine majesty with a punch line: why would anyone oppose such a powerful deity?

In its description of the character of God, Nah 1:2 employs a series of present participles: Yahweh is "the jealous one," "the vengeful one," "the one who rages." In Nah 1:3a, adjectives perform the same durative function: "Yahweh [is] slow of anger, and [is] great of strength." The one verbal form ("he will indeed not acquit," 1:3a AT) is imperfect, that mood in Hebrew reserved for incomplete, and often continuing, action. By their style, these verbs suggest eternal, changeless features of Yahweh's character.

A series of literary techniques further focuses the reader's attention on Yahweh's vengeance. "Repetition" situates vengeance as the structural and topical center of Nah 1:2: "the vengeful one [is] Yahweh" (AT) appears three times. Allusion also highlights Yahweh's vengeance. Nahum 1:2-3 quotes the most frequent and fundamental characterization of Yahweh in the Hebrew Bible. Found in Num 14:18; Joel 2:13; Jonah 4:2; Pss 86:15; 103:8; 145:8; and Neh 9:17 as well, its classic formulation appears in Exod 34:6-7:

Yahweh, Yahweh, a God merciful and gracious, slow to anger, and abounding in steadfast love and faithfulness, keeping steadfast love for the thousandth generation, forgiving iniquity and transgression and sin, yet by no means clearing the guilty, but visiting the iniquity of the parents upon the children and the children's children, to the third and the fourth generation.

In comparison with Exod 34:6-7, Nahum omits mention of God's mercy, covenant loyalty, and forgiveness and focuses solely on God's vengeance. Nahum 1:3 draws a strong dichotomy between God's friends and God's enemies: God is "slow to anger" *and* "will not acquit." Further underscoring the dichotomy, 1:6-7 explains that no one can withstand the inferno of God's anger *and* that God is a place of safety for those who take refuge in divine protection.

Vivid imagery and simile assist the unit in portraying Yahweh as a fierce, unstoppable warrior. Nature itself trembles before Yahweh's advance: mountains quake, the earth lifts up, and rocks break. Yahweh's anger is like fire (1:6), and those who oppose Yahweh are like intertwined thorns and drunkards (1:10). Together, these features stress Yahweh's power. Even though problematic to translate, Nah 1:10 is highly alliterative. Literally reading "like unto intertwined thorns and like their drinking, drunkards, [they are] eaten up like chaff dry full," the verse in Hebrew is full of s, b, and k sounds *(sĕbūkîm ûkĕsobʾām sĕbûʾîm)*.

Exegetical Analysis

Nahum 1:2-8 constitutes a theophany—a description of a visible appearance of God. Here, as in similar Old Testament passages (Judg 5; 2 Sam 22; Ps 18; Hab 3; Amos 1; Isa 29), God appears in a storm: mountains and hills shake, and the earth heaves (Nah 1:5). This imagery of cosmic shaking is frequent in biblical texts that describe God as the Divine Warrior. As helpfully schematized by Hiebert (1992), the Divine Warrior motif evolved over time. Although early Divine Warrior texts (such as Exod 15 and Deut 33) draw from common ancient Near Eastern mythological motifs to portray a deity who triumphs against cosmic forces, and although during the monarchy the images were used to bolster the praise of the Davidic king (as in Ps 18), the distinctive contribution of the prophetic materials was to portray the Divine Warrior as fighting against anyone—both foreign nations and the people themselves. The description in Nahum certainly fits the prophetic model: the Divine Warrior storms in to defeat all opposition.

Here, as in Hab 3, the language resonates with ancient Near Eastern mythological motifs. In both Canaanite and Babylonian mythologies, the world was formed as the result of combat between gods. In the Canaanite account, the god Baal fought and defeated Yamm (Sea) to create order in the world; in the Babylonian myth, the god Marduk slew the chaos monster Tiamat and created the heaven and the earth from her body. In Nahum, Yahweh exerts might by rebuking the sea and drying up rivers. Yahweh also withers Bashan, Carmel, and Lebanon, areas famed for fertile land.

Nahum 1:8 is difficult to translate, literally rendered "in a flood overflowing an end he will make, her place, and his enemies he will pursue darkness." Attempting to read with the MT, ASV translates the verse "he will make a full end of her place," and similar translations are NASB ("its site") and NKJV ("its place"). The NIV assumes that "her place" refers to Nineveh and adds the proper name to the text. Both RSV and NRSV follow the reading of the Septuagint: "He will make a full end to his adversaries." These translations, however, do not solve the problem of 1:8. Elsewhere in the Hebrew Bible, when used with an object, the phrase "make an end of" takes a "helping" preposition. In cases such as this one in which the phrase appears without a preposition (Isa 10:23; Neh 9:31), it takes no object. As elsewhere in Nahum, the reader is kept guessing about identities and about the precise message of the passage, unclear about the target of Yahweh's anger.

The flood imagery of 1:8 fits well with the Divine Warrior motif. "The flood" represents unstoppable devastation, as in Dan 11:10 and 9:26, the latter close in wording to Nahum: "The troops of the prince who is to come shall destroy the city and the sanctuary. Its end shall come with a flood, and to the end there shall be war" (Dan 9:26). Numerous Divine Warrior texts, including Jer 47:2, also describe devastation as a "flood" (NRSV: "torrent").

Nahum 1:9-10 introduces a problem that plagues the book: pronouns shift in gender and number and often lack clear antecedents. Who, for example, are "you" (1:9), "he" (1:8, 9), and "they " (1:10)? Different than in the unit to follow, "you" is here masculine plural and best understood generically: given Yahweh's impressive might, what can *anyone* plot against the deity? "He" most logically refers to Yahweh, the one who pursues and makes an end to enemies.

Theological Analysis

Literarily, if not historically, the problem underlying the book of Nahum is the perceived evil of the Assyrians. In a cultural world in which the defeat of a city was seen as defeat of its god, the success of the Assyrian armies was a theological problem: can Yahweh be in charge if hostile armies threaten Judah? Other biblical books wrestle with similar questions and offer diverse answers. Isaiah, for example, claims that the Assyrians are successful because God is temporarily using them as an instrument of punishment against Judah. Habakkuk maintains that those who wait patiently will see the similarly evil Babylonians punished. Apocalyptic materials such as Daniel suggest that the ultimate defeat of evil will come in a future time.

As the book progresses, Nahum responds to the might of the Assyrians by claiming that Nineveh is about to be defeated; indeed, its defeat is so sure that a picture of the devastation can already be painted. But rather than immediately announcing God's punishment against the Assyrians, the book instead opens by talking about who God is and how God (always) acts: God is powerful, and God will respond to *all* friends and *all* enemies in ways that are consistent with God's character. Only later, in chapters 2 and 3, do we learn that Judah is the friend and Nineveh the enemy, and how each will fare in light of these larger truths about God.

By opening with a description of God's (enduring) character, Nahum provides a framework for understanding the harshness of Nineveh's treatment in chapters 2 and 3: since God punishes enemies and rewards friends, Nineveh must indeed be an enemy.

In this light, God's response to Nineveh is not a capricious act of revenge, but the appropriate response of one who rewards the righteous and punishes the guilty.

While the opening poem focuses on God's general character, the reader knows from the superscription that the book is targeted at Nineveh; and hence the mention of Nineveh in the superscription has multiple effects. On the one hand, Judah's experience of the brutality of the Assyrians would in some ways explain why the vengeful side of God is being highlighted: certainly such brutality requires strong opposition. On the other hand, the brief mention of Nineveh also spoils the generic nature of the opening theophany; though striving to talk about God's character before describing God's concrete action with the Assyrians, the book is already anchored in a concrete time and place in its current form by the superscription. Hence, a reader who may take "comfort" in separating general truths about God from the concrete images of violence against Nineveh is "burdened" by knowing, all along, that the book cheers on Nineveh's destruction.

This focus on Nineveh, however, should not blind the reader to the reality that Nahum was not a book Assyrians would have read. Although it is *about* Nineveh, it was not written *for* Assyrians. Nahum's goal was not likely the changing of the Assyrians' behavior or their thinking, but rather Nahum was a book written and read by Judeans. For such readers, the opening chapter of Nahum, with its nonspecific mention of friends and enemies, both vindicates those who are confident of their status as Yahweh's friends and forces the recognition of how unstable the status of friend always is. By portraying the severity of the consequences for angering God, the chapter implicitly threatens the community itself, should it breach religious and social norms. Although clearly defending God's power and might, Nah 1 both comforts and implicitly challenges the reader.

YAHWEH'S RESPONSE TO EVIL (1:11-14)

The general description of Yahweh in Nah 1:2-10 is followed by a short unit that directs the deity's power and anger against a specific target. The identity of this target, difficult to determine, is likely the king of Assyria.

Literary Analysis

The identities of the unit's addresses are difficult to determine, given that it employs numerous pronouns that lack antecedents—"you" in 1:11, 12, 13, and 14; "they" in 1:10 and 12; and "him" in 1:13. The gender and number of these pronouns, however, provide some clues to the sense of the unit and suggest that "you" refers to at least two different groups.

In 1:12-13, "you" is promised protection by Yahweh: although "you" has been afflicted, Yahweh will cease the affliction and break the offending yoke. The fate of this "you" is contrasted with the fate of "they" and "him," who are depicted as having been oppressors. Several clues suggest that, in 1:12-13, Judah is the "you" being promised protection and against the Assyrians and their king. First, the second-person pronoun in these verses is feminine singular. Although Judah is a masculine noun, Judah is addressed in 1:15 (Heb. 2:1) with a feminine singular imperative. Second, the larger context of the book of Nahum contrasts Judah's fate with that of the Assyrians (see especially 2:1 [Heb. 2:2] and 3:18): the destruction of the enemy benefits Judah.

That a new "you" is addressed in 1:14 is suggested by the shift to the masculine singular and by the observation that this "you" receives Yahweh's punishment. Given that the king of Assyria is also addressed in the second masculine singular (3:18-19), one might assume that the king is also the subject of 1:14. Floyd (2000, 49) bolsters this assumption by arguing that the punishments outlined in 1:14 befit a royal figure.

Exegetical Analysis

The identification of "you" in 1:11, however, is more complex and intertwined with the translation of the verse as a whole. The pronoun is feminine singular, as in 1:12. But these two verses describe differently the fate of the feminine "you": in 1:12, she is promised salvation, but in 1:11, "plotting" against the deity is clearly a negative activity (as seen in 1:9, in which plotting is attributed to a masculine plural subject). If "you" is being accused of producing the plotter, then either (1) 1:11 and 1:12 refers to different feminine subjects, or (2) the same subject is both criticized and promised relief.

The first option is chosen by the NIV, which interprets "you" as Nineveh, mentioned in the superscription and described in feminine terms in Nah 3. Indeed, NIV supplements the translation to read "you, O Nineveh," as it also does in Nah 1:8. Such a solution has the advantage of explaining the verse's apparent condemnation, though other mentions of Nineveh are far removed from this verse.

Taking the second option, "you" in 1:11 may be Judah. This interpretation has the advantage of treating the feminine pronouns consistently, but, as translated in KJV, NASB, and NRSV, the verse appears to blame Judah for an undisclosed crime: accusing Judah for producing a plotter seems out of place in a unit in which Judah is promised protection from her enemy.

Floyd (2000, 50-51), however, argues that the verse may not be accusatory at all. In Hebrew, the verb translated as "come out" also can mean "depart from," and hence the verse may recount something positive that happened in the past: "From you an evil plotter departed." Floyd reads 1:11 as reminding the community of the departure of Sennacherib from the gates of Jerusalem in 701, seen in Isa 37 as Yahweh's gracious response to king Hezekiah's prayer. This historical reference is far from clear, but Floyd's reading does allow the possibility that the feminine singular "you" is used consistently in this unit to refer to Judah, while the masculine referents are to the Assyrians.

In its reference to a plotter and in its direct address the king of Assyria, the unit bears the marks of historical specificity. And, yet, the generic way in which the characters and events are described leaves readers with few clues from which to reconstruct the background of Nahum. Even more unclear is whether the problem of recreating Nahum's time period is only one for contemporary readers or whether the feeling of historical specificity is a literary illusion created by the book's author.

Theological Analysis

The opening theophany of 1:2-10 sets up an important distinction between the deity's friends and enemies: Yahweh is good to those who seek protection (1:7) but rages against adversaries (1:8). This unit furthers the distinction by contrasting the hopeful fate of a feminine singular "you" and the dishonorable end of "they/he."

Nahum 1:12*b*, however, destabilizes this simplistically dualistic world. In a single Hebrew word, Yahweh reveals that he himself is responsible for the addressee's current suffering: "I have afflicted you." For the first time in the book, Nahum suggests that Judah's suffering at Assyria's hands is Yahweh's doing.

Other prophetic materials, such as Hos 11:5 and especially Isa 1–39, describe Assyria as the disposable instrument of Yahweh's destruction of Judah: the deity will use Assyria to destroy Judah and then will destroy Assyria itself. Nahum is less clear than Isaiah about God's participation in Judah's affliction. Indeed, 1:12 is the only verse in Nahum that suggests that Judah's own sin led to the problems that Yahweh now promises to resolve.

Thus, although Nahum is usually seen as an unbridled tirade against the Assyrians, the book also acknowledges—however briefly—the complications of assigning the role of "innocent victim." In Nahum as well as in the contemporary world, the line between victim and perpetrator is rarely fixed and immutable.

When read as a whole, Nah 1 underscores Yahweh's power over all opposition. As elsewhere in the prophets, the Divine Warrior wages battle not only against the nations but also against rebellious Judah.

THE ASSAULT OF NINEVEH (1:15–2:13 [HEB. 2:1-14])

This unit contrasts the fates of two female figures: Judah is called to celebrate her deliverance and Nineveh is besieged by an invading army. Highly crafted poetry evokes the horror of war and the animosity of Yahweh toward the wicked city.

Literary Analysis

A new unit is signaled by the shift in attention to Judah, who is addressed in the second-person feminine singular and named for the first time in the book. In keeping with the previous unit, Judah is told to celebrate the end of her subservience, but, immediately in 2:1, another second-person feminine subject is addressed.

This new "you" is the target of a military siege, the description of which dramatically builds in suspense and intensity through 2:10. The advancing enemy is sighted and "you" are commanded to defend yourself (2:1); parenthetically, Jacob is identified as the beneficiary of the destruction (2:2); an army pours through city streets (2:3-5); in a grand climax, the city, finally named as Nineveh, falls (2:6-8); the destruction is surveyed (2:9-10); the ruined city is taunted (2:11-12); and (anticlimatically) Yahweh announces punishment (2:13).

The unit bears much in common with Nah 3. As discussed more fully in the literary analysis of Nah 3, these two final chapters of Nahum follow a similar structure, use common literary devices, and advance many of the same themes.

Numerous literary devices are employed in 2:1-4 to create a bold image of the siege of Nineveh. The appearance of the army is described with vivid colors (2:3) and with numerous similes (2:4). Nahum 2:2 also shares many of the literary features of 1:10, utilizing nouns and verbs from the same roots ("like drunkards drunk," "like emptiers emptied"). Like the chariots they describe, phrases in 2:4 flash like lightning, giving the reader glimpses but not the totality of the scene.

Terseness of style characterizes 2:8-10. Clipped commands, issued to no one in particular, approximate the panic of looting in 2:9; and in 2:10, staccato sentences, some without verbs, fire in rapid succession. The NRSV well captures the initial alliteration of 2:10: "Devastation, desolation, and destruction!" *(bûqâ ûmĕbûqâ ûmĕbullāqâ)*. Attention then turns to the body's response to terror: heart melts, knees totter, loins anguish, faces pale (KJV: "blacken").

Nineveh is named in 2:8 for the first time since the superscription. The Assyrian capital is depicted as a woman, through the use of the feminine pronoun and through being described as one who has handmaids. Although the personification of a city as a woman is a frequent motif in the ancient Near East and in biblical materials, the book of Nahum capitalizes on and extends this feminine imagery in pointed and dramatic ways, especially in chapter 3. In Nah 2:7, the reader hears the rhyming, onomatopoetic sounds of the handmaids' grief, as they moan (*měnahăgôt*) and beat their breasts (*mětōpěpōt*).

The imagery of the lion explored in 2:11-13 functions on several levels. On the one hand, it parallels Jer 51:38 and Amos, which depict lions as a picture of terror and ravenousness. On the other hand, the well-known use of the lion in Assyrian iconography and literature renders it particularly ironic. Tauntlike, it asks the whereabouts of the fierce Assyrians, who boast their strength. Different Hebrew words are used here (translated in NRSV as "lions," "young lions," "lionesses"); and though some have attempted to identify each with a role within Assyrian royalty (king, prince, queen), the metaphor need not be so forced. Even though the great Assyrian lion has taken prey and provided a protected den for its dependents, he is now defeated by one more powerful. In a clear summary statement (2:13), the destruction of Nineveh, so powerfully described in this chapter, is explicitly attributed to Yahweh God of Israel: God is the one who burns the chariots (2:3), vanquishes the lions (2:11-12), gives up the possessions of the Ninevites as booty (2:9), and cuts off the Assyrian messengers (2:13).

Exegetical Analysis

Several problems of translation and identification run through this unit. The "scatterer" of 2:1 is not named, nor are the "you" of 2:1 and 2:13, the "he" of 2:3, or the "she" of 2:7. Commentators offer diverse understandings of each.

Because the term "scatterer" appears throughout Divine Warrior texts as an epithet for Yahweh (Hab 3; Zech 13; Pss 18,

68, 144; 2 Sam 22), a coherent explanation is that in Nah 2 the Assyrian armies are ironically called to defend themselves against the oncoming invasion of the troops of Yahweh, the Divine Warrior, the "he" of 2:3. Providing further support for this interpretation are the strong connections between this unit, as well as other parts of Nahum, to Jer 51, which describes the destruction of the oppressor Babylon at the hand of the Medes. In both Jeremiah and in Nahum, revenge is waged to redress Judah's dishonor (Jer 51:24, 49; Nah 2:2). The assurance in 51:24 that Judah will see revenge against Babylon "before your very eyes" correlates strongly with Nahum picturing Nineveh's fall as a word of salvation to Judah, although Jeremiah stresses far more explicitly than Nahum that God first used the oppressor to punish Judah (Jer 51:5, 20). Like Nahum, Jer 51:15-16 links the theophany of the Divine Warrior with the fall of a specific wicked empire.

Other connections between Nahum and Jeremiah abound. Both picture the dead lying in the streets (Jer 51:4; Nah 3:3); shout imperatives to the armies (Jer 46:3-4, 9; 49:14, 28-29; 50:14, 26-27; 46:9; 51:8, 11, 12; Nah 2:1; 3:14-15); liken enemy troops to locusts (Jer 46:23; 51:14; Nah 3:15); describe the weakness of warriors as having "become women" (Jer 48:41; 49:22, 24; 50:43; 51:30; Nah 3:13); utilize lion imagery (Jer 49:19-20; 50:17, 44; 51:38; Nah 2:11-12); describe the chaos of war as drunkenness (Jer 48:26; 51:7, 39, 57; Nah 3:11); portray vanquished leaders as sleeping (Jer 51:39, 57; Nah 3:18); describe the oppressor's wound as incurable (Jer 51:8; Nah 3:19); and picture flood waters as symbolic of destruction (Jer 50:42; 51:36, 42, 44, 55; Nah 1:8; 2:6).

These connections between Nahum and Jeremiah do not necessarily argue for the dependence of one book upon the other. Rather, by highlighting the stock nature of the language employed by Nahum to describe the victory of the Divine Warrior, they strengthen the perception that Nah 2 is describing the invasion not of a human army, but instead that of the Divine Warrior. The cosmic Divine Warrior who marched to vanquish all foes and save all friends in 1:2-10 here fights an earthly battle against a particular enemy. Nineveh will be destroyed not by human hands, but by the vengeance of Yahweh.

The "his" of 2:3 likely refers to Assyrian king, given that the army described in 2:6 begins to stumble and that the verse refers to a defensive structure ("mantlet"). Dressed in impressive uniforms and equipped with calvary and chariots, the Assyrians scramble to defend Nineveh against the advance of Yahweh's troops.

The mention in 2:6 of the bursting of water gates is treated literally by some interpreters, based on the much later testimonies of Diodorus Siculus and Xenophonon that Nineveh fell by the flooding of its water supply. Parallels with similar documents, however, suggest that the imagery is metaphorical. In Jer 51, the fate of the city is described both as flooding (v. 42) and as drought (v. 43); and in the Mesopotamian Lament over the Destruction of Ur, that city's fall is described as a storm (Kramer 1940, lines 198-203). Moreover, the language of the theophany in Nah 1:8 attributes to the Divine Warrior the power of an overwhelming flood.

Nahum 2:7 has proved problematic for interpreters. The first two Hebrew words are *huṣṣab gullĕtâ*. The second verb clearly means "[she] is exiled," but translations of the first word *(huṣṣab)* range from the name of a princess (KJV) to "it is determined" (NRSV, NASB, NIV, NKJV). If the latter translation is adopted, then the "she" whose exile is determined is not specified. Although Sanderson (1992, 218) identifies "she" as Ishtar, the city goddess of Nineveh, a more logical identification is Nineveh itself, addressed with a feminine pronoun in 2:1 and named explicitly in 2:8. Various translations add a word to the verse to indicate that "she" is indeed Nineveh. RSV and NAB add "its mistress," and NIV and NRSV add "the city." No longer directly addressed, the feminine target of Yahweh's attack is now described in the third person, in a detached, distanced way.

The "you" of 2:13 is feminine singular. Given that the verse addresses punishment to this subject, the referent is likely the "she" of 2:7—that is, Nineveh. While Nah 1 and Nah 3 end with an announcement of punishment against the (masculine) king of Assyria, Nah 2 announces punishment on Nineveh itself.

Theological Analysis

Nahum 1:15–2:13 is powerful poetry. Although more evident in Hebrew, most English translations approximate its artfulness. The facetious imperatives addressed to the doomed Assyrian soldiers, the vivid colors of their uniforms, the variety of verbs describing the movement of the horses, the comparison of the women of the city to mourning doves and the city to receding water, the aggressive language of the invading army, the alliteration of language, the ironic treatment of Assyrian lion imagery, and the rhetorical, mocking questions thrown at Nineveh—all allow a reader to feel the scene described, to imagine a city in the process of being destroyed. Even those who decry the book as devoid of any valuable theology acknowledge its literary artistry.

For Wessels (1998), the power of the poetry is not an incidental feature of the book, but indeed a key to its meaning. He considers Nahum "resistance poetry." Like poetry arising from oppressed cultures such as South Africa under apartheid, its function is to produce an imaginative world that stands in opposition to the present one. Nahum's ability to evoke the sense of immediacy and bloody detail serves a political purpose: envisioning the possibility that Assyrian might can be broken by the power of God, Nahum offered to a downtrodden Judah hope and the will to resist Assyrian hegemony.

Wessel's approach, however, does not take into account the "dark side" of resistance movements, how oppressed groups treat their own causes as pristine and manifest little capacity for acknowledging their own acts of oppression. The tendency to reverse the tables, for the oppressed to fashion themselves after the image of their oppressors, is well documented in ancient and contemporary resistance movements. Ironically, Nahum's poetry reinforces the ideology of brutalization—the logic of retaliation. Even if Judah were in no position to exact the vengeance that is here imagined, the images are only comforting and hope producing because they so effectively reproduce the realities of war that the author—and the author's audience—must have suffered.

Although parenthetical in the structure of 1:15–2:13, verse 2 seems core to its ideology: the defeat (and, later in chapter 3, the humiliation) of Nineveh functions to restore the pride and honor of Jacob. Although Judah has been destroyed, it will be vindicated by the destruction of Nineveh; Judah will regain face from shame.

And yet, underlying the explicit attention to Judah and Nineveh, personified as females, is the concern with male honor. In 2:2, Judah's restoration serves to restore not her own honor but that of Jacob/Israel. Similarly, in the lion's den analogy in 2:1-13, the male lion is mocked for being unable to care for his den, an apparent analogy to the pending fate of the king of Assyria at the hands of Yahweh the Divine Warrior. For both the king of Assyria and Yahweh, the humiliation of the female is a matter of male shame.

Although Nineveh is personified as a woman in 1:15–2:13, she is addressed with no gender-specific derogatory language. This unit, however, sets the stage for the graphic violence against women that characterizes Nah 3. These issues—gender and violence—will dominate our attention in the following section.

AN ORACLE AGAINST NINEVEH (3:1-19)

Nahum 3 describes the assault of Nineveh in bold, often disturbing terms. It personifies Nineveh as a prostitute, brutally punished for her crimes, and raises contemporary concerns about the danger of gendered metaphors and of violent images in the Bible.

Literary Analysis

While chapter 3 continues the description of Yahweh's attack on Nineveh in chapter 2, it stands as a distinct unit, signaled by the "woe" that introduces the unit and by the intensification of derogatory language against Nineveh. Nahum 3 parallels Nah 2 in several ways.

Structurally, both chapters follow similar patterns. Each

begins with a description of the city's siege, stops to describe Nineveh in metaphorical terms, returns to the images of the siege, compares the Assyrians to animals, and ends with an announcement of disaster. The unit develops in this way:

3:1-3	Images of the city's destruction
3:4-7	Nineveh described as a prostitute
3:8-10	Nineveh compared to Thebes
3:11-17	Nineveh further threatened/taunted
3:18-19	King of Assyria taunted

Stylistically, the chapter uses many of the poetic features employed in chapter 2. The verbless sentences of Nah 3:1-3 (compare Nah 2:1) throw at the reader disjointed images of Nineveh's destruction without context; one of the most haunting verses of the book, 3:3 scatters "piles of dead, heaps of corpses, dead bodies without end!" Nahum 3:5 uses direct address to Nineveh, who is consistently described as a woman (compare Nah 2:1). Numerous comparisons, in the form of simile and metaphor are drawn: Nineveh is compared to Thebes, troops are like women, the army is called to become like locusts, the Assyrian leaders are shepherds, and the Assyrians themselves are like scattered sheep (compare the descriptions of Yahweh's army in 2:3-5). In an image frequent in the Prophets, Nineveh will reel as though drunk (Jer 13:13; 25:15-29; 48:26; 49:12; 51:7, 39; Obad 16; Hab 2:15-16; Zech 12:2; Lam 4:21; Ezek 23:31-34), and her fortresses will fall as easily as ripe figs fall to the ground.

The analogy drawn in 3:15b-17 explores various aspects of the locust. Locusts swarm in large numbers, underlying the ironic command for the Assyrians to multiply like locusts. Locusts shed their skin and quickly fly again, giving rise to the taunt that Assyrian guards are also undependable.

Thematically, Nah 3 repeats many of the motifs of Nah 2 (and Nah 1). The assault against Nineveh outlined in Nah 2 is again described, in greater detail and with more graphic violence; as earlier, the defenses of the city are described as vulnerable to invasion (cf. 2:6 and 3:12-13). Like Nah 1, chapter 3 ends with a taunt against the king of Assyria.

Like Nah 2, Nah 3 also personifies Nineveh as a woman. In its recapitulation, however, chapter 3 intensifies Nineveh's feminine personification. Here, Nineveh is not just a woman, but a *zônâ*—a prostitute. Her punishment is not just exile, but the sexual humiliation of a whore. Indeed, it is the graphic depiction of the punishment exacted against Nineveh that has attracted the most attention of contemporary commentators.

Exegetical Analysis

The term *zônâ* carries multiple nuances in the Hebrew Bible. Literally, it refers to a professional prostitute, one who receives money for sexual acts. The term describes the activities of Tamar (Gen 38) and Rahab (Josh 2), and its prohibition is paralleled with that of a male prostitute in Deut 23:18. Figuratively, however, *zônâ* refers to any promiscuous woman. In Deut 22:21, for example, a young woman found not to be a virgin is called a *zônâ*, and Ezek 23:3 uses the term to accuse young women of promiscuous behavior.

Its figurative sense of "promiscuity" extends further to describe religious unfaithfulness. In the Pentateuch, the Deuteronomistic History, and occasionally in the Psalms, verbal forms of *zānāh* describe the worship of deities other than Yahweh (Exod 34:5-16; Lev 20:5-6; Deut 31:16; Josh 2:1; Judg 2, 8; Pss 73, 106). In the prophetic literature, *zônâ* is used frequently in the marriage metaphor, in which God's relation to Israel/Judah is compared to a man's relation to his wife and in which religious unfaithfulness is compared to adultery. In Isa 57:3, Jer 3:8, and Hos 4:13-14, the roots *nāʾap* ("commit adultery") and *zānāh* stand in synonymous parallelism; and in the lengthy expositions of the metaphor in Ezek 16 and 23 and Hos 2, both charges are made against unfaithful women.

Such usages suggest that *zônâ* refers to any woman who does not meet societal expectations of sexual conduct. It serves to demean the object of scorn by equating him or her with a woman who sells her sexual services. Hence, although some interpreters have attempted to specify Nineveh's acts of promiscuity, identifying them as her treaties with multiple partners, the reference may be a slur more than an analogy. Nahum, having inherited the tradition of personifying cities as women, uses the culture's definition of the worst kind of woman—the whore—as an aspersion against Nineveh.

Although, by analogy, *zônâ* can be used for the activity of males (Israel/Judah and their male inhabitants can be accused of being [like] a *zônâ*), the slur is distinctively female in orientation. In a patriarchal society, a woman's sexuality is owned by her father until it is transferred to her husband; a man's sexuality is problematic only when its exercise threatens the sexual property of other males. Patriarchal marriage provides the context for the accusation of *zônâ*, as Bird explains: "*znh* is not used for incest or other prohibited relationships, such as homosexual relations or bestiality. It focuses on the absence of a marriage bond between otherwise acceptable partners" (1989, 90, n. 13).

The punishment that awaits the promiscuous Nineveh is outlined in 3:5-7. The first verb in 3:5 is usually translated as the "uncovering" of the skirt, although the verbal root *gāḥāḥ* is the same one in 2:7, translated in the NRSV as "exile." The exposure of a woman's genitalia as a means of humiliation is well known from the prophetic literature, as in Isa 47:2-3 in which daughter Babylon is stripped and humiliated and in Hos 2:2-3 in which stripping is preliminary to the death of the woman. "Uncovering" also often carries the sense of sexual violation: in Lev 18:18, it is paralleled with taking a woman as rival to her sister; in the description of Israel's whoring in Ezek 16:36, it is paralleled with the outpouring of lust; and in Jer 13:22, Judah is not only exposed, but also "violated."

Significantly, it is Yahweh who exacts this punishment on Nineveh. Yahweh is imaged as a man who sexually humiliates Nineveh in return for her promiscuity, as other nations, imaged as men, gaze at her nakedness so that she becomes a "spectacle"—something to observe. Yahweh throws excrement on her and despises her. This motif of a woman—described as both attractive and a whore, being sexually humiliated while others watch—is one known from pornographic literature; some feminist scholars, in turn, have designated these biblical passages as "pornoprophetics." Different from most prophetic literature, however, Nahum directs the punishment of one called a whore against a nation other than Israel or Judah. Uniquely here, Yahweh punishes the promiscuity of one with whom he is not in covenant/marriage relationship.

The taunt of Nineveh in 3:8-12 compares her to another humiliated female character: Thebes, a well-defended Egyptian city conquered by the Assyrian king Ashurbanipal in 663 B.C.E. As traced in the introduction, the mention of Thebes's fall as having already taken place is often seen as a clue to the dating of Nahum, given the assumption that a human author cannot write before an event that is described as having taken place in the past.

The phrase "gates are wide open to your foes" in 3:13 may be a *double entendre,* promising the horror of sexual violation: Magdalene, for example, translates "gates" as "vagina," read in conjunction with Isa 3:26 (1995, 333). Sanderson, who explains both the social setting from which the rape/war connection arises and its problematic character for modern readers, highlights the irony of this passage: Assyria's brutal warfare was perpetuated by men, and when women were involved at all they were victims (1992, 219).

Attention turns away from Nineveh in 3:18-19 to the king of Assyria, referred to in the masculine singular. The leaders of Assyria are described as shepherds, common Near Eastern vocabulary for describing those charged with oversight of the population. Ironically, the king who is described as a predator in 2:11 is mocked in 3:18 for having shepherds who slumber; the one whose people are described in 3:18 as scattered sheep is depicted in 2:12 as bringing strangled prey into the den.

For any reader, the literary style of Nah 3:1-3 captures the horror of mass death. For ancient readers, the image may have been additionally brutal: ancient Near Eastern treaty curses threatened that those who broke agreements would suffer the shame of unburied bodies; and biblical narratives such as that of the deaths of Saul and Jezebel underscore the shame of not having a decent burial.

Theological Analysis

Women and Metaphor

This section is perhaps the most disturbing in the book of Nahum, due to the graphic detail in which Nineveh's destruction is described and, at least for some readers, to the sexual violence envisioned. Recognizing that the one who lifts up the skirts and invites others to gaze at the woman's body is God adds to the "burden" of reading.

Not surprisingly, women readers and male readers who can imaginatively read as women find this language especially horrific. As Exum (1995) has explained, the "politics of identification" leaves women readers of these images in a double bind: on the one hand, they are expected to identify with God's perspective, which for women means a vicarious participation in violence against women/themselves; and on the other, when women feel sympathy for or identify with the woman in the text, they place themselves in solidarity with an object of abuse and shame.

For the metaphor of "Nineveh the Justly Punished Whore" to be effective, readers have to share several assumptions with the author:

> that prostitutes are seductive, enticing men to act
> against their will;
> that a woman's choice of partners is not hers to
> make; and
> that sexual violence is proper punishment for
> perceived improper sexual behavior.

Many modern readers do not share these assumptions. Particularly, contemporary views of rape and domestic violence posit that no behavior justifies physical abuse, and sociological studies of prostitution demonstrate how often the practice itself arises out of and perpetuates the victimization of women (for a fuller discussion of these issues, see O'Brien 2002).

Nahum's image of Nineveh the Prostitute, then, confronts the modern reader with the larger question of how to read and appropriate biblical metaphors (for God, for nations) that arise from cultural assumptions that they do not wish to perpetuate. Does continuing to use the language of "whore" for Nineveh reinforce the notions that women's sexuality is dangerous and that it deserves violent punishment? At the very least, recognizing the cultural assumptions of ancient Israel may help our contemporary readers recognize their own. It is not only in the book of Nahum that anger burns away "polite" facades of civility to expose the bedrock of assumptions about women (and minorities and all "others"), mediated through slurs and fantasies of others' suffering.

Revenge and Retaliation

The fundamental belief that brutality is deserving of brutal punishment runs throughout the book of Nahum. The opening theophany praises God's power by offering assurances that God can vanquish enemies; the repeated contrasting fates of Judah and Nineveh promise that the punishment of God's enemies is inevitable; and the punishment of Nineveh the Whore assumes that sexual impropriety is deserving of sexual violence. The book ends on this note as well, reminding the reader that Nineveh's treatment is the punishment for Assyria's endless cruelty: "All who hear the news about you clap their hands over you. For who has ever escaped your endless cruelty?" (Nah 3:19).

The definition of justice as avenging wrongdoing by exacting equivalent punishment—"the punishment fitting the crime"—is, indeed, one of the most consistent ideologies of the Hebrew Bible. It undergirds the legal reasoning of the Pentateuch, for which payment is made "eye for eye" *(lex talionis)*; the Deuteronomistic History's presentation of God's work in history, in which Israel's and Judah's falls are explained as just punishment for their idolatries; the piety of the Psalms, in which worshipers ask for vindication against enemies; and, most especially, the theology of the Prophets, in which Judah and foreign nations are punished for their crimes.

This theology of repayment is both familiar and also acceptable to many modern readers. It forms the basis for certain Christian understandings of Jesus' atonement and provides the conceptual frame for many interpersonal relationships.

For other readers, such thinking is problematic. The mentality of revenge feeds a never-ending cycle of brutality, as a century of conflict between Albanians and Serbs, Tutsis and Hutus, Israelis and Palestinians attests. Even if Nahum is imaginative literature and even if its focus is on God's action and not that of humans, it nonetheless relies on the ideology of revenge to offer good news and comfort.

Simply dismissing Nahum as morally inferior, however, fails to take seriously the way in which this book is itself a response to human suffering. No one can deny the cruelty of the Assyrians, the terror that they carefully manufactured, the lives that they took.

In 1962, the Jewish theologian Abraham Heschel argued that God's anger against injustice is a sign of God's goodness, that a God who cares about humanity must be angered at its suffering. According to Heschel, the prophets perceived God's wrath not as a fundamental characteristic of God, but as a temporary response to human sin—humans provoke God's anger and humans can choose not to provoke God's anger. Indeed, Heschel quotes a rabbinic commentary on Nahum to underscore his point: "The Lord must punish, but He will not destroy, for He is the master of His anger [Nah 1:2], in control of His anger" (Heschel 1962, 294). To dismiss Nahum, according to Heschel, would be to dismiss the belief that God cares about injustice.

> The message of wrath is frightful indeed. But for those who have been driven to the brink of despair by the sight of what malice and ruthlessness can do, comfort will be found in the thought that evil is not the end, that evil is never the climax of history. (Heschel 1962, 284)

Perhaps what is problematic about Nahum, then, is not its

attribution of anger to God, but rather how the book envisions God's *expression* of that anger. Difficult to embrace is the apparent pleasure the author takes in imaging the pain of Nineveh—reproducing a picture of a pile of corpses like an impassive death camp photographer, registering no horror that, like the children of Thebes, the children of Nineveh will be smashed against a rock, gazing along with the nations at Nineveh's nakedness. None of the pathos of God is directed to the slaughter of the average Assyrian man, woman, and child—complicit or not with Assyrian imperial policy.

A balanced ethical response to the book of Nahum is a simultaneous yes and no—yes to the belief that tyrants stand under the judgment of God and no to taking pleasure in sexual violation, humiliation, and death, and no to any response to evil—including the reader's own—that perpetuates the very ideology of brutality that it seeks to oppose.

INTRODUCTION: HABAKKUK

In moving from Nahum to Habakkuk, the reader makes several shifts. The historical situation is no longer the period of Assyrian oppression, but that of Babylonian (Chaldean) control. The tone is no longer one of bold confidence that God will destroy the wicked, but one of pointed skepticism about God's justice and care. Underlying both books, however, is the desire to understand God's response to oppression and the conviction that, ultimately, the Divine Warrior will march on Judah's behalf.

The book of Habakkuk has engendered much scholarly debate. Both ancient and modern translators have struggled with numerous words and phrases, and scholars have suggested various paths by which the book took its current shape. Most of all, liturgical features within the book (especially the musical notations in chapter 3) have led to various understandings of the relation between prophecy and corporate worship in ancient Judah.

Despite these contested features, however, Habakkuk communicates in an accessible, contemporary way. Its topic is a timeless one: how can God be understood as just and caring if the wicked prosper? Although Habakkuk poses this question of theodicy within a concrete historical situation—the oppression of the Babylonians—it has remained poignantly relevant in various situations of hopelessness and despair.

LITERARY ANALYSIS

The book may be outlined as follows:

1:1	Superscription	
1:2-17	Encounter between the prophet and Yahweh	
	1:2-4	The prophet speaks
	1:5-11	Yahweh speaks
	1:12-17	The prophet speaks
2:1-20	Another encounter between Yahweh and the prophet	
	2:1	The test
	2:2-5	Yahweh's response
	2:6-20	Yahweh's response, extended: five woes to the wicked

	2:6-8	Woe
	2:9-11	Woe
	2:12-14	Woe
	2:15-17	Woe
	2:18-20	Woe

3:1-19	Prayer of the prophet	
	3:1	Superscription
	3:2	The prophet's petition
	3:3-15	The march of the Divine Warrior
	3:16-19	The prophet's response, ending with a psalm-like subscription

One of the most striking features of the book of Habakkuk is its autobiographical style. In most prophetic books, the personality of the prophet is obscured behind his role as Yahweh's messenger: the prophet speaks for God, his speech punctuated by "thus says Yahweh." In Habakkuk, however, the prophet begins speaking in the first-person singular immediately after the superscription: "How long, Yahweh, shall I cry?" Indeed, the prophet consistently speaks in his own voice throughout the book. It is a style that Habakkuk shares with the psalms of individual lament (for example, Ps 22) and with the book of Job, as well as with the confessions of Jeremiah (Jer 11:18–12:6; 15:10-21; 17:14-18; 18:18-23; 20:7-18).

In the case of the book of Jeremiah, Terence Collins (1993, 118) has well argued that the "personal" nature of the book is the result of conscious redactional crafting of the book and cannot be taken as evidence that the reader has been given a snapshot of the "historical" Jeremiah. Robert Carroll has gone as far as claiming that Jeremiah is a fictional character created for the purposes of the book (Carroll 1988, 25). The "personal" style of Habakkuk, similarly, is not necessarily an indication that the book has preserved the actual words and thoughts of the historical prophet. The *literary* effect of the autobiographical style, nonetheless, is important. This style imbues Habakkuk with the poignancy of personal struggle, creating the sense that we are hearing the heartfelt dilemmas of an individual.

In Habakkuk, however, the personal is also the communal. The prophet is shown as caring about the cosmic nature of evil, as in the general complaint about the fate of humans in 1:14, and God's responses to the prophet extend beyond the problem of the Chaldeans to address the larger fate of the proud in 2:4-5. The prophet also seems to speak for the community, posing not individual complaints, but concerns about the fate of his people.

The dialogical style of the book also grants it a sense of immediacy. The prophet complains; God responds; the prophet continues to complain. Although the book does end on a confident note, the prophet is not silenced by God, as is the central character in the book of Job.

Whether chapters 1 and 2 technically constitute a dialogue is debated. Floyd, for example, has argued that the prophet's complaint in 1:2-4 only makes sense if it is in response to the claims that the deity makes in 1:5-11 (2000, 95-96). He suggests that 1:2-4 is Habakkuk's response to a prophecy that is quoted in 1:5-11. Floyd is correct in pointing out the problematic relationship between 1:2-4 and 1:5-11, but calling Habakkuk dialogical is nonetheless in order. The first two chapters are structured according to alternating speakers, incorporating two voices.

Although in chapter 1 the prophet speaks at length, the voice of Yahweh predominates in chapter 2. Following the vision that Yahweh grants in 2:1-4, the "woe" (NRSV: "alas!") oracles that run from 2:6-20 elaborate upon Yahweh's perspective on the wicked.

In Hab 3, the question about God's justice culminates in an appeal for God to march as the great Warrior; just as the deity conquered the forces of chaos in the past, so too the prophet calls Yahweh to act again on the people's behalf. The musical notation that begins and ends the chapter may bear clues for its historical background, but of equal importance is the literary effect of the piece. Habakkuk's final response to Yahweh is not argument, but prayer; and his hope comes as much from remembering what God has done in the past as from concrete promises for the future.

SOCIAL AND HISTORICAL ANALYSIS

The superscription to Habakkuk gives no indications of its historical setting, though the book is usually dated to the seventh century B.C.E. based on the reference to the power of the Chaldeans in 1:6. The Chaldeans, a population group in southern Mesopotamia, rose to prominence under Nabopolassar, who defeated the Assyrians in 626 and founded the neo-Babylonian or Chaldean empire. In the seventh and sixth centuries, "Chaldean" and "Babylonian" were virtually interchangeable terms, as seen in the synonymous usage of the terms in Isa 47:1 and Jer 25:12.

Judah began paying tribute to Babylonia after the latter's decisive victory against the Egyptians at Carchemish in 605. In 601, however, the Judean king Jehoiakim rebelled against Babylonian control in favor of Egypt, contrary to the advice of the prophet Jeremiah; and, in response, the Babylonians attacked Jerusalem in 597 and deported the royal family and prominent citizens. Although the next Judean king, Zedekiah, initially supported Babylonian rule, his eventual revolt led to the return of the Babylonian armies, who destroyed Jerusalem in 587 or 586 and put an end to the Judean state.

Precisely when in the neo-Babylonian period Habakkuk is set

remains unclear and is related to the contested interpretation of Hab 1:2-4 (as noted above). If Habakkuk's initial complaint is about the cruelty of the Babylonians themselves, then a date after Babylonian control of Judah is indicated (after 605). If, however, the prophet refers to another domestic or international enemy from whom the Babylonians are offered as relief, then the identity of the original enemy would determine the setting of the passage: if the original enemy was the Assyrians, a date prior to the fall of Nineveh in 612 is in order; if the Egyptians, who were heavily involved in the power struggles between the Assyrians and Babylonians, then a date of 609–605 is likely.

Haak sets Habakkuk between 605 and 603, when tensions between those Judeans encouraging alliance with Egypt and those touting a pro-Babylonian policy were high. Tracing in Habakkuk the same pro-Babylonian stance as Jeremiah, Haak argues that the enemy of Habakkuk is an internal one—the Judean king Jehoiakim and his pro-Egyptian supporters. Indeed, Haak sees the entire book as concerned with this Judean enemy, in contrast to most interpreters who see Habakkuk protesting the wickedness of the Babylonians (beginning either in 1:2 or in 1:12) (Haak 1992, 111-49).

The debates about the identity of the "enemy" in Habakkuk (always the Babylonians? always the Judean king? first the Judean monarch and then the Babylonians?) are fueled by the generic nature of Habakkuk's rhetoric. Apart from the mention of the Chaldeans in 1:6, references remain to the "wicked," to "destruction" and "violence" (1:3), and to the perversion of justice (1:4)—terms all sufficiently elastic to describe a variety of internal and external crises in Judah. Indeed, this generic style is one of the features that allows Habakkuk to communicate powerfully at different times and places.

Parts of the book of Habakkuk assume the shape of literary forms that appear elsewhere in the Old Testament in connection with corporate worship. Most striking is the beginning and ending of Hab 3, which give it the form of a psalm. The superscription sounds much like that of Ps 7, both in linking the psalm to an individual personality and in indicating that its musical setting is *šigyōnôt;* and the subscription bears features of Ps 6, in being addressed to the music leader and in calling for stringed instruments.

Chapters 1 and 2 may also bear features of corporate worship. Numerous psalms of lament begin with "How long?" (Pss 13, 35, 74; cf. Hab 1:2), and Haak has pointed to other structural similarities between Habakkuk and this genre of psalm, finding, for example, two cycles of Invocation and Complaint, an Oracle of Salvation, Expression of Certainty, and Hymnic Elements (Haak 1992, 13-16).

Do these *literary* features indicate that the book derives from the *social setting* of the Temple? The very idea of a "cult prophet" (defined as one who works within the structures of Israel's religious or governmental institutions) goes against the common understanding of prophets as "outsiders" who criticized religious and political institutions. Prophets, however, are depicted in the Old Testament in a wide range of roles, and figures such as Nathan (2 Sam 7, 12; 1 Kgs 1) and Haggai are shown as working within institutional structures. Was Habakkuk a "cult prophet," leading his community in lament of its fate? Does the book preserve a liturgy used in corporate worship?

Although such a scenario certainly is possible, the book provides little basis on which to confirm the suggestion. Recent work in form criticism has well demonstrated that prophets use a variety of literary styles that may evoke the feeling of a particular setting: the use of the lament form may be a literary device, as much as the indicator of a particular social location. At the very least, the book of Habakkuk links prophecy and worship literarily and uses the style of worship forms to communicate the profundity of the prophet's lament.

THEOLOGICAL ANALYSIS

Theodicy, a primary theme of the book of Habakkuk, is a problem more often addressed in the biblical Wisdom literature than in prophecy. Most prophecy defends the justice of God, insisting that Israel's and Judah's tribulations are God's punishment for their wrongdoings. Like the books of the Deuteronomistic History (Joshua–Kings), the prophets claim that Yahweh rewards the righteous. In its complaint that the righteous do not always prosper, the book of Habakkuk expresses a view more common to Ecclesiastes and Job than to Isaiah and Amos.

At first glance, Habakkuk seems very different from Nahum, which precedes it in the canon. Nahum is very clear about the identity of the wicked and the righteous and in its certainty that God will punish the wicked; the author revels in imagining the nature of that punishment. Habakkuk defines the wicked and the righteous in much fuzzier terms, complaining that even God is not clear on the distinction between the two.

The apparent differences between Habakkuk and Nahum, however, obscure their common underlying concern. Both express the confidence that God will act. Both imagine God as a Divine Warrior who will trample foes. And, importantly, both attempt to defend God's justice. The very confidence with which Nahum depicts God's defeat of Nineveh arises from the perceived need to convince those who doubt God's power and care. Both Nahum and Habakkuk affirm God to the skeptical.

The theme of theodicy grants Habakkuk a contemporary feel. Readers reeling from the Holocaust, from the ethnic wars of the twentieth century, and from the seemingly intractable violence of the twenty-first century can find common voice with the prophet's cry: "Justice never prevails. The wicked surround the righteous—therefore judgment comes forth perverted" (1:4). Readers in the past have also found Habakkuk meaningful to their own struggles. The pesher of Habakkuk, a commentary on the book found at Qumran, interpreted the text as about the author's own day in a direct and immediate way: the "wicked" was the "wicked priest" (perhaps Jonathan or Simon from the Maccabean family), and the "righteous" was the community's own revered teacher (see Horgan 1979).

Habakkuk's "answer" to the problem of injustice is often seen in 2:4: the righteous will live by living faithfully and patiently. But the style of Habakkuk suggests another "answer" as well: Habakkuk gives not only permission, but also the words, for believers to complain and question, to petition God to act on behalf of the oppressed.

COMMENTARY: HABAKKUK

SUPERSCRIPTION (1:1)

In a short, simple phrase, the introduction to the book of Habakkuk indicates that what follows is an oracle that the prophet saw. Using standard prophetic vocabulary, it stresses the divine origin of the message.

Literary Analysis

Habakkuk and Nahum are the only two prophetic books of which the superscriptions describe the material to follow as an "oracle" *(maśśāʾ)* that the prophet has "seen" *(ḥāzāh;* Nahum uses the noun form *ḥāzôn).* As suggested in the commentary to Nah 1:1, the use of the term "vision" does not necessarily indicate that the material was received visually; rather, the term is often used synonymously with "prophecy." In the case of Habakkuk, however, the visual component of the received message is underscored by the reappearance of *ḥāzôn* in 2:3, in which Yahweh instructs the prophet to write down the vision.

Unlike Nahum, Habakkuk is designated as a prophet. Although Habakkuk's is not the only superscription to make the prophetic role explicit (Haggai and Zechariah are also called prophets in their superscriptions), it is fitting that a book in which the prophetic personality is so prominent should call attention to the prophetic role early on.

Exegetical Analysis

No information about Habakkuk's family background, geographical location, or time period is given. He is known only by his title and by his name, which may be related to the Hebrew root *ḥābaq*, which means to clasp or embrace.

The name does not appear elsewhere in the Bible. The prophet is mentioned in the Greek version of the book of Daniel (a portion also known as Bel and the Dragon), where he is transported to Babylon to feed Daniel in the lion's den.

Theological Analysis

Like other prophetic books, Habakkuk presents divine communication as revealed through an individual, historically specific human. By stressing Habakkuk's role as a prophet, the superscription highlights the mediating function of prophecy: prophets speak not only for themselves, but also for God. Thus, all that is to follow in the body of the book is framed not as the prophet's own idiosyncratic complaint, but rather as a message from God to humans.

ENCOUNTER BETWEEN THE PROPHET AND YAHWEH (1:2-17)

After the superscription, the book of Habakkuk turns immediately to the prophet's complaint that God is silent in the face of violence. In the ensuing dialogue, God claims that the Babylonians act at divine command, and Habakkuk further challenges God's justice.

Literary Analysis

This first encounter between the prophet and Yahweh is structured as a dialogue, initiated and concluded by the prophet:

1:2-4	The prophet speaks
1:5-11	Yahweh speaks
1:12-17	The prophet speaks

The encounter begins with the prophet's abrupt address of Yahweh. This style is unexpected in a prophetic book. Other prophetic books present the prophet as one caught off guard by a revelation from Yahweh and compelled to speak on the deity's behalf; predominantly, prophets utter divine oracles and use the form of messenger speech ("thus says Yahweh"), speaking *for* God. In contrast, Habakkuk is presented as initiating an encounter with the Divine and speaking, in a bold way, to (and even against) God.

In 1:2-4, the prophet complains that the deity is apathetic toward injustice. The first two verses are in the form of questions: "How long will I cry and God be silent?" and "Why does God cause me to see trouble?" The questions are followed with a declarative indictment: justice is "bent" (AT).

Although Yahweh speaks in 1:5, the deity does not respond on the terms set by the prophet in 1:2-4. Habakkuk had framed his complaint as an individual one ("How long shall *I* cry for help?"; "Why do you cause *me* to see trouble?"), yet the imperatives in 1:5 are common plural, addressing a broader audience than the prophet. Similarly, the deity offers no self-defense against the prophet's original complaint but instead announces a new turn of events. God is rousing the Babylonians, who are described as bitter and "hurrying" (NRSV: "impetuous"), those who take possession of that which belongs to others. Beginning in the second half of 1:6 and continuing throughout this unit, the Babylonians are described with the singular masculine pronoun "he" (NRSV: "they"), leading some interpreters to suggest that the king of Babylon is being described, even though the personification of a nation as an individual is also a reasonable explanation of the form.

Yahweh's response is generally understood to continue through 1:11. Haak, on the contrary, maintains that the deity's speech stops with 1:6 and that the prophet resumes the address at 1:7 (Haak 1992, 14), based in part on a particular reading of 1:7. In the middle of 1:7, the Hebrew text reads *mimmennû,* which can mean either "from us" or "from him." Most translations, including the NRSV, take the second translational option and connect it with the second part of the verse: "their justice and dignity proceed from themselves" (making "him" plural). Haak instead translates "from us" and links it with the first part of the verse: "He is terrible and fearful *against us*." This reading leads Haak to see 1:7 as the resumption of the prophet's speech, complaining about the fierceness of the Babylonians (Haak 1992, 41).

Haak's interpretation, however, does not account for the nature of the prophetic response in 1:12 to what has just been said. Understanding 1:7-11 as Yahweh's voice highlights the shocking nature of the deity's response. By underscoring the rapaciousness of Babylon, its disregard for others, and its worship of its own might, the speech intensifies rather than solves the prophet's problem.

The third speech of the cycle, 1:12-17, does seem to respond to the speech that has preceded it. Although the prophet's first complaint protested wickedness in a general way, this second complaint speaks often of "him," likely referring to the Babylonians of 1:5-11; that is, the prophet now protests the unsatisfactory nature of Yahweh's response.

Habakkuk 1:12 is usually read as a series of affirmations of Yahweh: Yahweh is eternal and will (eventually) punish the Babylonians. The verse may also be read, however, as the prelude to the complaints that follow in 1:13-17: (1) Yahweh does not have to worry about dying, as humans do, and thus seems removed from human pain; and (2) rather than being marked as *objects* for judgment, the Babylonians have been appointed *for carrying out* justice and as the *agents* of rebuke, which leads the prophet to protest the use of a wicked nation as an agent of punishment.

The prophet's use of ʾādām (humankind) extends concern to the broader human condition, though the enemy is still described as "he." In contrast to the image in Gen 1 of humans as having dominion over the fish of the sea and the creeping things of the earth, humans here are shown as fish caught in a net. "He" (likely still the Babylonians) ensnares all of the earth and worships his own net (1:16), just as he does his own might (1:11).

The literary device of comparison is used frequently in this unit. In 1:8, horses are swifter than leopards and keener than wolves; horsemen fly like eagles. In 1:9, captives are gathered like sand. In 1:14-17, the comparison of humans to fish caught in a net provides a haunting image of helplessness and pending doom.

Exegetical Analysis

The primary question in this unit is about whom the prophet is complaining. Is the prophet complaining about the same problem in both of his speeches? Who is the "wicked" of whom he speaks?

Perhaps the most common way of understanding the book suggests that Habakkuk initially complains about an enemy other than the Babylonians but then laments the Babylonians after God's announcement in 1:5-11 of their role in the divine plan. The initial wicked one is sometimes identified as the Assyrians or Egyptians but most often as the Judean monarch. Hiebert, for example, identifies the corrupt Judean king as Jehoiakim, who is also criticized in 2 Kgs 23 and in the book of Jeremiah and whose rule was overturned by the Babylonians (Hiebert 1996, 631). The complaint in 1:4 that Torah is perverted (NRSV: "law") resonates well with the identification of the enemy as Judean. According to Hiebert, God's plan to rouse the Babylonians leads to a second complaint: that the means by which God responds to the initial oppressor is equally problematic.

Haak also sees the enemy of 1:2-4 as Jehoiakim, but he argues that the entire book addresses the Judean ruler and the international powers that supported him—especially Assyria and Egypt (Haak 1992, 134). The prophet's second complaint elaborates on the first, by critiquing the supporters of the king.

Floyd, on the contrary, believes that the entire book addresses the oppression of the Babylonians. The unit is not a sequential dialogue, he maintains, but rather the prophet's complaint about a prior prophecy regarding the Babylonians, which is quoted in

1:5-11. For him, 1:5-11 is the basis for the prophet's complaint, not God's response to it (Floyd 2000, 95-96).

As suggested in the introduction, these various interpretations arise because of the general and elastic nature of Habakkuk's language. The "wicked" and the "righteous" can refer to internal and external enemies; many historical settings could be described as those of "violence" and "contention." This unit exacerbates the problem further, however, by sending mixed signals about the object of its scorn. On the one hand, the two complaints (1:2-4 and 1:12-17) use much of the same language: both lament God's silence, speak of the "wicked" and the "righteous," and even use the same word to describe God's "looking" on oppression (*tabbîṭ* 1:3 and 1:13). In many ways, the second complaint sounds repetitive of the first, suggesting that the intervening speech of Yahweh is irrelevant to the prophet's monologue. On the other hand, certain features of the second complaint seem to depend upon Yahweh's speech in 1:5-11. The third-person masculine subject ("he") that appears in 1:12 (NRSV: "them") and 1:15 (NRSV: "the enemy") relies on the identification of "him" as the Babylonians in 1:5-11, and the description of the fisher making sacrifices to his net in 1:16 resonates with the description of the Babylonians as worshiping their own might in 1:11.

Perhaps even more important for the reader, Yahweh's description of the Babylonians in 1:5-11 itself marks them as wicked. They come for violence (1:9), just as the prophet complained about violence in 1:2. Having learned from Yahweh that the Babylonians are fierce and violent, it is hard not to think of the Babylonians when the prophet resumes his complaint about violence. The second complaint has ties both to the first complaint and to the new information that God shares about the Babylonians.

These multiple resonances suggest that the speeches of the prophet and Yahweh are not a direct dialogue—one speaking, the other offering a direct response. Rather, somewhat like the speeches of Job, each articulates a position that resonates in indirect ways with the surrounding material.

What are the implications of these observations for understanding the social and historical setting of Habakkuk? At the very least, they caution against overconfidence in any historical reconstruction. The general nature of the descriptions and the various internal resonances, whether the intention of the original author or the result of the book's transmission, serve to prioritize the larger theme of evil rather than any particular form that evil might take.

The translational issues of the unit also complicate its interpretation. The second phrase of 1:9 is difficult to translate. The noun that stands in construct to "faces" is *měgammat,* found nowhere else in the Hebrew Bible. The NASB translates the phrase as "their horde of faces," though many translations ignore *měgammat* altogether. The final word of the phrase can mean "eastward" or "forward," such that NJB reads "their faces scorching like an east wind" and RSV reads "with faces pressing forward."

Several verses use unexpected pronouns. In 1:3, the MT reads, "Why do you cause me to see trouble and *you* regard toil?" By omitting the subject of the second verb, NRSV implies that the *prophet* is the one who regards toil. In 1:6-8, singular and plural pronouns alternate in the description of the Chaldeans, though the NRSV smoothes over this difficulty by consistently using the plural.

The most famous case of pronoun shift in Habakkuk is in 1:12. Rabbinic writings report that the original reading of "*you* shall not die" was altered to "*we* shall not die," one example of ancient emendations called *tikkunim sopherim,* or "restorations of the scribes." The pious change would have avoided the very possibility of God's death or, as Floyd suggests, remedied the sarcasm of the statement (Floyd 2000, 108). The NRSV retains the original text ("you will not die"), while the majority of modern translations read with the scribes ("we will not die"). The NAB omits the phrase completely.

The form of this unit has been variously assessed. Hiebert draws connections between 1:2-4 and 1:12–2:1 and the psalms of lament, and he identifies 1:5-11 as a prophetic announcement of judgment (Hiebert 1996, 630-38). Other commentators have described the whole unit as a communal liturgy of lament, suggesting the social setting of the Temple. As Floyd well argues, however, the style of lament does not necessarily point to a single social setting, since prophets could imitate liturgical forms and since the ritualized, predictable outcome of the psalm of lament finds no parallel in Habakkuk's open-ended complaint (Floyd 2000, 99). That is, Habakkuk's use of forms from the Temple liturgy does not indicate that the book was itself used in the Temple.

Theological Analysis

From start to finish, Hab 1 is concerned with the question of theodicy. Why is there injustice in the world if God is good and God is powerful? The prophet never questions the assumptions that underlie his concern; he does not question the existence of God, the power of God, or even the goodness of God. Rather, the prophet questions God's *willingness* to act.

That God does not directly answer the prophet's charges, but rather announces the appearance of the "fierce" Babylonians, may disturb some readers. God offers no self-defense, and, in fact, God's speech never explicitly claims that the Babylonians are the answer to Habakkuk's initial complaint. The prophet draws that conclusion in 1:12, but God's description of the Babylonians is one of terror, not comfort. Habakkuk does not present a God who immediately and compassionately responds to human cries of pain.

In both form and content, this unit speaks both to individual injustice and to the issues of the community. Although the prophet appears to speak on his own behalf, God's response is communal, and the comparison of humans to fish caught in a net indicates that the issues are broader than those of individual suffering.

Habakkuk 1 models the acceptability of protest, even—perhaps especially—to God. God may not answer Habakkuk's complaint directly, but neither does God chastise Habakkuk for voicing it.

ANOTHER ENCOUNTER BETWEEN YAHWEH AND THE PROPHET (2:1-20)

The prophet again confronts God, demanding a response to perceived injustice. Yahweh replies with assurances of comfort and of punishment for the wicked.

Literary Analysis

Like chapter 1, chapter 2 begins with the prophet's initiative. *He* determines to wait for Yahweh's response and to decide if the divine answer is acceptable. Yahweh does respond, although, as before, refusing to answer the prophet's complaints directly. The unit then turns to a series of "woes" against the wicked and ends with a call to recognize the power of Yahweh.

The unit may be outlined as follows:

2:1	The test
2:2-5	Yahweh's response
2:6-20	Yahweh's response, extended: five woes to the wicked
2:6-8	Woe
2:9-11	Woe
2:12-14	Woe
2:15-17	Woe
2:18-20	Woe

The literary setting of the unit is that of the military watch-post. The expression "my watchpost" depicts the prophet as a sentinel, and the parallel term "rampart" (or better, "siege-works") evokes the sense of a city in distress, under attack. The language of Yahweh's response also draws from the world of military communications: the vision that Yahweh will reveal is to be made legible to a runner, the information-bearer of armies and kings. As in Isa 21, the prophet is one who scans the horizon for information; but although in Isaiah the watcher strains to learn of the fate of Babylon, in Habakkuk the prophet awaits— and actively seeks—the word of Yahweh.

In response to Habakkuk, the deity promises a *ḥāzôn*, a "vision" (2:2). This noun is often used elsewhere for prophecy and derives from the same root as *ḥāzāh* ("see"), used in the superscription of Habakkuk ("the oracle that the prophet Habakkuk saw"). Habakkuk 2:2-3 sets the stage for Yahweh's reply, explaining the nature of the vision to come. What remains unclear is whether the deity's speech moves from preliminary instructions to the actual content of the vision. Specifically, does the call to steadfastness in 2:4 (translation discussed below) (1) constitute the *answer* to Habakkuk, or does it (2) encourage the prophet to *continue waiting* for the divine response?

Whereas Floyd (2000, 123) and the majority of interpreters follow the first of these options, Roberts argues for the second. His translation of 2:3-4 is as follows:

> For the vision is a witness to the appointed time;
> It is a testifier to the end, and it does not lie.
> If it seems slow, wait for it.
> For it will surely come; it will not delay.
> Now the fainthearted, his soul will not walk in it,
> But the righteous person will live by its faithfulness.
> (Roberts 1991, 105)

Roberts argues that 2:2-4 recounts the prophet's reception of a vision, the content of which is revealed in chapter 3. While the translational basis for this interpretation will be discussed below, his understanding well accounts for the general nature of the unit—the way in which it does not answer the prophet's complaint. As in chapter 1, Yahweh speaks at the prophet's instigation, but the divine reply does not directly answer the hard questions about justice that the prophet has posed.

In 2:4-5, Yahweh ironically calls the prophet to recognize the very truth that he has complained of being unable to see: that the arrogant falter and will not endure. Yahweh's attempt to provide comfort by underscoring that the arrogant gather nations for themselves (2:5) is likewise ironic, since it mirrors the description of the Chaldeans whom Yahweh is arousing ("who march through the breadth of the earth to seize dwellings not their own," 1:6).

Habakkuk 2:6-17 expands upon Yahweh's description of the dismal fate of the wicked in a series of five "woes." All use the Hebrew term *hôy* (NRSV: "alas"), the first four in their opening verses (2:6b, 9, 12, 15), and the fifth in the midst of the subunit (2:19). The implied speaker of the woes is "everyone" (2:6). These speeches are presented as the common perspective of all people: all recognize the folly of the arrogant.

Like the earlier speeches of Yahweh, the woes respond *generally* to complaints that the prophet has expressed *specifically*. In its concern with lending practices, the first woe does not immediately fit the Babylonian context, though the plundering of nations mentioned in 2:8 resonates well with Babylonian oppression. Similarly, the second woe could apply to enemies either internal or external to Judah, in its concern both with houses built by iniquity and with "cutting off many peoples" (2:10). The metaphor of drunkenness in 2:15 is common to prophetic rhetoric, as is the image in 2:16 of God's wrath as a cup to be drunk. Habakkuk 2:15-16 bears many similarities with Obad 15-17 and with the parallel oracle against Edom in Jer 49:7-22, in which Edom will be punished in kind for its treachery, will drink the cup of God's wrath, and will be stripped bare. The complaint in Hab 2:9 that the arrogant set their nest in high places also finds parallel in Jer 49:16 and Obad 3-4. The one specific accusation that the wicked have done violence to Lebanon (2:17) stands out against the other generic descriptions of wrongdoing.

The final woe is unique from the others in its diatribe against idol worship. Although other prophets also mock those who worship stone and wood, the concern seems out of place in Habakkuk. Habakkuk 1:16 does describe the Babylonians as offering sacrifices to the net with which they catch nations, but little else in the book has depicted idolatry as their primary flaw: elsewhere in Habakkuk, the Babylonians' rapaciousness and self-reliance are stressed (1:6-7).

Two calls to praise Yahweh interrupt the woes. Habakkuk 2:14 affirms that all will acknowledge Yahweh, and 2:20 bids all the earth to keep silence in God's presence.

Exegetical Analysis

Each of the three subunits of this section (2:1, 2:2-5, and 2:6-20) raises translational and interpretative issues. In 2:1, understanding *who* will answer is complicated by a textual matter. The MT reads "what *I* will answer," though many English translations (NRSV, NJB, NAB) have adopted the Syriac reading of "what *he* will answer," attempting to retain the parallelism of the verse ("what he will say"//"what he will answer"). The MT reading fits well with the tone of the book, however, in that the prophet is shown throughout Habakkuk as talking back to God's response. The translation of the United Bible Societies' Hebrew Old Testament project is perhaps the best: "What I will have to answer to the complaint which I have presented" (United Bible Societies 1980, 355-56).

In 2:2-5, textual and translational issues range from minor to substantive. Renderings of 2:2 (regarding the nature of the tablet written) and 2:3 (regarding "the end") differ in nuance though not in essential meaning, but the translation problems of 2:4 are more substantive. The first phrase literally reads "she is lifted up"; the NRSV translation of "the proud" relies on an emendation of the text. The meaning remains unclear.

The core affirmation that ends 2:4 traditionally has been translated as "the righteous live by their faith," based in part on the apostle Paul's use of the verse in Gal 3:11 and Rom 1:17 to stress the importance of belief in Jesus. Two aspects of the verse, however, challenge this traditional translation. First, the Hebrew word *ʾĕmûnâ* less denotes belief than it signifies steadfastness. Throughout the Psalms, for example, *ʾĕmûnâ* is an attribute of God: God's constancy. Second, the pronoun suffix of "faith" is masculine singular and as such can refer back either to the righteous one or to the vision of which Yahweh is speaking. That is, the verse legitimately may be rendered as "the righteous one will

77

live by his steadfastness" or, as in Roberts's translation noted above, "the righteous one will live by its [the vision's] reliability."

In 2:5, the first noun is "wine" *(hayyayin)* in the MT but appears as "wealth" in the Qumran Habakkuk pesher. The MT reading is to be preferred, against Roberts's claim that "one can do nothing" with the reading of "wine" (Roberts 1991, 113). Although the mention of "wine" initially seems out of context, the motif of drunkenness that dominates both the fourth woe (2:15-17) and also the prophetic books in general accounts for its usage here.

In the subunit of 2:6-20, translational issues also arise. At 2:16, the second imperative in the MT is "have your foreskin uncovered," while the Septuagint reads "stagger." The MT reading well parallels the ending of the previous verse: just as the wicked exposed others' nakedness, so will their nakedness (in this case, of one uncircumcised) be exposed. As noted above, both Jer 49 and Obadiah connect drinking with bodily exposure. By following the Septuagint in reading "stagger," the NRSV ignores both this common prophetic vocabulary and also the connections between 2:16 and the previous verse.

The unit bears two different form-critical genres, one in 2:1-5 and another in 2:6-20. Floyd deems Hab 2:1-5 a report of an oracular inquiry, since, like Jer 21 and 42–43, it depicts Yahweh responding to a prophet's bequest (Floyd 2000, 125). Similarly, Mason notes the similarity between 2:1-5 and Isa 21, in which the prophet is prepared for a divine communication (Mason 1994, 89).

The formulaic repetition of *hôy* in 2:6-20 leads some to discern within these verses the particular form of the "woe oracle," linked by early form critics with funerary or mourning rites in ancient Israel and Judah. Floyd's lengthy discussion of the woe oracle argues that *hôy* expresses "a [wide] range of reactions appropriate to a calamity" (Floyd 2000, 133), and not just the setting of mourning. He links the woe sayings to Wisdom speech, given their concern with reproof (Floyd 2000, 138). Hence, as noted earlier, although Habakkuk uses stereotypical prophetic forms (such as the woe oracle), there is little basis on which to reconstruct the social setting out of which those forms initially may have arisen.

In describing the recording of a prophetic vision, this unit may provide information about the connection between prophecy and writing in the ancient world. Although the Hebrew Bible presents prophecy primarily as something received by the eye or ear, in several places the prophet is instructed to write down the message for the future. In Isa 30:8, for example, the prophet is to write an oracle on a tablet as a future witness, and the superscription of Nahum designates the book as a *sēper*, a "writing." Such connections may suggest, as Floyd maintains, that "this text was produced by a scribal group that recorded and studied prophetic lore, a group with which the prophet himself had some association, or to which he perhaps even belonged" (2000, 128; see, too, Floyd 1993). Such a possibility is bolstered by recent prophetic study that stresses the significant amount of redactional activity in the prophetic books: at least in their final forms, the books do testify to prophecy as something to be read and contemplated. Habakkuk 2:2 does not necessarily provide corroborating information regarding the written nature of ancient prophecy, but it would hold a special meaning for the scribes who transmitted (and even composed) prophetic books.

Theological Analysis

The traditional translation of 2:4 sets this verse as the answer of God to the problem of injustice: in response to the prophet's observation of the injustice of the world, God declares that (despite outward appearances) the wicked are doomed to failure and the righteous live by their trust in God. The resultant message is one voiced throughout the prophetic books and throughout the Bible as a whole; it serves to assure the victims of injustice that God ultimately controls the world and wills justice for the faithful.

When 2:4 is read as underscoring the faithfulness of the vision rather than of the individual, the theological import of the verse is not altered radically, in that it still stresses the trustworthiness of God. This alternative translation, however, does not see 2:4 as God's answer, but rather as the instruction that precedes the vision. In this interpretation, Hab 2:1-20 still leaves unanswered the charges posed by the prophet in chapter 1 and leaves the reader in anticipation of further divine response.

Both readings affirm the faithfulness of God, but both also leave open-ended the means and timing by which God will address injustice. The woes, although clear in the attitudes and behaviors that engender God's wrath, do not explain how the punishments that the wicked deserve will be carried out.

In its affirmation of God's care, then, Hab 2:1-20 also underscores the mystery of divine retribution and cautions against anyone who would claim to pinpoint exactly how God is working in the world. In many ways, Hab 2 is a statement of faith rather than a justification of God. In it, God and, indeed, all people of the world affirm the truths of divine compassion and justice but do not explain how those attributes manifest themselves in daily affairs.

In many ways, the book of Habakkuk finds similarities in the book of Job. In both, the specific complaints of the sufferer are answered with nonspecific affirmations about the power and goodness of God. Job is convinced, or at least humbled, by the manifestation of God's power. As we turn to the final chapter of Habakkuk, we will consider whether the prophet is equally assured.

PRAYER OF THE PROPHET (3:1-19)

Presented in the style of a psalm, this chapter looks both backward and forward to the dramatic appearance of Yahweh the Divine Warrior, who will set all aright. As such, it offers the hope of Yahweh's decisive response to the prophet's challenging of Yahweh's justice.

Literary Analysis

The beginning of this unit is marked by a new superscription, which labels the material to follow as a prayer of the prophet. It may be outlined as follows:

3:1	Superscription
3:2	The prophet's petition
3:3-15	The march of the Divine Warrior
3:16-19	The prophet's response, ending with a psalm-like subscription

Like earlier chapters, this unit addresses Yahweh in the second person. The tone of the preceding material was that of complaint, but the attitude of chapter 3 is of praise and petition.

The unit is clearly crafted to be read as a psalm. It begins with a psalmic superscription: as in Pss 17, 86, 90, 102, and 142, it is called a "prayer," and the musical setting *šigyōnôt* is similar to the one prescribed for Ps 7. Interspersed throughout the piece is the refrain *selâ*, a term that appears frequently in Psalms, though its meaning is uncertain; and the unit ends with the type of musical direction found in Pss 4, 6, 54, and 55. The description of the worshiper in 3:19 as one with deer's feet finds an almost exact parallel in Ps 18:33 (so, too, 2 Sam 22:34).

Yahweh is portrayed as a cosmic Divine Warrior, charging onto the earth, fomenting mountains and rivers (3:3-15). This image of Yahweh appears elsewhere in the Bible, such as in Nah 1, but the depiction in Hab 3 is extended and detailed. Yahweh's might obscures the sun; pestilence and plague precede him; his steps shatter mountains; his arrows stop the moon. Throughout, the unit portrays God in bold, mythic terms; its connection with the mythologies of the ancient Near East will be explored below.

The temporal nature of the Divine Warrior's activity is debated. Is the prophet recounting the *past* deeds of Yahweh as the basis of a request for present intervention? Or do the verses describe a theophany *now being experienced* by the prophet himself, providing the content of the vision promised in 2:1-5? Clues point in both directions. On the one hand, the petition of 3:2 supports the first of these understandings: the prophet has heard of God's action in the past and now asks God to make the same work known in the present. On the other hand, the verbs of 3:3-5 are predominantly imperfects (with the exception of "covered" in 3:3), which usually (though not always) denote present or continuing action, as captured in the NAB and NASB (though not the NRSV). In the MT, the verbs do not shift to the perfect until 3:6.

The response of the prophet in 3:16 adds further weight to the second interpretation. Just as the prophet had heard *(šāmaᶜtî)* past reports of Yahweh's action in 3:2, so, too, the prophet claims in 3:16 to have heard *(šāmaᶜtî)* information that terrifies him and convinces him to trust that God will soon act. Something has transpired between 3:2 and 3:16 that enables the prophet to believe that, although justice is still not done, God will act on the people's behalf. He will wait quietly for God's recompense on the enemy.

These interpretations need not be sharply distinguished from each other, however. The prophet's present vision could be of Yahweh's past action: the prophet's encounter with the awesome nature of God's ancient deeds could inspire him to recognize God's power in his own present situation. Perhaps it is no accident that in Hab 3, the past and the present seem indistinguishable.

Exegetical Analysis

Although language describing the Divine Warrior is ancient, it served different functions at different times in Israel's history: in early texts as a creation motif, in the time of the monarchy as a support of Davidic kingship, and in the prophets as an image of the deity who punishes both the nations and the covenant people (see Hiebert 1992). Habakkuk 3 highlights the early cosmological aspects of the image of the Divine Warrior, drawing from the well of ancient Near Eastern mythological motifs.

In both Canaanite and Babylonian mythologies, the world was formed as the result of combat between gods. In the Canaanite account, the god Baal fought and defeated Yamm (Sea) to create order in the world; in the Babylonian myth, the god Marduk slew the chaos monster, Tiamat, and created the heaven and the earth from her body. Parts of the Hebrew Bible use similar imagery in describing Yahweh's creation of the world: in Ps 74, God breaks the head of dragons and of the beast Leviathan; and in Ps 89, God rules the sea and crushes the mythical Rahab.

Habakkuk 3 reflects this language in several ways. Roberts, for example, suggests that "horns" of light (NRSV: "rays") in 3:4 draws from ancient Near Eastern iconography (Roberts 1991, 153). In order to capture in English the strong mythological nuances of Hab 3, many modern commentators render the elements of nature in this unit as proper rather than common nouns (River, Sea, Pestilence, Sun, Moon).

The precise description of River and Sun, however, is complicated by several difficulties in translation. In the MT, Hab 3:9 is packed with nouns, unclearly related to one another: literally, it reads, "Nakedness your bow was exposed, oaths staffs speech. Sela. Rivers you divided the land." Two attempts at literal renderings are the KJV ("Thy bow was made quite naked, *according* to the oaths of the tribes, *even thy* word. Selah. Thou didst cleave the earth with rivers.") and the NASB ("Thy bow was made bare. The rods of chastisement were sworn. Selah. Thou didst cleave the earth with rivers."). Roberts (1991, 139-40) offers several emendations, and Hiebert (Hiebert 1986, 25-27) attempts to discern ancient spelling changes that may have led to scribal confusion. The NRSV rendering, "sated were the arrows at your command," reflects the consonantal text of the MT but not its vowel pointing.

The exact translation of 3:10-11, which uses these nouns, is also complicated. Because the verb "raised high" at the end of 3:10 has no apparent subject, many translations link it with the first noun of 3:11. The NRSV, for example, reads, "The sun raised high its hands; the moon stood still in its exalted place." The RSV and NASB attempt to retain the MT reading: "It lifted high its hands. Sun *and* moon stood in their places." Readers are encouraged to consult Roberts (1991) and Hiebert (1986) for detailed discussions of textual and translational problems, which go beyond the selective treatment given here.

Recognizing that Hab 3 resonates with early elements in the evolution of the Divine Warrior motif, Hiebert argues that Hab 3 was an ancient hymn that was later edited and adapted to meet the needs of a much later time period (Hiebert 1996, 654-55). He sees the current form of the hymn as expressing the

apocalyptic view that the only answer to the problem of historical evil is God's intervention on the people's behalf. Unlike Isaiah
or Amos who affirm that God directs human armies to order the
world, Hab 3 sees the only hope for justice in the march of the
Divine Warrior. What distinguishes Habakkuk from full-blown
apocalyptic, however, is that its mythological motifs are not
directly related to the historical evil that the prophet experiences.
The poem, for all of its power, does not explain to the prophet
how—or when—his own oppressor will fall.

Hiebert's claim that the Divine Warrior hymn existed prior to
its inclusion into the book is echoed by Nogalski. He maintains
that the poem itself was composed during the late exilic or early
postexilic periods and was incorporated into the book in the
Persian period as part of the process of creating the Book of the
Twelve. He finds connections between Hab 3:16-19 and Joel, as
well as between the Divine Warrior hymns in Habakkuk and
that in Nahum (Nogalski 1993b, 159-81).

The difficult language and syntax of the chapter would support the theory of the poem's independent history. Most important, however, the poem now stands as the "answer" to the
prophet's complaint and the content of the "vision" given in 2:1-
5. In its current form, the march of the Divine Warrior is now
the assurance of God's power and will to save. Although Yahweh
may be described in terms akin to those of other ancient Near
Eastern deities, Hab 3 insists that Yahweh—not Baal or Marduk
—rules the cosmos.

Theological Analysis

The depiction in Hab 3 of Yahweh as the Divine Warrior is
both comforting and problematic for believers. On the one hand,
the insistence on the raw power of God underscores that God is
not powerless in the face of evil; both in the past and in the present, Yahweh has the power to overthrow pervasive evil. For
audiences suffering oppression, the affirmation that God is
stronger than the oppressor is good news.

On the other hand, the image also raises issues of gender and

violence. By depicting God as a warrior, Hab 3 not only reinforces the male identification with God, which many feminists
have seen as dangerous for both women and men, but also cele-
brates the violent defeat of enemies. Although some interpreters
claim that images of a violent God actually work against human
violence by limiting such activities to the divine realm, human
history has shown how easily human armies claim to fight for
God. The violence of the Divine Warrior stands in tension with
Habakkuk's complaint that "violence" surrounds him (1:2-3).

In Hab 3, the vision of the Divine Warrior does lead to a
change in the prophet: he no longer complains, but instead vows
to wait silently. Strikingly, however, the vision never addresses
directly the charges that Habakkuk has leveled against God.
God's power has been defended, but Habakkuk had never questioned God's power—only God's justice.

The primary message of Habakkuk is that those who are
faithful must trust that God will act, but it does not make clear
whether there is any role for human opposition to injustice.
Should one only wait for God to act against wrongdoing? The
model of the prophet Habakkuk gives one clue: in times of injustice, the faithful (such as the prophet) may, and perhaps are
encouraged to, protest, to complain, to petition God for change.

INTRODUCTION: ZEPHANIAH

THE PROBLEM WITH ZEPHANIAH

The general theme of the book of Zephaniah is easily described. The book announces the coming Day of Yahweh, a day of distress and fury, a day of punishment for wrongdoers. The details of this punishment, though, are more difficult to discern. In the course of its three short chapters, Zephaniah describes in a variety of ways *who* will be punished, *why*, and *when*.

These shifts are found in all three chapters of the book. Chapter 1 begins and ends with punishment to be meted out indiscriminately to all inhabitants of the earth (humans and animals), though the middle of the chapter concerns Yahweh's punishment on Judah for its idolatry. Chapter 2 launches a general diatribe against Judah, turns to the punishment of the nations who are accused of crimes against Judah (2:10), and then promises that a remnant of Judah will inherit the territory of others (2:7, 9). Chapter 3 first accuses Jerusalem of rebellion, then turns to a mixture of punishment and promise for the nations, and concludes with a paean of salvation for Judah. At times, these changes appear to be expected in the course of historical events (2:4-5), at other times, in the realm of a perfect future (2:9; 3:20). Indeed, as Adele Berlin suggests, "Zephaniah gives the impression, more than other prophetic books, of moving erratically between messages of chastisement and comfort, between descriptions of the fate of Israel and the nations" (Berlin 1994, 9-10).

Various interpretative frameworks have been advanced to explain these shifting perspectives within the book of Zephaniah. One approach is to discern within Zephaniah some type of thematic structure that accounts for its diverse blocks of material. Many scholars discern in Zephaniah a three-part scheme common to many of the prophetic books—that of Judgment on Judah, Judgment on the Nations, and Salvation to Judah—though they disagree on precisely where those themes begin and end. The merits of this tripartite schematization of the book will be explored below in my discussion of Zephaniah's structure.

A quite different approach has been taken by Paul House, who treats Zephaniah as a prophetic drama, divided into three acts. Within the acts, multiple scenes are delineated on the basis of alternating voices, and the whole follows a dramatic flow of Exposition, Complication, Climax of Crisis, Resolution of Crisis, and Falling Action and Conclusion (House 1988, 126). House's treatment remains unconvincing, both because of the historical problems of positing dramas in ancient Israel (see Roberts 1991, 161-62) and because of its inability, as other schemes, to account for the multiple perspectives within single speeches.

Another approach is to abandon the search for unity and to explore instead the historical processes by which the book took on its current shape. James Nogalski, for example, argues that the original core of Zephaniah was focused on the fate of Judah; but as the book was edited for its inclusion in a developing Book of the Twelve, it took on a more universal scope (he sees similar expansions toward a universal message in Nah 1 and Hab 3; Nogalski 1993, 178). Margaret Odell, too, views Zephaniah as a composite collection, "integrated into a single exhortation to acknowledge the sovereignty of Yahweh" (2000, 671). Such an approach is helpful in acknowledging the tensions within Zephaniah but does little to consider the *result* of the redaction, what the book's final form now conveys.

My own interest is to read Zephaniah as a literary whole while honoring as carefully as possible its shifts in mood, theme, and perspective. I take seriously its difficulties and ask what sense one may make of them. What effect on a reader (or at least on me as a reader) does this particular literary style have? Throughout, my interests are primarily ideological and rhetorical. I am interested in how this book, explicitly and implicitly, configures the ethical landscape, how its rhetoric and symbolic world encourages its readers to think and behave. The style as well and the explicit message of Zephaniah may have something to say about the complex interrelationship between Judah and the nations.

My approach is, whenever possible, to read the Masoretic Text (MT) as it stands. I do not read with the MT out of an illusion that it is a pristine or "original" text, or even with the understanding that it is the final form of the text. The MT does, however, witness to an *extant* textual tradition. Unlike reconstructed, eclectic texts, it stood as a literary whole at some stage of its history. Out of curiosity, I am interested in how the difficult language within that literary whole might function: how can a text's ambiguities and puzzles be seen to function in their larger context? What do shifts in pronouns and tenses do to the reading process?

Although the text of Zephaniah is not particularly problematic, it nonetheless contains some difficult passages. As a comparison of English Bibles will reveal, the rendering of Zeph 2:2, 3:10, and 3:17 varies a great deal, as do the names of the particular animals named in 2:14. I will explore significant translational concerns in the body of the commentary.

LITERARY ANALYSIS

Zephaniah follows the standard features of the prophetic genre. It begins with a superscription that names the prophet, locates him genealogically and temporally, and labels the material as the "word of the LORD." The book contains announcements of judgment and of salvation, consistently using poetic form. Messenger speech marks Zeph 1:2, 3, 10; 2:9; and 3:8, 20. Throughout, Zephaniah presents itself as the report of what a prophet heard from God and invites its reader to accept the book as an accurate report of God's will.

Just how typical of the prophetic genre the book is can be seen by tracing its similarities with other prophetic books. Its concern with the coming fury of the Day of Yahweh is paralleled in Isa 13; 22; Jer 46; Joel 2–3; Amos 5; Obad 15; and Mal 3:2. Like Ezek 30:3 and Joel 2:2, Zeph 1:15 describes the Day as one of "clouds." Many of the threats that Zephaniah inveighs are common to other prophets: not being allowed to enjoy the fruits of one's own labor (Zeph 1:13; Amos 5:11), being made like Sodom and Gomorrah (Zeph 2:9; Isa 1:9; 13:19; Jer 23:14; 49:18; 50:40; Amos 4:11), and being made into a deserted place (Zeph 2:13-15; Isa 17, 18, 25). Along with the Oracles against the Nations series in Isa 13–23, Jer 46–51, Ezek 25–32, and Amos 1:3–2:3, Zephaniah lists nations whom Yahweh will punish (Zeph 2:4-15). Nations are accused of pridefulness (Zeph 2:10; Ezek 7:24; 30:6, 18; Zech 10:11)—especially Moab (Zeph 2:8; Isa 16:6; Jer 48:29). In both Zeph 1:12 and Jer 48:11, the accused are described as those who thicken on their "dregs" or "lees." Moreover, like most of the prophetic books, Zephaniah ends on a note of hope.

Zephaniah, indeed, reads like a prophetic primer. Mason well observes that "Zephaniah encapsulates in miniature almost the whole range of Old Testament prophecy" (Mason 1994, 17). Its accusations against Judah are general and typical (idolatry, not drawing near to God, and so on), a feature that, as we shall see below, has rendered difficult the determination of the book's origin.

The structure of Zephaniah is debated. Not only do ancient manuscripts differ in their division of its units (see the chart in Berlin 1994, 18), but also modern commentators organize the book in various ways. As noted above, a common division of the book is into three parts, based on theme. Roberts (1991, 162-63), for example, outlines Zephaniah as follows:

1:2–2:3	Judgment against Judah and Jerusalem
2:4-15	Oracles against foreign nations
3:1-20	Judgment and deliverance of Jerusalem

Others concur in discerning these three parts of the book, though they differ in where they discern section breaks. Robert Bennett (1996), for example, defines the Oracle against Judah as 1:2–2:4; the Oracles against the Nations as 2:5–3:8; and the Oracles of Promise as 3:9-20.

For all of its aesthetic appeal, this three-part outline of Zephaniah appears forced. Such a rendering requires interpreters to ignore certain features of individual sections (Zeph 1 is concerned not only with Judah, but also with "all the inhabitants of all the earth," v. 18) and to posit an overly general theme (while chapter 3 may be focused on Jerusalem, its range from judgment to deliverance indicates that it does not focus on a single aspect of the city's fate). Advancing a three-part scheme for Zephaniah also fails to account for the formal features of the text that may suggest its logical breaks.

Michael Floyd's division of the book (2000), on the contrary, pays much attention to formal stylistic features. He divides the book into the following major units:

1:2-18	Announcement of the Day of Yahweh
2:1–3:7	Exhortation for the people to prepare for the coming Day of Yahweh; various motivations are given (Floyd gives an extensive outline)
3:14-20	Exhortation to rejoice

Floyd's outline is attentive to rhetorical shifts (the imperatives in 2:1 and 3:14 are taken as indicators of new units), and he attempts to categorize the flow of Zephaniah's argument.

My own outline differs somewhat from that of Floyd, both due to my attempt to provide a simple outline suitable for a commentary and due to my different understanding of individual verses.

1:1	Superscription
1:2-18	Coming punishment
2:1-3(4)	Call to repentance
2:5-15	Judgment on the nations

3:1-13   Woe and salvation to Judah (and the nations)

3:14-20   Promises of restoration for Judah (and the nations)

This outline is based on several observations. First, chapter 1 seems a self-contained unit: the chapter begins and ends with "all the inhabitants of the earth," and chapter 2 begins with an imperative, marking a shift in rhetorical style. Second, Zeph 2:4 serves to bridge the call for Judah's repentance in 2:3 and the punishment of the nations in 2:5. Having introduced the fall of the nations as a motivation for Judah's repentance, Zephaniah can then turn full attention to the fate of the nations. Third, after the curse against Nineveh that ends chapter 2, chapter 3 turns to a new subject, Judah, and beings with "woe" (NRSV: "ah"), suggesting a shift in rhetorical style. Fourth, concern remains with both Judah and the nations until 3:14, which shifts to direct address of Zion.

SOCIAL AND HISTORICAL ANALYSIS

The history *in* the text of Zephaniah—the period in which the prophecy is set—is that of the Assyrian period. The superscription dates the activity of the prophet to the days of Josiah, who reigned over Judah from 640–609. According to 2 Kgs 22–23, Josiah came to the throne while still a child. When he was eighteen, he undertook a sweeping religious reform—destroying all shrines outside of Jerusalem, reinstituting the Passover, and calling Judeans to live according to a book of the Law rediscovered in the renovation of the Temple. Josiah was killed at Megiddo during his attempt to prevent Necho, king of Egypt, from aiding Assyria.

The history *of* the text—the date of its actual composition—may be the Josianic period as well. Roberts suggests that the book was written before Josiah's reform of 622, since it rails against Judah's idolatry (Roberts 1991, 163), as does Szeles, who dates the book to circa 630 (1987, 61). Corroborating such a date, Christensen argues that the nations lambasted in Zeph 2–3 represent those territories targeted by Josiah's policy of political expansion (1984, 678).

Ben Zvi, to the contrary, maintains that Zephaniah derives from the postmonarchic period. Although he concurs that some various themes and details in the text fit the time of Josiah, he also identifies aspects of the book that fit a later time period: particular late words and linguistic usages, apocalyptic ideas, references to a "remnant" and "survivors," and dependence upon biblical traditions (Wisdom, other prophets) that are themselves late. Ben Zvi does not provide extensive arguments for this position but does offer a compelling image of a writer in the postmonarchic period drawing upon the authority granted premonarchic prophets to gain authority for his own sense of his community's failings and its future (see his conclusions at Ben Zvi 1991, 347-58).

Other interpreters find no basis on which to date Zephaniah. Mason suggests that though Zephaniah would fit the time of Josiah, it would fit various other times as well (1994, 21-22). The statements against idolatry are general, and the list of nations seems stereotypical: they range from the west (Philistia) to the east (Moab and Ammon) and from the south (Egypt) to the north (Assyria).

I agree with Mason that Zephaniah's generic features render difficult a determination of its date. My own approach aligns with that of Berlin who focuses on the Josianic period as the *literary* (and not necessarily the *historical*) setting of the book of Zephaniah (Berlin 1994, 37-39). That is, the period of Josiah is important not for what it may reveal about the book's production, but for how its author intended readers to envision the message it conveys.

Berlin suggests that the period of Josiah was chosen for the literary setting of Zephaniah because it was remembered as a mini golden age (Berlin 1994, 47). The Deuteronomistic History (Joshua through Kings) describes the period of Josiah in glowing terms, downplaying (as Berlin notes) the extent to which Assyrian control circumscribed Josiah's political control. Chronicles further exalts Josiah by repeatedly comparing him to David (2 Chr 34:2, 3) and by underscoring his leading role in Temple worship.

Reading the book of Zephaniah against the implied background of the time of Josiah has several effects. First, it strengthens the book's stance against idolatry. The tirade in Zeph 1 against idolatrous priests and those who worship both Yahweh and other deities strengthens (and is strengthened by) the 2 Kings description of Judah prior to Josiah's reform. And the obscure mention of those "who leap over the threshold" in 1:9 can be seen as those involved in foreign rituals when read alongside the list of practices condemned in 2 Kgs 23.

Second, a Josianic context for Zephaniah forges a relationship between the book and other prophetic materials set by their superscriptions in the Assyrian period. Zephaniah becomes a contemporaneous voice with Nahum, a book whose call for the downfall of Nineveh gains a sympathetic reading when set within the context of Assyrian hegemony. Similarly, Jeremiah's superscription explicitly links the prophet with the reign of Josiah, in turn highlighting the book's concern with syncretistic worship.

The possibility that the book of Zephaniah may reflect African concerns is raised by its mention of "Cush" (NRSV: "Ethiopia"). In the superscription, "Cushi" (the Cushite) is listed as the prophet's father; Zeph 2:12 indicates that "Cushites" will be killed by the sword; and 3:10 promises that scattered ones from beyond the rivers of "Cush" will bring offerings to Yahweh. While the Hebrew $kûš$ traditionally has been translated "Ethiopia," arguments have been advanced that it refers to Egypt, the Kassite kingdom, the descendants of Ham, and an Ethiopian outpost south of Judah. Most convincing is the identification of Cush with the Sudan, south of Egypt (Crocker 1986).

Does "Cushi," the name of Zephaniah's father, suggest that the prophet had Sudanese background? Berlin sees little connection, interpreting Cushi as a personal name and not an ethnic marker, akin to the Cushi of Ps 7:1 (Berlin 1994, 66). Others such as Rice (1979), Anderson (1990), and Bennett (1996) argue the importance of recognizing the presence of non-Israelites in the biblical record.

The case is difficult to decide. Elsewhere in the Bible, the term "Cushi" sometimes appears with a definite article, as an ethnic marker: Num 21:1 speaks of "Moses' wife, the Cushi (one)" (AT); the runner in 2 Sam 18:21 is called "the Cushi"; in Jer 38:7, Ebed-melech is called "the Cushi." The term appears without an article in Jer 36:14, where the reference is to "Shelemiah son of Cushi," and in Jer 13:23, where it appears to stand for Cushites in general. A reasonable conclusion is that Cushi is an ethnic designation that could also serve as a personal name.

Tracing Zephaniah's lineage to an African, however, depends on supplying additional information than the superscription provides. Zephaniah lists four generations of the prophet's ancestors: prior to "Cushi" in the genealogy stand Gedaliah and Hezekiah, two Israelite names. Obviously, Zephaniah did not get his African lineage through the male line. Rice's proposal that Hezekiah's wife was Cushite and gave their son a name that would reflect his African heritage is highly conjectural (Rice 1979, 28).

Anderson's reminder that ancient Israel was ethnically diverse is an important one, a helpful corrective to the notion of a pure Israelite race (Anderson 1990). The inclusion of "Cushi" in Zephaniah's genealogy may, indeed, attest to such diversity. But the evidence is far from conclusive. The interest with Cush, however, is not incidental to Zephaniah: it is also mentioned in 2:12 and 3:10.

THEOLOGICAL ANALYSIS

From its opening verses, Zephaniah focuses heavily on Yahweh's retribution against wrongdoing. The Day of the Yahweh is described in harsh terms: it is a day of ruin, devastation, and darkness, in which people's blood is poured out like dust.

This image of an angry, punishing God is disturbing, even distasteful, to those who prefer to dwell on the deity's forgiveness, patience, and mercy. But, as explored in the commentary on Nah 3, a compelling case can be made for the ethical necessity of God's anger, God's stance against injustice. A moral God cares about what happens to the world.

What makes Zephaniah even more difficult than Nahum, however, is the generic way in which the sins of the people are discussed. Although in Nahum, God's wrath is against the Assyrian empire, easily seen as the oppressor of the ancient world, in Zephaniah, the crimes of the people are not specific. Judah is clearly accused of idolatry, but the sins of the nations are not so clear. At times, the nations seem punished because of their pride; at others, the fact that their loss is Judah's gain raises the question of whether their primary crime is being "other" than Judah.

The book's consistent yet multifaceted concern with the relationship between Judah and the nations speaks to the tension between understanding Yahweh as equally concerned with all the earth and as especially invested in the nation of Judah. One way to understand this tension is to see it as between universalism and particularism within ancient Judaism, a concern often of interest to Christian commentators. But perhaps a more helpful—and sympathetic—reading is to see in Zephaniah the affirmation that the God who is ultimately sovereign over all of the earth is also passionately involved in the life of a particular community. Readers who identify with Judah in the text are allowed to affirm God's oversight and concern for them: even though "we" might stand in need of judgment, God's final word is that of restoration. And those readers who might see themselves in the "nations" also are presented with words of divine chastisement and care.

COMMENTARY: ZEPHANIAH

SUPERSCRIPTION (1:1)

The book of Zephaniah opens with a typical prophetic superscription. The book receives a genre title ("a word"), an attribution of speaker (Zephaniah), the speaker's genealogy (traced back four generations), and a temporal setting ("in the days of Josiah").

Literary Analysis

Like Jeremiah, Hosea, Joel, Amos, Jonah, Micah, Haggai, and Zechariah, the book of Zephaniah is designated as "the word" of Yahweh, indicating that it is to be understood as divine speech. The divine word is mediated by an individual human being, marked by name and by genealogy, and the message is set within a particular historical context. The superscription thus instructs its reader to understand the material to follow as God's message to a past community.

Exegetical Analysis

The names that fill Zephaniah's superscription have engendered much discussion. The prophet's name means "Yah(weh) has hidden" or "Yah(weh) has stored up" and is shared by other characters in the Old Testament. The identities of Zephaniah's four male ancestors are variously assessed. Cushi can be a personal name or an ethnic designation, though little evidence for either interpretation is available (see introduction to Zephaniah).

Of the remaining names, Hezekiah is noteworthy, since a man of the same name ruled Judah three generations before Josiah. Second Kings devotes less space to the religious reforms of Hezekiah than to those of Josiah: two verses report that Hezekiah abolished high places and tore down the image of the serpent Nehushtan, to whom the people brought offerings (2 Kgs 18:4-5). And yet, the same text lavishes praise on this first of the great reformers. He is compared to the great king David (2 Kgs 18:3), and he acquires even higher stature than Josiah: "There was no one like him among all the kings of Judah after him, or among those who were before him" (2 Kgs 18:5). Second Chronicles gives an expanded account of Hezekiah's reform, showing the king overseeing Temple worship and leading the people in the celebration of the Passover (2 Chr 29–31). According to Sir 49:4, all of the kings of Judah were sinners except David, Hezekiah, and Josiah. King Hezekiah belonged to the appropriate generation to be Zephaniah's great-great-grandfather, though the name refers to other persons in the Bible as well (1 Chr 3:23; Ezra 2:16; 2 Chr 28:12). If a royal connection were being made, one might expect an explicit labeling of Hezekiah as king, as in Isa 1:1 and Hos 1:1.

Concerning the other names of the genealogy, Gedaliah is also the name of the governor appointed by the Babylonians after the destruction of Jerusalem in 586, and Amariah is the name of various men in the books of Ezra, Nehemiah, and 1 Chronicles; either these names were common in various time periods of ancient Israel, or the book is evoking the postexilic setting. Ben Zvi points out that the names that appear prior to Cushi in Zephaniah's genealogy all end in "Yah(weh)," and he suggests that the names have been chosen to counteract the stigma of Cushi's non-Israelite status (1991, 49).

The rest of Zephaniah provides no clues by which to settle these genealogical uncertainties. Although the book does criticize royal figures in 1:8, it demonstrates no more awareness of the royal court than do other prophetic works; and while Cush appears elsewhere in the book, it does not receive a disproportionate amount of attention.

Some scholars seek a precise date for Zephaniah, debating whether the prophet spoke before or after Josiah's reforms: does Zephaniah outline the sins of the community that led to the need for reform, or does it indicate that the people continued to stray even after the reforms were instituted? These *historical* dimensions of the genealogy of Zeph 1 are difficult to resolve, but the *literary* dimensions of the list function to set the tone for the book. The foreign element of the name Cushi followed by four Yahwistic names introduces the theme of Judah's relation to the nations, and, by invoking the names of Judah's two greatest champions of religious purity (Josiah and Hezekiah), Zephaniah reminds the reader of the zeal of those who sought to abolish syncretistic worship. The mention of Josiah's father, Amon, however, reminds the reader that, even in times of reform, idolatry is but one step removed.

The superscription also implicitly sets the book of Zephaniah in the late Assyrian period, along with Nahum and Jeremiah. In stark contrast to Nahum, which depicts Assyria as the brutal, cosmic foe, the destruction of which is necessary for Judah's salvation, Zephaniah blames the Judeans for accommodation to foreign control. Their adoption of foreign dress and worship practices is attributed to sheer volition, not to the pressures of a colonial empire. In the same way that 2 Kings makes Josiah sound much more free to act than the political context of the day would have allowed (Berlin 1994, 45), so, too, Zephaniah never directly addresses Assyrian control of Judah.

Theological Analysis

By opening with concrete details, the superscription of Zephaniah suggests the importance of reading this book (and perhaps all prophetic books) within a specific historical setting. Although the time of Josiah may not be the period of the book's composition, it is the implied setting in which the book is to be read.

By extension, the superscription suggests the concreteness of the divine word. Here, as elsewhere in the prophets, God's message is historically specific. The book does not claim to be the atemporal word of Yahweh for all times and places, spoken directly to every individual. Rather, it is a word spoken to a community in the past that lived in a specific political, religious, and social context. Modern readers who seek what Zephaniah might mean to the present, then, are called to a humble appropriation of the book: recognizing that this book was not written directly for any contemporary community encourages means of interpretation that honor other readers and that acknowledge individual interests.

COMING PUNISHMENT (1:2-18)

Zephaniah opens with a scathing announcement of punishment. It addresses both Judah and the world at large, announcing the coming Day of Yahweh as recompense for idolatry.

Literary Analysis

By its chiastic structure, the unit stresses that God's punishment, while focused on Judah, extends to all of the earth. It begins by announcing that God is about to sweep away "everything from the face of the earth" and ends with the threat that God will make an end of "all the inhabitants of the earth" (1:18). In the middle, focus remains on the destruction of Judah and the dire consequences of the coming Day of Yahweh. The section may be outlined as follows:

1:2-3	Destruction of the world
1:4-6	Destruction of Judah
1:7-13	The effect of the Day of Yahweh on Judah
1:14-18	The effect of the Day of Yahweh on "all the inhabitants of the earth"

The unit opens with a difficult phrase, translated by NRSV as "I will utterly sweep away." In Hebrew, one usually gives strength to a verb by using it twice in succession, once in a regular form and once in the infinitive absolute. Zephaniah 1:2, however, binds together two verbs that sound alike but come from different roots (the infinitive absolute of *ʾāsap* and the hiphil form of *sûp*). In order to have the phrase fit more standard grammar, some emend the text. A more interesting possibility is that the author is using language creatively, jarring the reader from its very first pronouncement.

Various techniques give the impression that the destruction envisioned in 1:2-3 is total. The vocabulary echoes that of the creation narratives of Gen 1–3 ("humans, beasts, and birds"; and "God formed man [*ʾādām*] from the dust of the ground [*ʾădāmâ]*"; Gen 2:7), as well as that of the flood narrative in Gen 6 ("I will blot out from the earth the human beings I have created—people together with animals and creeping things and birds of the air"; Gen 6:7). Zephaniah also echoes Genesis in the frequent use of *kōl* ("all, every") to underscore the extent of God's reach (de Roche 1980, 107). Zephaniah 1:2 and 1:3 are punctuated with messenger speech ("thus says the Lord"), reminding the reader that the message being delivered carries divine weight. Zephaniah 1:6 speaks of the deity in the third person, providing an additional reminder that the divine word is mediated by a prophetic spokesperson.

Although 1:4 marks no change in style (God continues to speak in first person), it shifts the brunt of the deity's anger from the whole world to Judah in particular. Language distinctive to the Deuteronomistic materials (Deuteronomy through Kings) appears in the mention of "idolatrous priests" in 1:4 (see 2 Kgs 23:5). The repeated use of the conjunction "and" (Heb. *wĕ*) gives the unit a breathless, run-on feel.

The interjection "hush" or "shh" in 1:7 marks the beginning of a new subunit, and attention turns to a general description of the Day of Yahweh. The Day will mark the punishment of those who are involved in syncretistic practices and who doubt the deity's power (1:8-13). The description of the Day in Zeph 1:14-16 is developed in striking poetic form. Repetition is seen in the use of the word "day" (Heb. *yôm*) in 1:7; 1:14 (two times); 1:15

(five times); and in 1:16. The piling up of nouns in 1:15 lends weight to the dire nature of the wrath to come: "wrath, distress, anguish, ruin, devastation, darkness, gloom, clouds, thick darkness, trumpet blast, and battle cry."

Direct, nonmetaphorical language dominates this section. The deity speaks in forceful declarative statements ("I will . . . "; 1:2-4, 9, 17), and the scope of the destruction is underscored by all-inclusive vocabulary ("humans and animals, birds and fish"; 1:3). Intensity is maintained throughout the section by the piling up of phrases (1:15-16) and by the gradual revelation of information (1:7-8 reveals that Yahweh has prepared a sacrifice before revealing who will be slaughtered). Figurative language, though sparse, does appear. Zephaniah 1:17 employs various similes ("like the blind"; "blood poured out like dust"; "flesh like dung"). In 1:12, God's exhaustive campaign against evil is compared to a night search with lamps, and the complacent are compared to wine left too long in its sediment. A further characterization of the faithful is created by the rhetorical device of the granting of voice to their attitudes: Zephaniah claims to know what the sinful say in their hearts ("those who say in their hearts, 'Yahweh will not do good, nor will he do harm'"; 1:12), just as the book of Malachi creates the speech of the people in order to refute it (see Mal 1:2, 6, 7, 13). The contrast between the people's doubt that God will act and the forcefulness with which the deity announces the punishment to come underscores just how unexpected is the dawning Day of Yahweh.

Exegetical Analysis

English translations treat differently the rendering of 1:3. In this verse, God is said to sweep away not only humans and animals, but also others who are described as *hammakšēlôt ʾet horšāᶜîm*. The Hebrew word *hammakšēlôt* is a feminine plural noun that can be translated "stumbling blocks." The *ʾet* that follows can be taken as the preposition "with"; Berlin, for example, translates the phrase "the stumbling blocks along with the wicked" (a similar translation is found in KJV and NJV); and she suggests that the "stumbling blocks" are images of the animals that are mentioned earlier in the verse, the worship of which is prohibited in Deut 4 (1994, 73). The term *'et* can also stand as the marker of the direct object, and numerous modern translations emend the verb to preserve a continuity in speaking voice: in NRSV, RSV, and NAB, for example, God declares "I will make the wicked stumble" (similar translations are found in RSV and NAB).

The effect of these translational differences is a disagreement regarding the point in the unit at which idolatry is introduced as Judah's sin: is it mentioned in 1:3, as in Berlin's translation, or not until 1:4, as in the NRSV? Both translations, however, introduce new information into the account of pending destruction: God's punishment is due to wickedness.

The center of this passage is concerned with syncretistic practices. At least initially, the people are accused not of abandoning the worship of Yahweh, but rather of worshiping Yahweh and other deities at the same time (1:5). "The remnant of Baal" (1:4) is often interpreted as evidence that the book was written after Josiah's reforms and indicates ongoing apostasy, though it could refer to any period in which a small but insistent group worships the Canaanite deity. Bowing "down upon the roofs" to "the host of the heavens" (1:5) refers to the worship of astral deities, as similar usage of these phrases in Deut 4:19; 2 Kgs 17:16; 23:5; Jer 8:2; 19:13; and 32:29 suggests. Some link "all who leap over the threshold" (1:9) with the practices of the Philistines described in 1 Sam 5:4-5, while Ben Zvi suggests that the phrase refers to all people—anyone who walks over a threshold (1991, 102). Given the litany of worship practices here being condemned, the phrase likely signifies some specific practice, the precise meaning of which is lost to us.

Most modern translations (NASB, NAB, NRSV, NJV) translate the end of 1:5 as "[those] who bow down to Milcom," an Ammonite deity, reading (along with several ancient Versions) the Hebrew *malkām* as a variant of the god's name. Other possible translations of *malkām* are "their king" (human or divine) and "Molekh," traditionally understood as the name of a deity to whom children were burned in sacrifice. Recent discussion suggests that Molekh was not the name of a specific god, but Heider makes a good case that the Molekh cult was practiced by several Judean kings and that the sacrifices involved were part of the worship of dead ancestors (Heider 1992, 897).

Clearly, a reconstruction of the practices to which Zephaniah is referring is difficult, though several elements help shape the impression that foreign worship is addressed. First, the mention of Baal early in the section leads the reader to assume that idolatry is the primary basis for the accusations. Second, the description of the royal court as clothed in "foreign vestments" (1:8) supports the impression that, throughout, the passage is lambasting those who have incorporated into their daily lives ideas and practices brought from outside of the community. Third, this section shares much vocabulary with that used to describe religious reform and apostasy in 2 Kgs 21–25. Manasseh, remembered in the Deuteronomistic History as an evil king, erected altars for Baal (2 Kgs 21:3; Zeph 1:4) and for the host of heaven (2 Kgs 21:3; Zeph 1:5), and he made his son pass through fire (2 Kgs 21:6; giving weight to the translation of "Molekh" in Zeph 1:5). Josiah, the religious reformer, abolished the altars of Asherah and Baal (2 Kgs 23:4; Zeph 1:4), deposed the idolatrous priests (2 Kgs 23:5; Zeph 1:4), outlawed the worship of the hosts of heaven (2 Kgs 23:4; Zeph 1:5), and forbade any to pass their children through fire as an offering to Molekh (2 Kgs 23:10; Zeph 1:5). Indeed, the punishment that Zephaniah announces resonates with the insistence in 2 Kings that even the righteousness of Josiah did not turn Yahweh from punishing Judah for the sins of Manasseh. Perhaps coincidentally, the final chapter of 2 Kings mentions a priest named Zephaniah (2 Kgs 25:18; Zeph 1:1) and a governor named Gedaliah (2 Kgs 25:22-25; Zeph 1:1).

Second Kings also makes clear that worship practices were political issues in the ancient world. King Ahaz, who notoriously set up foreign images and practices in the Temple, is said to have done so "because of the king of Assyria" (2 Kgs 16:18), and Hezekiah's religious reforms and his rebellion against the king of

Assyria are closely related (2 Kgs 18:3-8). Just as Josiah's religious reform was an act of national self-assertion, so, too, Zephaniah's call for pure worship would have necessitated a policy of independence from Assyria.

The crimes that Zephaniah discerns in the community are wide ranging. Zephaniah 1:9 speaks of those who practice deceit and violence, and 1:10-11 may address commercial interests. The Fish Gate (mentioned in Neh 3 and 12) and the Mishneh (the Second Quarter, 2 Kgs 22) were wealthy districts in Jerusalem; the Makthesh (Mortar) is not mentioned elsewhere but also was likely a place of business. The MT of 1:11 refers to the "people of Canaan," which most translators render as "merchants," based on Isa 23:8, Ezek 16:29, Hos 12:7 and on the apparent parallelism with "those laden with silver" (1:11). The coming punishment will especially affect the wealthy: those who have wealth, houses, and vineyards (1:13) will not be able to enjoy their fortunes, and neither their silver nor their gold will be able to save them (1:18).

The Day of Yahweh, the announcement of which dominates this section, is a multifaceted image and has engendered much scholarly discussion. The term "Day of Yahweh" appears thirteen times in the Hebrew Bible and only in the prophetic books. Related vocabulary, such as "that day," is much more frequent. General references to the "day" occur more than two hundred times in the prophets (Hiers 1992, 82). In all of these occurrences, the Day seems to refer to a specific time in which God will act decisively to right wrongs and establish justice. In some passages, the establishment of justice requires the punishment of foreign nations; in others, the punishment of Israel or Judah; in yet others, the salvation of the downtrodden covenant community.

For scholars who attempt to trace the development of the idea chronologically, Amos 5:18 stands as an important piece of evidence. According to Amos, his community is wrong to look forward to the Day of Yahweh since it will be a day of "darkness" rather than "light," leading many interpreters to conclude that the Day was originally seen as one of vindication for Israel but was turned by the prophets into an image of Judah's own punishment. But, given that most of the classical prophets use Day of Yahweh language against their own people, this developmental argument is tenuous, relying on the rhetoric of Amos to have depicted accurately the views of every member of his community. A more reasonable conclusion is that ancient persons, like modern ones, held diverse ideas about what God must do to establish justice. As Crenshaw well concludes, "YHWH's self-manifestation portends either blessing or curse, depending on whether the deity comes in favor or wrath" (1995, 49).

Scholars also debate about the setting in which the concept of the Day of Yahweh arose. Its origins have been found in the ancient Israelite tradition of holy war, in the ceremonies of the Israelite New Year festival, in the curses used in ancient Near Eastern treaties, and in the language used to describe Yahweh's theophany. (For an outline of these positions, see Crenshaw 1995 and Hiers 1992.) Each of these theories highlights and accounts for some—though not all—of the elements of the Day of Yahweh materials, suggesting that the materials as they are now presented to us encompass a range of motifs, themes, and images.

Zephaniah shares many of the themes and much of the vocabulary of other passages that discuss the Day of Yahweh, or "that day" (*denotes passages that are especially close in wording to Zephaniah):

near, Zeph 1:7, 14	Isa 13:6; Jer 48:16; Ezek 7:7; *30:3;
	Joel 1:15; 2:1, *3:14; *Obad 1
darkness, Zeph 1:15	Amos 5:18, 20
darkness *and* gloom, Zeph 1:15	Exod 10:22; Joel 2:2
make an end, Zeph 1:18	Nah 1:8; Isa 10:23; Jer 4:27
wrath, anger, Zeph 1:18	Isa 13:9, *13; *Ezek 7:19; 38:19
all the earth, Zeph 1:18; 3:8, 19	Isa 13:5
military images, Zeph 1:14, 16	Isa 13:4-5; Joel 2:2
a day of sacrifice, Zeph 1:7-9	Isa 34:6; Jer 46:10

This list, not exhaustive, indicates that Zephaniah has much in common with other Day of Yahweh texts, especially Isa 13. Its power comes not from the uniqueness of its description, but rather from the power of its variation on this pervasive theme. For example, although the vision of the Day of Yahweh as a time of sacrifice appears both in Isa 34 and Jer 46, Zeph 1:7-9 heightens the intensity of the scene by not immediately revealing the identity of the sacrificial victim.

Zephaniah 1 ends with a cry of judgment against "all the inhabitants of the earth," raising the question of just how universal is the message of chapter 1. Such a question is bound up with an understanding of the oracle's opening, "I will utterly sweep away everything from the face of the earth" (1:2). How is the reader to understand the relationship between the apparent global scope of the chapter's frame and the more specific focus on Jerusalem in its center?

Various ways of correlating the universal and particular in Zeph 1 are possible:

1. *The focus is really on Judah.* According to this interpretation, Zeph 1 is ultimately concerned with Judah and uses "global" language in the service of addressing its specific target. Just as Micah and Amos begin with addressing the larger world before concentrating on the sins of their own communities, so, too, Zephaniah may be using universal language to intensify the sense that Judah's punishment is inevitable. According to Berlin: "While the main focus of God's wrath is Judah, the Judeans are warned that they cannot escape because God's wrath will encompass the whole earth" (1994, 92).

2. *The sin of Judah will cause the whole earth to be destroyed.* In the understanding of Bennett, the ring structure of Zeph 1 indicates that "the sinfulness of . . . one community has consequences for all creation" (1996, 676). Judah's sin leads to the disruption of the cosmic order, the entire ecological system. Floyd suggests that Zephaniah shares with the Primeval History (Gen 1–11) the conviction that "some wicked persons can bring about the destruction of the underlying social and ecological relationships on which all sentient life depends" (2000, 190).

3. *The destruction of the earth and of Judah are two separate topics that have been joined into a literary whole.* Another way of understanding this material is to suggest that Zeph 1 envisions *both* a universal *and* a particular devastation, which are linked in the literary structure of the chapter. According to Nogalski, this dual focus of Zeph 1 is the legacy of an editor; the addition of the opening verses (like the additions of theophanies to Nahum and Habakkuk) expanded the narrow attention on Judah to a broader view of God's pending interaction with the world (1993, 199).

Deciding on one of these options is difficult, given the language of Zeph 1. Although the NRSV translation of Zeph 1:2 sounds unambiguously universal ("I will utterly sweep away everything from the face of the earth, says Yahweh"), the word for "earth" here is *ʾādāmâ*, more frequently translated "ground." It is the term used, for example, for the "ground" on which the creeping animals move (Gen 1:25) and for the origin of the dust from which the first human was formed (Gen 2:7). The Hebrew word *ʾādāmâ* occasionally refers to geographical territory as well (Gen 12:3; 28:14; Deut 14:2; Amos 3:2). Hence, 1:2 can, though does not necessarily, denote a global dimension.

The use of *kōl* ("everything") is ambiguous as well. The word *kōl* is most often an adjective, and, when linked with a noun, it signifies "every" or "all of." In passages such as 1:2, in which *kōl* is used as a noun and appears without an article, literary context usually suggests the extent of its scope. At the end of Gen 9:3, for example, it refers to all of the "moving things" that are mentioned earlier in the verse, whereas it signifies "all people" in Isa 30:5 and "all things" in Ps 8:6. *Kōl* is as common and variously used in Hebrew as is the word "all" in English, providing little basis on which to establish the extent of the punishment envisioned by Zephaniah.

The ending of chapter 1, "a terrible end he will make of all the inhabitants of the earth," uses a different Hebrew word for earth (*ʾereṣ*). Unlike *ʾādāmâ* as used in 1:2, *ʾereṣ* has as its primary meaning the whole earth, though it is sometimes used to describe particular countries or territories (1 Sam 9:4-5) and even the ground (Gen 18:2). In turn, the whole phrase "all the inhabitants of the land" can be used to refer to all humanity (Ps 33:14; Jer 25:29-30) or to those who live in a particular geographical area (Num 33:52; Josh 2:9; Jer 1:14; 47:2). In the powerful Day of Yahweh material in Joel, the phrase refers to Judahites (Joel 1:2, 14; 2:1).

The vocabulary of Zeph 1, then, is open-ended, allowing both universal and particular interpretations, though most readers have been drawn to the universal dimensions. One possible factor for the broader interpretation is the chapter's allusions to the creation narratives in Genesis. Although words such as "human," "beast," "fish," and "bird" appear elsewhere in the Bible, they are most famous for their inclusion in Gen 1. For contemporary readers familiar with the dramatic poetic account of the creation of the world in Genesis, an encounter with Genesis-like vocabulary in Zephaniah easily leads to the impression that it, too, deals with the entire creation.

Or perhaps Zephaniah more subtly intertwines the fates of Judah and of the world. In 1:3, the vocabulary inspired by Genesis is interrupted by the mention of the wicked, suggesting even in the "universal" opening frame of the chapter that the wicked are not only in Judah. Similarly, the closing frame blurs the distinctions between Judah and the world. Even as attention returns to the "whole earth" and even as language drawn from Genesis resumes (ʾădāmâ, "dust"), remnants of the accusations against Judah remain: the inability of silver and gold to save points back to the criticism of the wealthy earlier in the chapter.

The opening chapter of Zephaniah has raised important issues: the relation of Judah to the world and the nature of the Day of Yahweh. The exploration of the remaining chapters will allow a fuller consideration of Zephaniah's understanding of these themes.

Theological/Ethical Analysis

God's Punishment

Zephaniah's description of the Day of Yahweh has incited the religious imagination in various time periods. Its translation in the Vulgate is the starting point for the *Dies irae,* a Latin poem of fifty-seven lines, which, until the reforms of Vatican II, served as the sequence in the Mass for the Dead in the Western Church. The haunting mid-thirteenth-century tune, which repeats the music of its first two phrases no fewer than twelve times, "has a melody which perhaps more than any other plainchant has seared itself onto the musical consciousness of later centuries" (Kerman 1980, 84). Famous musical settings include Mozart's *Requiem,* Verdi's *Requiem,* Berlioz's *Symphonie fantastique,* and Liszt's *Totentanz.* The description of the Day also carries a weighty connotation for Jewish readers after the Holocaust: underlying the NRSV translation of the Day as one of "ruin" is the Hebrew word *šô'â* (Shoah), the name given in the twentieth century to the destruction of European Jewry.

Although the remaining chapters of Zephaniah explore additional dimensions of the Day of Yahweh, it is important to note that the book's first presentation of the Day in chapter 1 does not attempt to balance judgment with mercy. Yahweh's intentions are solely toward punishment, a punishment that is total and far-reaching. According to Calkins, Zephaniah's voice of doom makes it "the saddest book in the whole Bible" (1947, 69); but, as stressed in the commentary on Nahum, many theologians have found its insistence on punishment for evil to be a valuable corrective to theologies that focus only on divine forgiveness. Liberation theologians such as Jose Miguel Bonino and classic Reformed thinkers such as John Calvin alike have stressed that punishment of evil is prerequisite to understanding God as both sovereign and just.

The Poor

On its own, Zeph 1 does not clearly manifest a liberationist concern with the rights of the oppressed. The note of universal destruction on which the chapter ends reminds readers that a critique of the wealthy need not translate into the vindication of the poor. Calkins goes too far in calling Zephaniah a spoiled young aristocrat with no concern for the poor (1947, 68); but in Zeph 1, all perish—the wealthy and the poor alike. Zephaniah's attitude toward the poor will be considered further in the commentary on 2:3.

Idolatry

The Assyrian setting of Zephaniah, if only literary, works against a narrow understanding of its concern with idolatry. The call for the abolishment of images is not merely a call for religious purism, denigrating particular types of worship at the exclusion of others. Rather, it serves a powerful voice against dividing one's allegiances out of the naive hope of avoiding social and political calamity. Judahites, especially the royal family, would gain by adopting Assyrian customs—a choice that likely involved self-interest.

Preachers and teachers attempting to modernize Zephaniah's message often produce their own list of contemporary "idolatries," ways in which the hearts of contemporary people are led astray—ways that often mirror those actions the preacher usually finds personally repugnant. In contrast to such approaches, it is helpful to observe that, at least in Zeph 1, the prophet is not calling for repentance, but rather preparing people for the punishment to come. The point of Zephaniah is not that individuals or religious communities can avoid the fate of the Judeans by simply refraining from the modern equivalents of idolatrous Judean practices. Rather, the book calls readers to take responsibility for the daily compromises that humans make, even the ones that seem most practical and savvy.

Indeed, the generic nature of Zeph 1 works against any exact correlation between ancient and modern practices. The sins of which the people are accused—idolatry, deceit, violence, indifference—fit no particular stage of Judah's history better than another. The challenge that Zephaniah provides to contemporary theologians, then, is of seeing God at work in "ordinary" times, those not marked by major political upheaval.

The Earth

Zephaniah is certainly not an environmental tract. It neither calls humans to greater care for the earth nor grants animals a value independent of and equal to humans. The book does, however, work out of the assumption that human sin disrupts the cosmos: both humans and animals suffer as a result of human wickedness. Hence, although Zephaniah is not a manifesto for the concept of the global village, it does model by its very literary style the interconnectedness of Judah and the rest of the world.

CALL TO REPENTANCE (2:1-3[4])

After the announcement of punishment in chapter 1, delivered in the third person, chapter 2 shifts to direct address. A nation, unnamed, is addressed in the second-person plural. Following a series of phrases that are difficult to translate, the humble of the land are called to repent, given further motivation to do so by God's power over the cities of Philistia.

Literary Analysis

By literary context, the unnamed nation of 2:1 may be Judah. No other nation has been mentioned since the superscription, and the last place name to have been explicitly mentioned is Jerusalem (1:12). The fact that the imperatives in 2:1 and 2:3 are plural, even though Judah is singular, follows the lead of chapter 1 in devoting attention to the activities of all of the nation's inhabitants. Moreover, the literary repetition of "all" the humble of the earth in 2:3 (translated in NRSV as "land," though the noun is the same as in 1:18), draws a connection between chapters 1 and 2.

Given the thoroughgoing condemnation of all of the earth in chapter 1, the call to repentance in 2:1-3 comes as a surprise. And yet, only the humble are called to repent, and the ability of repentance to avert the deity's wrath is not assured: *perhaps* they may be hidden on the day of Yahweh's wrath. In this way, Zephaniah joins the book of Joel in calling the nation to repent even in the face of a punishment that is almost assured: "Yet even now, says Yahweh, return to me with all your heart, with fasting, with weeping, and with mourning; rend your hearts and not your clothing. Return to Yahweh, your God, for he is gracious and merciful, slow to anger, and abounding in steadfast love, and relents from punishing. Who knows whether he will not turn and relent, and leave a blessing behind him, a grain offering and a drink offering for Yahweh, your God?" (Joel 2:12-14).

Commentators disagree as to whether 2:4 belongs with 2:1-3 or 2:5-15. The verse opens with the particle *kî* (NRSV: "for"), which is used in a wide variety of ways in the Hebrew Bible. The word *kî* can be emphatic ("indeed") or causal ("because"), and hence it is variously understood in 2:4 as beginning a new section or as linked grammatically with 2:3. Because 2:5 begins with an interjection, "woe" *(hôy)*, 2:4 is best understood as transitional verse between 2:1-3 and 2:5-15: Yahweh's destruction of the Philistine cities concludes 2:1-3 with a motivation to repent and introduces the theme of foreign nations, which will be fully explored in 2:5-15.

These few verses employ numerous literary devices. The most frequent is that of repetition. "The anger of Yahweh" appears three times: twice in 2:2 and again in 2:3. "Seek" is repeated three times in 2:3; and in 2:2, "before" begins three phases. An additional literary device is paranomasia, the stringing together of similar-sounding words. Paranomasia is especially evident in 2:4, in which the fates of the Philistine cities resonate with the city's names. Gaza *(ʿazzâ)* is forsaken *(ʿăzûbâ)*; Ashkelon *(ʾašqělôn)* is ruined *(šěmāmâ)*; and Ekron *(ʿeqrôn)* is uprooted *(tēʿāqēr)*. The aural connection between Ashdod *(ʾašdôd)* and its fate of being driven away *(yěgārěšûah)* is less clear, though some commentators emend the verse to intensify the assonance (Zalcman 1986, 366).

Zalcman goes further to suggest that the adjectives chosen for the cities have double meanings: each describes not only the fate that can befall a city, but also "four of the most bitter fates a woman can endure: abandonment, spinsterhood, divorce, and barrenness" (1986, 367). Gaza will be abandoned/an abandoned wife; Ashdod will be a desolation/a woman deserted by her finance; Ashdod will be driven out/a divorced woman; and

Ekron will be uprooted/a barren woman. This suggestion is intriguing, but the words he describes are used with varied nuances in the Old Testament, and determining what precise connotations the words carry is difficult. The verbs are in feminine singular, so some level of feminine personification (even if only that cities are seen as female) is being employed.

The section serves the function as exhortation. The humble of the nation are called to seek Yahweh in hopes that they might survive the inevitable Day of Yahweh's wrath, here described in an intensive way. The phrase "the heat of the anger of Yahweh," 2:2, also appears in Num 25:4; 32:14; Jer 4:8; 25:37; 30:24; and 2 Chr 29:10 (AT).

Exegetical Analysis

This section bears many translational difficulties, which are handled in various ways by modern interpreters and translators.

The imperative opening the section, translated in the NRSV as "gather together," appears in two Hebrew stems or forms. One form does not appear elsewhere in the Hebrew Bible, though the other bears the meaning of gathering sticks or stubble and is used in Exod 5:7 and 12 to describe the requirement of the Hebrew slaves of gathering straw for making bricks. Sweeney, who connects Zephaniah's exhortation to the agricultural festival of Sukkoth (Tabernacles), suggests that the verb was chosen to imply that Yahweh will gather Judah as the harvest is gathered (2000, 511). It also connects well with "chaff" in 2:2.

The description of the nation that is addressed in 2:1 is not entirely clear. The verb "desire" *(kāsap)* appears here in a form often used for the passive, and hence the KJV translates "O nation, not desired." Elsewhere, however, this form of *kāsap* does not carry a passive meaning: in Gen 31:30 and Ps 84:2 it is used in an active sense, so that a resultant reading for Zeph 2:1 would be "O nation not longing," with the object being implied ("not longing Yahweh," according to Ball 1988, 114). The common translation "shameless nation" (NAB, NIV, NRSV, RSV) relies on understanding the verb in light of its meaning in Aramaic.

The translation of 2:2 is extremely difficult. The KJV comes close to a literal rendering of the MT: "Before the decree bring forth, before the day pass as the chaff, before the fierce anger of Yahweh come upon you, before the day of Yahweh's anger come upon you." In his attempt to stay close to the MT, Ball assumes that much of the verse is understood: "Before the decree is established, (and you become) like chaff (which) passes away (on that) day" (1988, 100). Responding both to the difficult syntax of the phrase and to the difficulty in determining the nature of the "decree" that is begotten, NRSV omits both "the decree" and "the day," leaving "before you are driven away like the drifting chaff." Clearly, readers do well to approach the verse with humility.

A subgroup of the nation is addressed in 2:3. The word ⁽ānāw (NRSV: "humble") refers both to the physically poor (as in Amos 2:7) and to the spiritually humble (as in Num 12:3). Sweeney suggests that the word "invokes the image of poverty or at least contrasts the audience with wealthy wrongdoers identified in Zeph 1:2-18" and suggests that Zephaniah supports the economic dimensions of the Deuteronomic reforms by asking the "people to identify with the poor rather than [with] the rich in supporting Josiah's reform" (2000, 512).

While a concern with the poor would certainly fit in the larger message of Zephaniah, such an orientation is not clear. In the syntax of 2:3, the "humble" are defined as those "who do his [God's] commands," and they are told to seek "humility" (from the same verbal root as the earlier adjective). These clues suggest a more attitudinal than socioeconomic interpretation of ⁽ānāw in Zeph 2.

The cities mentioned in 2:4 are four of the five major cities of the nation of Philistia. Gath is mentioned alongside Ekron, Gaza, Ashdod, and Ashkelon in biblical accounts of the early years of Israelite occupation (Josh 13:3; 1 Sam 6:17), and 2 Kgs 12:17 records that the king of Aram marched against Gath in the eighth century. The city disappears from the biblical record after the Assyrian period and is noticeably absent from the list of the Philistine cities here and in Jer 25:20. Sargon II of Assyria destroyed Gath around 712.

Theological Analysis

Repentance and Judgment

This short section raises the important issue of the relationship between repentance and judgment. Even though Zephaniah is insistent that Judah deserves God's punishment, it leaves open the (slim) possibility that repentance might alter God's decrees. Zephaniah, like many other prophets, suggests not only that the deity can have a change of heart, but also that God's mercy might outweigh divine justice.

Salvation for the Humble

In its address to the humble of the land, Zeph 2:3 suggests that not all of Judah will be saved: only those who work Yahweh's justice have the possibility of avoiding the wrath to come. Here, Zephaniah not only advances the "remnant theology" shared by many of the prophets, but also names the exercise of justice as the fundamental requirement of the one who desires God's favor. Just what counts as "justice" is left vague in Zeph 2, as were the descriptions of "violence and deceit" in 1:9.

Zephaniah 1 does, however, list various activities that provoke God's anger: idolatry (1:4-6) and a trust in wealth (1:9-11, 18). With a sequential reading of the book, in which each chapter is read as building upon the previous one, Zeph 2:1-4 thus calls its hearers to avoid the actions described in chapter 1: to trust in Yahweh and not in other deities or in economic security. This section also implies the religious danger of pride, a theme that will be explored further in the next unit.

JUDGMENT ON THE NATIONS (2:5-15)

Following the promise of the destruction of Philistine cities in the previous section, this unit treats, in turn, Canaanites (2:5-7), Moabites and Ammonites (2:8-11), Cushites (2:12), and Assyrians (2:13-15). From its opening word of lamentation *(hôy)*, the unit maintains a critical stance toward the nations, who are accused of mistreatment of Yahweh's own.

Literary Analysis

The subunits within this section are not uniform. Although Canaan and Cush are addressed directly, in second person, the other oracles describe the fate of the nations in the third person. Moreover, the oracle against Cush stands out, not only because it is significantly shorter than the other units, but also because it offers no explanation of the nation's offense.

The literary technique of repetition operates within some of the subunits. *Hebel*, meaning "measured area" and translated here by most interpreters as "coast," appears three times in the oracle against Canaan (2:5, 6, 7), and forms of *ḥārap* ("reproach, taunt, scoff") are found in 2:8 and 2:10. The unit employs numerous images of pasturing sheep—to denote both rest and contentment (2:7) and also to suggest that the urban areas of the nations will be reduced to pastureland (2:6, 14).

In keeping with the tradition of ancient Near Eastern treaty curses (explored below), each unit promises a reversal of fortunes. The inhabited seacoast (2:5) will become pastureland (2:6); boastful Moab and Ammon (2:8) will become as desolate and as detestable as the infamous Sodom and Gomorrah (2:9); and the exultant city of Nineveh (2:15) will become the haunt of wild animals (2:14).

Directing God's judgment and punishment on a series of foreign nations, Zeph 2:5-15 takes the form of the Oracles against the Nations (OAN), a common type of speech within the prophetic books. Isaiah 13–23, Jer 46–51, Ezek 25–32, Amos 1:3–2:3, Nahum, and Obadiah are widely recognized to fit this category, though some have suggested that the OAN are ubiquitous in the prophetic materials, absent only from Hosea.

Despite various attempts to discern a specific literary form of the OAN, most scholars now agree that thematic rather than structural similarities link these materials. Their distinguishing characteristic is their announcement or envisioning of the destruction of a nation other than Judah or Israel at the hands of Yahweh, God of Israel. Most of the texts describe the reason for this destruction in general terms. Occasionally lambasted for their treatment of Israel and Judah, the nations are more often accused of nonspecific pride.

The turn to Nineveh at the close of chapter 2 sets the stage for chapter 3, which launches a lengthy diatribe against the Assyrian capital. As elsewhere in Zephaniah, Yahweh's attention rests both on Judah (as in 2:10) and on all the nations of the earth.

Exegetical Analysis

This unit bears many translational difficulties, the first of which is the identity of the Cherethites addressed in 2:5. The term itself may refer to "Cretans," but often in the Hebrew Bible it appears in connection with the Philistines (e.g., Ezek 25:16), suggesting that the Cherethites may have been a subgroup within Philistine society (Roberts 1991, 196). In 2 Sam 8:18, they appear as foreign mercenaries within David's army. Given that attention seems to remain on Philistine territory (the seacoast) from 2:5 to 2:7, the Cherethites may be synonymous with "Philistines."

Why does Zephaniah focus on this particular roster of nations (Philistines, Moabites and Ammonites, Cushites, and Assyrians)? Edom is conspicuously absent, since it often appears in OAN lists alongside Ammon and Moab. Christensen posits a historical explanation. He argues that Zeph 2 provided a theological rationale for Josiah's plans for military expansion into Philistia and the Transjordan at the expense of Assyrian aims. Because Edom was currently occupied by Egyptian troops, it was not a site of Assyrian-Judean conflict (1984, 678).

Sweeney similarly views Zeph 2 as a reaction against pervasive Assyrian control in Philistia and the Transjordan, from which many of the Judean elite may have benefited financially (Sweeney 2000, 513-15). His explanation accounts not only for the culminating oracle against Nineveh that ends Zeph 2, but also for the short mention of Cush, since Egypt made inroads against Assyria in the early years of Josiah's reign: "During the early years of

Josiah's reign, the emergence of Egypt and its overrunning the Philistine plain would be interpreted by Zephaniah as evidence that YHWH had begun to make good on the promise that Assyria would be punished for its actions against Israel" (Sweeney 2000, 514).

Such a historical setting also accounts for the concern the unit shows for the remnant of Judah and its return. Though many interpreters view the mention of exiles in 2:7 (although many modern translations read "restore their fortunes," the phrase may also be read as "return their captives") as indication of a postexilic date, Sweeney argues that Assyrian relocation of Judeans from the Shephelah into Philistia and the transfer of Tranjordanian territory from Judah to the Ammonites and Moabites would have produced in the seventh century a sizable number of exiles and a yearning for the return to the Judean homeland (Sweeney 2000, 515-16).

Although Sweeney and Christensen discern historical reasons behind the particular list of Judean enemies, Berlin and Floyd point to literary factors. According to Berlin, the principle of inclusion is mythopoetic, drawing from the Table of Nations in Gen 10 (1994, 120-24): the overlapping vocabulary between Zeph 2 and Gen 10 suggests that Zephaniah drew from Genesis, editing it to fit the prophet's own political situation. Floyd suggests that a constellation of factors accounts for the list of nations in Zeph 2: large and small nations are chosen, as are those who stand north, south, east, and west of Judah and (reading with Berlin) those that bear some connection to Gen 10 (2000, 211).

Although the literary connections Floyd and Berlin identify are intriguing, this unit fits well the historical scenario Sweeney describes. Additional support for its Assyrian period background is the unit's building to a speech against Assyria, who receives the greatest attention of the nations lambasted. The strong concern about territory is evident in 2:9, which promises that Judah will benefit from the redistribution of land.

As noted above, these oracles employ many of the stereotypical features of the Oracles against the Nations (OAN). As in other OAN, the nations are accused of pride (Isa 10:12; 13:19; 16:6; Jer 48:29; 49:16; 51:41) and threatened with becoming like

Sodom and Gomorrah (Deut 29:23; Isa 1:9; 13:19; Jer 23:14; 49:18; Amos 4:11). Similarly, Zeph 2 follows the OAN in drawing from the language of ancient Near Eastern treaty curses. For example, Delbert Hillers traces in various ancient treaties the imprecation that the land of those who break treaty will become fit only for habitation by wild animals (1964, 44). Hillers also traces the connection between shaking the fist and hissing in Zeph 2:15 with the curse formulae of many treaties (1964, 76).

The translation of 2:14 is difficult, both in identifying the animals that are named and in understanding the second half of the verse. The two animals of 2:14a (qā'at and qippōd) are variously rendered as "pelican and hedgehog" (NASB); "screech owl and desert owl" (NAB) (the two terms are reversed in NIV and NRSV); and "vulture and hedgehog" (RSV). Both terms appear in Isa 14:23 and 34:11 (the latter of which Hillers connects to the treaty curses), though no evidence is available for a precise determination of the meaning of these terms.

The translation, though not the basic understanding, of 2:14b also varies greatly. Literally, the MT may be rendered, "A voice will sing in the window, Dryness in the bowl (or threshold) because cedar (he) laid bare." Understanding the "voice" as referring back to the animals of the previous verse, NAB reads, "Their call shall resound from the window, the raven's croak from the doorway," and NRSV renders, "The owl shall hoot at the window, the raven croak on the threshold; for its cedar work will be laid bare." Ben Zvi, like the NASB, attempts to remain close to the MT by rendering ḥōreb ("dryness") as "Desolation." All of these translations extend the image of this section, in which mighty cities will be destroyed, inhabited only by wild animals. Much like the figure of Babylon in Isa 47, mighty Nineveh sits in the dust.

Theological Analysis

As elsewhere in the prophetic books, the genre of the Oracles against the Nations raises issues of nationalism. Does the book of Zephaniah claim that God favors only Judah?

That Judah will benefit from God's activity against Philistia,

Cush, the Transjordan, and Assyria is clear in this section. Zephaniah 2:7 is explicit: "The seacoast shall become the possession of the remnant of the house of Judah, on which they shall pasture, and in the houses of Ashkelon they shall lie down at evening." Zephaniah 2:9 extends the thought: "The remnant of my people shall plunder them, and the survivors of my nation shall possess them."

The historical background that Sweeney reconstructs, however, sets the concern with Judah's territorial integrity in context. Having suffered at the hands of its neighbors, Zephaniah's community expresses its conviction that God cares about its plight and will restore the people to their homes.

Within the larger book of Zephaniah, the concern for Judah's welfare does not translate into a blindness to Judah's own problems. As seen clearly in chapter 1, God's judgment comes against *all* nations, including Judah.

WOE AND SALVATION TO JUDAH (AND THE NATIONS) (3:1-13)

After the Oracles against the Nations that dominate 2:5-15, Zeph 3 returns to concern with Judah and its sins that characterized 2:1-4. The nation is first criticized and then, as the unit progresses to its close, promised salvation.

Literary Analysis

The Judean focus of the chapter is not immediately made clear, since the chapter leaves the "stubborn and polluted" city unnamed. Given that the previous chapter also ended with reference to an unnamed city (which, in literary context, seemed to be Nineveh), a reader might initially wonder if the same city is addressed in both chapters. The opening verses, however, give clues that the city is one in Judah: in 3:2-4, it is accused of not trusting in God, and her priests are lambasted for profaning Torah—charges most naturally referring to a Judahite locale. Most interpreters, in turn, identify the addressee of 3:1 as Jerusalem (Floyd 2000, 230).

The resumed concern about Judah does not, however, indicate that Zephaniah has abandoned its consideration of the nations. Indeed, this unit bears an envelope structure, in which the fate of Judah and that of the nations is intertwined, even as the section finally ends with its eye on Judah:

3:1-5	Woe to Judah
3:6-7	The nations are punished as a warning to Judah
3:8-10	The nations are first punished, then restored
3:11-13	Judah is restored

The subject of the woe against Judah, begun in 3:1, continues through 3:5. The faithlessness of the city is contrasted with the faithfulness of God; unlike the one who knows injustice, Yahweh is righteous (3:5).

Zephaniah 3:6-7 provides an important interpretive key to the book of Zephaniah, tying together the book's concern with the nations and with Judah. God's actions against the nations have been undertaken with Judah in mind. The destruction of the nations (which comprises much of Zeph 2) should have led Judah to acknowledge the power of Yahweh and to repent of its own misdeeds.

God's full intention for the nations, however, moves beyond their punishment, as 3:8-10 makes clear. After God pours out wrath on the nations, then their language will be turned into pure speech (overturning the curse of Babel in Gen 11), and all of them will serve God as one (lit., "with one shoulder").

The nations having been restored, 3:11 announces the pending restoration of Judah, addressed as "you." The rebellion and the pride that mark Judah's current behavior (3:1-4) will be overturned in the days to come. A remnant of the humble will be spared (3:12).

Literary echoes bind Zeph 3 with previous chapters. Zephaniah 3:1, which announces woe against Judah, mirrors 2:5, which announces "woe" against the inhabitants of the seacoast; and the promise in 3:13 that Judah will pasture peacefully on its own land repeats the image of 2:7, though both verses stand in contrast to 2:14, which inveighs the turning of the nations into pastureland as a threat. As in chapters 1 and 2, Zeph 3 expresses God's intentions toward "all the inhabitants of the earth" (1:18; 2:4-15) and toward Judah specifically (1:12; 2:1).

Exegetical Analysis

The punishment announced in the first half of the unit addresses not only the city as a whole, but also the leaders of the community. Like other prophets, Zephaniah blames the leaders of the community for leading the people astray (for example, Jer 2:26 and Hos 9:15). In its criticism of "officials," Zeph 3:3 returns to the concern of 1:8 with those in command.

The shift to promises of salvation in the second half of the unit is striking, though a clear understanding of Zephaniah's vision for the restoration of Judah and the nations is complicated by the translational difficulties of 3:10 and following. In the MT of 3:10, the phrase *ʿătāray bat pûṣay* literally reads, "my supplicants, daughter of my dispersed ones." KJV, ASV, and RSV attempt to retain this reading, while NIV, NASB, and NRSV omit "daughter." In keeping with the LXX, NJB omits the phrase "the daughter of my dispersed," and NAB renders the entire phrase "as far as the recesses of the North," based on a conjectural reading given in BHK. Berlin renders the problematic terms as a geographical proper name: Atarai Fair Puzazi (1994, 135). The verse leaves ambiguous just *whom* Zephaniah is envisioning as bringing offerings to Yahweh. Interpreters agree that by 3:13 attention has shifted from the nations to Judah, though they differ on whether that shift begins at 3:10 or 3:11. Are the "dispersed" of 3:10 to be understood as Judean exiles returning from everywhere (from as far away as Cush), supporting Sweeney's claim that the verse "conveys the restoration of the people of Israel and Judah at the Temple in Jerusalem" (2000, 522)? Or will *all* people (even those beyond the rivers of Cush) become worshipers of Yahweh, in keeping with Floyd's understanding that the verse envisions all people becoming God's supplicants (Floyd 2000, 235)?

The usage of the verb *pûṣ* does not resolve these difficulties. Elsewhere, *pûṣ* is used for both scattered Judah (Jer 9:16) and the scattering of other nations (Gen 10:18). Clearly, the meaning of the verse cannot be resolved on lexical grounds, but only inferred based on an understanding of its literary context.

Several clues suggest that the shift between the concern for the nations and that for Judah occurs between 3:10 and 3:11. (1) The phrase "on that day" is a common transitional phrase in the Hebrew Bible. The presence of the phrase in 3:11 signals a minor disjunction between 3:10 and 3:11, allowing for a change in subject. (2) And 3:11 also marks a shift from the third to the second person: the nations are *described* in 3:10, but Judah is *addressed* in 3:11. (3) Both Zeph 3:9 and 3:10 evoke the language of Gen 11. Not only does Zephaniah envision the return of humanity to a state of common language (3:9, see Gen 11:1), but it also uses the same word to describe the scattering of humans as does Gen 11:4 and 8 *(pûṣ)*. These clues suggest that 3:10 imagines all inhabitants of the earth bringing offerings (see, too, Mal 1:11), though it does not explain the meaning of "daughter" in the phrase, which remains an enigma.

Zephaniah 3:10 marks the third reference to Cush in Zephaniah. In Zeph 1:1, Cushi is listed among the ancestors of Zephaniah. In 2:12, Cush seems to assume a historical dimension: the prediction that Cushites will be killed by the sword is sandwiched between announcements of punishment against Moabites and Ammonites and Assyria. Such references suggest that here, in 3:10, Cush is not merely an hyperbole for "far away" (as in Ps 68:31 and perhaps in Isa 45:14), but likely reflects the book's distinctive concern with this distant nation.

In 3:12, Zephaniah promises that Yahweh will rescue a remnant of the "humble" *(ʿānî)* and the "lowly" *(dāl)*. Some translate *ʿānî* as "poor" and suggest that Zephaniah treats the economically disadvantaged as the remnant of Israel (see, too, exegetical remarks on Zeph 2:3). Such a nuance to the term is not clear, however. Elsewhere in the Hebrew Bible, *ʿānî* is used for various types of affliction: though it at times refers to those without economic resources (Exod 22:25), it also describes those who are childless (Gen 29:32), defeated in war (Lam 1:9; NRSV: "affliction"), or forced into submission (Exod 10:3). *Dāl* refers generally to those who "lack," in contrast to the rich (Exod 30:15; Ruth 3:10) and to the great (Lev 19:5). According to Rodd, in the Hebrew Bible, "the ethics of poverty is subsumed under that of oppression" (2001, 184). The contrast being made in Zeph 3:12-13 between the *ʿānî* and the *dāl*, on the one hand, and the haughty and prideful, on the other, suggests that the humility that Yahweh will reward is attitudinal, not socioeconomic.

Theological Analysis

This unit, as previous units in the book of Zephaniah, points to a complex relationship between Judah and the rest of the world. On the one hand, Yahweh's care extends to the nations: they will be restored and will offer sacrifices to Yahweh. On the other hand, the nations' punishment is not for their own wrongdoings as much as for the instruction of Judah, and Judah remains the primary focus of Zephaniah's remarks.

For ancient and modern communities that identify with Judah, Zephaniah embodies the dialectic (and occasional tension) between proclaiming that God has a special relationship with covenant communities and also that all humanity is interconnected. Zephaniah's words challenge both any attempt to limit the scope of God's power to the church or to synagogue, on the one hand, and cultural and religious relativism, on the other.

Zephaniah is insistent that not all who claim membership in the covenant community will survive. Voicing the theology of the "remnant" common to many of the prophets, Zephaniah offers hope only to those within the community who are humble. This humility is attitudinal and not necessarily economic, echoing the stance against pride that permeates Isaiah.

PROMISES OF RESTORATION FOR JUDAH (AND THE NATIONS) (3:14-20)

The book of Zephaniah closes with a "happy ending." In strongly gendered language, Daughter Jerusalem will be defended and cared for by Yahweh, her king and savior.

Literary Analysis

The beginning of a new unit is signaled by the shift to direct address in 3:14: Zion is called to rejoice because her judgment has been taken away. More technically, three subjects are addressed (Daughter Zion, Israel, Daughter Jerusalem), and although they seem to be equated, Israel is addressed with a masculine plural command while "daughters" Zion and Jerusalem are addressed in feminine singular.

The unit makes several temporal shifts. It begins with commands, calling Zion to rejoice *now*. Zephaniah 3:15 announces that God *has* turned away the enemy (perfect verb, completed action). Zephaniah 3:16 speaks of the salvation Jerusalem will *experience* in the future (imperfect verbs, incomplete action, best translated as future). These shifts, along with the vocabulary of the unit ("on that day" and "fear not"), mark it as a promise of salvation, a later development of the preexilic oracle of salvation that may have been uttered by priests (see Floyd 2000, 248-49). That is, the change in Judah's fortunes in 3:15 may not reflect a shift in historical circumstances, but rather indicate the confidence of the author that Judah will indeed be saved.

In strongly gendered imagery, the description of Zion/Jerusalem as a daughter is juxtaposed with that of Yahweh as a king in 3:15 and as a warrior in 3:17 (*gibbôr*, translated in NAB as "savior," and in NKJV as "Mighty One"). With a mighty (male) protector, she need not fear evil anymore (3:15).

Exegetical Analysis

As noted above, the indication in 3:15 that Judah has been saved from its enemy may be a literary device more than the reflection of a change in the historical conditions of the community. The enemy remains unnamed in this unit, though Zeph 2 clearly indicates that numerous nations stand as enemies of Judah. The Moabites and Ammonites will be punished because they reproached God's people (2:10), and the general enmity between Judah and the nations is indicated by their inverse fortunes. Hence, the book of Zephaniah, ever shifting in its description of the relationship between Judah and the nations, ends with Judah as distinct from, and triumphant over, others.

The translation of the second half of 3:17 is greatly disputed. The verb *ḥāraš* usually means "be silent or deaf" (as in Num 30:14; NRSV: "say nothing"), accounting for the NIV's "he will be quiet in his love." The NASB makes the verb causative: "he will quiet you with his love," similar to the JPS reading of "soothe." Assuming that "silence" does not fit the context of Zeph 3:17, especially since the next phrase claims that Yahweh will rejoice with a ringing cry, others emend the verb based on the readings of ancient Versions: Sweeney to "I will betroth" (2000, 524), and the RSV, NRSV, NAB, and NJB to "renew" (based on the Greek reading, emended to Hebrew *ḥādāš*). Ben Zvi argues for the MT reading, explaining that God is holding back rebuke (and, hence, is silent) out of love for the community (1991, 251-52). His reading has the benefit of honoring the MT and of accepting the most difficult reading, even though the verse remains enigmatic.

Similarly, the translation of 3:18 is unclear, literally reading, "the grieving ones from the assembly I will gather from you, they were a burden upon her a reproach." The first word, "grieving," is found at the end of 3:17 in the Septuagint, and NRSV omits it in translation. Despite numerous attempts to solve this textual puzzle (see Berlin 1994, 146), none remains convincing, leaving the verse unintelligible.

In 3:19 God promises to deal with Judah's "oppressors." Translated in English as a noun, "oppressors" is in Hebrew a participle, derived from the root *ʿānāh*, the same one translated as "humble" in 2:3 and 3:12. While the earlier two occurrences likely refer to spiritual attitude, the context in 3:19 implies a more physical dimension. Grammatically, the participle appears in a form that gives a causative effective: Judah will be saved from those who have *made* her humble—that is, humiliated her.

This verse, along with the mention of the enemy in 3:15, indicates a new concern in Zephaniah with Judah's punishment at the hands of a party other than Yahweh. As chapter 2 lambasted other nations for vaunting themselves over Judah, this unit states explicitly that Judah has suffered at the hands of enemies.

The last phrase of 3:20 says, "when I restore your captives before your eyes, says the LORD." Numerous contemporary commentators have rendered the promise more generally as "restore your fortunes," based on the general usage in Job 42:10, in which the same word describes the restoration of Job's former state. The more general meaning is promoted by those who see a reference to the return of exiles anachronistic, since Zephaniah spoke long before the Babylonian exile. The more literal reading of "captives," however, fits well with the concern about the dispersed ones in 3:10, and the phrase is common elsewhere in referring to the return of those scattered: Deut 30:3; Jer 29:14; 30:3, 18; 31:23; 32:44; 33:7; Joel 3:1; Amos 9:14.

The concern with returnees raises questions regarding the historical setting of the pericope. Those who accept a seventh-century setting for the book see attention to returnees as anachronistic and thus evidence that Zephaniah, like many of the prophetic books, has been edited to end with a promise of salvation. Nogalski, for example, lists numerous interpreters who treat all or parts of 3:9-20 as a postexilic addition (1993, 201-2). Ben Zvi agrees that the perspective of the unit is postexilic but claims that the entire book of Zephaniah derives from the postexilic community (1991, 324).

The passage does, indeed, have much in common with other prophetic passages considered postexilic:

Micah 4:6 In that day, says the LORD, I will assemble the lame and gather those who have been driven away, and those whom I have afflicted.

Zechariah 10:8-11 I will signal for them and gather them in, for I have redeemed them, and they shall be as numerous as they were before. Though I scattered them among the nations, yet in far countries they shall remember me, and they shall rear their children and return. I will bring them home from the land of Egypt, and gather them from Assyria; I will bring them to the land of Gilead and to Lebanon, until there is no room for them.

Isaiah 11:11-12 On that day the Lord will extend his hand yet a second time to recover the remnant that is left of his people, from Assyria, from Egypt, from Pathros, from Ethiopia, from Elam, from Shinar, from Hamath, and from the coastlands of the sea. He will raise a signal for the nations, and will assemble the outcasts of Israel, and gather the dispersed of Judah from the four corners of the earth.

Zephaniah 3:14-20 certainly resonates with the postexilic situation and with texts considered to date to that period.

Before the text is definitely dated to the postexilic era, however, several cautions are in order. First, this closing pericope is not the only part of Zephaniah to express concern with the ingathering of those scattered. As discussed above, 3:10 also speaks of the return of dispersed ones, either Judean or perhaps those of other nations. Moreover, Isa 11:11-12 (see above) bears many similarities (especially in place names) with Zeph 2, the latter usually identified as reflecting the Assyrian period.

Second, positing the pericope as a postexilic composition is based solely on the assumption that in no period other than in the Babylonian could a writer express concern about those living outside of the homeland. Although certainly the Babylonian exile marked massive demographic upheavals, earlier military campaigns of the Assyrians also dispersed members of the covenant community; the fact that Israel is named alongside Judah in 3:14 may indicate that the northern kingdom also factored into the author's hopes for a future restoration (see, too, 2 Chr 30:9, in which Hezekiah, during the Assyrian period, addresses those who are captives and who will be returned to their land). As noted above (see Exegetical Analysis on 2:5-15), Sweeney argues that during the Assyrian period, Judeans were relocated from the

Shephelah into Philistia, and Tranjordanian territory was transferred from Judah to the Ammonites and Moabites, producing a
sizable number of exiles (2000, 515-16).

The current book of Zephaniah, then, resonates in multiple
ways. (1) When read within the Assyrian context of its superscription, the book speaks to the restoration of the Judean community after the upheavals of the seventh century. In this reading,
the concern with restoration in 3:14-20 reiterates and expands
upon the hope expressed in 2:7 and 3:13. (2) When read within
its literary context in the larger prophetic corpus and in the Bible
itself, "exiles" takes on a Babylonian nuance and suggests that
an Assyrian-period prophet foretold events beyond his own life-
time. In their final form, many prophetic books speak of events
prior to their actualization. For example, the prophetic words
attributed to Haggai and Zechariah seem to address a contemporaneous building project, but the words of Amos and Jeremiah
are presented as delivered prior to the fall of their respective
nations, and the final form of Isaiah includes a mention of Cyrus
the Persian, who lived two hundred years after the date given for
Isaiah in the book's superscription. In the case of Zeph 3, the
mention of a return from the Babylonian exile by an Assyrian-
period prophet would give greater weight not only to the
prophet's reputation, but also to the promise itself. As Sweeney
well notes (2000, 493), Zephaniah's placement between
Habakkuk, set in the Babylonian context, and Haggai, set in the
Persian period, would invite a reader to infer that Zephaniah is
concerned with the Babylonian period.

The compositional history of the book is rendered even more
complicated by the evident overlap in verses 19 and 20. The two
share much vocabulary: "in that time," "to praise and a name,"
and "gathering." But, although in 3:19 God promises to return
the lame and the outcast, turning them to praise and a name,
3:20 extends the promises to "you," suggesting a larger and
more inclusive audience. The expansion of the promise may very
well be the work of a later editor.

Theological Analysis

The happy ending of the book of Zephaniah contrasts the strong word of punishment with which the book began. Although in chapter 1 God vows to wipe out everything from the face of the ground and to stretch out the hand against Judah, chapter 3 closes with God's promises to restore Judah and its renown.

Many interpreters consider the message of judgment incompatible with the message of salvation and explain their dual appearance in the book as a mark of its redaction. Zephaniah, however, at least in its final form, binds these two facets of God together: the God who punishes wickedness and idolatry is the same God who cares for the people and offers them comfort. In this affirmation, Zephaniah challenges modern readers against sentimentalizing the love of God. God's care for humans does not preclude—and in fact may require—God's action against oppression and wrongdoing.

Zephaniah, nonetheless, bears many of the same tensions with which the contemporary world wrestles. In its seemingly shifting understanding of the relationship between Judah and the nations, Zephaniah raises the issue of particularity and universalism: Do nations (and faiths) share a common destiny, or it is appropriate for some to understand themselves as closer than others to the heart of God? Zephaniah may be read to affirm both responses, but, perhaps most important, Zephaniah also insists that no nation or faith stands beyond the judgment—or care—of God. All are chastened for their pride and are called to "seek righteousness, seek humility" (2:3).

INTRODUCTION: HAGGAI

In turning to the final three books of the Prophets, the reader of the Jewish and Christian canons encounters a new set of concerns. Haggai, Zechariah, and Malachi are set in the Persian period, inaugurated when Cyrus the Persian conquered the ancient Near East in 538 B.C.E. and implemented a policy of governing subject peoples on their home territories. The books reflect the distinctive concerns of this period—the nature of Jewish identity and the role of the Temple and its priesthood in a nation living under colonial rule.

LITERARY ANALYSIS

The book of Haggai is punctuated by various date formulae, all within the second year of the reign of the Persian king Darius. These date formulae, along with shifts in topic, give the book the following structure:

1:1-11	Disputation over building; first day of sixth month
1:12-15	The community's response; twenty-fourth day of sixth month
2:1-9	An oracle in the midst of building the Temple; first day of seventh month
2:10-19	A request for a priestly ruling; twenty-fourth day of ninth month

2:20-23   Oracle regarding Zerubbabel; twenty-
            fourth day of ninth month

Most commentators recognize a similar outline, though they differ on the number of units defined. For example, Meyers and Meyers (1987, xlviii) delineate two units, and Petersen (1984, 32) distinguishes five. The only major disagreement involves 1:15. Since a date formula appears at 1:15*b*, many commentators see it as the beginning of a new unit (Redditt 1995; Floyd 2000) or even as belonging with the oracle in 2:15-19 (Mason 1977, 414). Meyers and Meyers (1987, 36-37) well argue, however, that the data provided by 1:15*b* complete the information given in the first chapter and that the mention of the "second year" applies both to chapter 1 and to chapter 2.

Although it contains oracular speech, the book of Haggai is primarily narrative in style. Even its opening does not constitute a standard prophetic superscription. Rather than being set apart from the book as other superscriptions are, Hag 1:1 is integrated into the story line of the book. The narrative orientation of Haggai is particularly evident in 1:12-15, which reports the response of the community to the prophet's words in 1:1-11.

A distinctive feature of the book is its repetitive, almost formulaic use of language. "Thus says Yahweh" appears five times (1:2, 4, 7; 2:6, 11); Haggai is called a "prophet" five times (1:1, 3, 12; 2:1, 10); "the word of Yahweh" appears five times (1:1, 3; 2:1, 10, 20); the deity is called "Yahweh of hosts" twelve times (1:2, 5, 7, 9, 14; 2:4, 6, 7, 8, 9, 11, 23); and the phrase "set your minds upon your ways" appears twice (1:5, 7). The entire phrase "the word of Yahweh by the hand of Haggai the prophet" is repeated in 1:1, 3 and 2:1; and the phrase "the word of Yahweh was unto Haggai the prophet" occurs in 2:10 and 2:20. The descriptions of the two primary characters, Zerubbabel and Joshua, likewise are formulaic: Zerubbabel is described not once, but three times by both his father's name and his title (1:1, 14; 2:2), twice more by his father's name (1:12; 2:23), and once more by his title (2:21); he is identified by name alone only in

2:4. Joshua is identified by both his father's name and his title in all four references (1:1, 14; 2:2, 4).

Commentators such as Mason (1977) have viewed much of Haggai's repetitive language as a clue to the book's compositional history, but perhaps even more interesting is its effect on the reader of the book's final form. As a result of its repetitive language, especially in describing the activity of Haggai, the book becomes self-consciously prophetic: few books in the canon draw so much attention to the prophetic nature of the material. Ironically, this hyperprophetic language itself raises the question of why its author or editor felt the need to stress the book's prophetic character.

This question becomes particularly pertinent in light of the book's retrospective character: Haggai describes the Temple project in the past. The verb tenses indicate that by the time of the book's completion, Haggai's activities were over, and the Temple was likely finished. The great stress that the book places on the prophetic credentials of Haggai and of the prophetic legitimation of the building project, then, serve not to encourage Temple rebuilding but rather to address issues of a later time.

SOCIAL AND HISTORICAL ANALYSIS

The Persian period setting of the book is clearly indicated by its date formulae and by its description of Darius as "the king." Darius ascended to the Persian (Achaemenid) throne late in the year 522, following Cambyses (530–522). The second year of Darius's reign corresponds to 520.

The Persian Empire was founded by Cyrus the Great, who assumed power over Babylon in 539. Cyrus's imperial policy, as documented in the Bible and on the Cyrus Cylinder, was to govern subject populations on their own soil. Hence, those who had been displaced by the earlier Babylonian policy of exile were not only allowed, but also encouraged to return to their ancestral lands. The Neirab archive from Aleppo, for example, found in the 1920s, contains numerous loan transactions that describe extensive movements of population groups under Persian rule.

Once population groups were properly relocated, they were kept under Persian control by a local governor who ensured the giving of tribute to the royal treasuries. In each community, a dominant elite would be identified, and its loyalty would help advance Persian interests. The Persians typically used local instruments in their effort to solidify their rule; in Egypt and elsewhere, they mandated and financed the restoring and building of temples to local deities, both to promote goodwill and also to establish an institution through which Persian policy could be administered.

The biblical account of the Return fits much of what we learn from other sources vis-à-vis Persian policy. The book of Ezra describes the rebuilding of the Temple as mandated (not just allowed) by Cyrus and the cost of rebuilding as funded through Persian treasuries (Ezra 1, 6). The book of Nehemiah also describes the burden of the heavy tribute that the community paid the Persians (Neh 9:36-37). Nehemiah's commission from the Persian government to return to Yehud (the name for the province under Persian rule) and rebuild the walls of Jerusalem may be seen as a military fortification of an area strategically important to Persian interests.

The description of the Temple rebuilding project given in Haggai and Zech 1–8 fits with the one outlined in the book of Ezra. According to Ezra 2:68–3:7, a first wave of return was initiated after Cyrus's Edict in 538. This group, which included the governor Zerubbabel and the chief priest Joshua, first set up an altar for sacrifices and then, in the second year of its arrival, began work on the Temple proper. The laying of the foundation of the Temple was a cause for great celebration (Ezra 3:10-11). After meeting opposition from various groups, the building of the Second Temple was completed in the sixth year of Darius's reign (= 516, Ezra 6:15).

Although the degree to which the books of Ezra and Nehemiah are historically reliable is disputed, their description of the Temple rebuilding project provides a helpful narrative background for the books of Haggai and Zechariah. The date formulae of both prophetic collections fall within the dates outlined in Ezra, and, when the materials are read together, Haggai and Zechariah appear to provide the impetus for the activities completed in Ezra. Haggai's description of a functioning sacrificial system and priesthood prior to the completion of the Temple (2:11-14) is understandable in light of Ezra's indication that the altar was established before the Temple as a whole.

The Jerusalem Temple had long been central to Judean worship, but it took on a new role in the Persian period. As noted above, recent study of Persian imperial administration indicates the great interest that the Persians took in the work of local Temples, likely using them as venues for the collection of taxes and the distribution of royal allotments. Joel Weinberg (1992) has argued that a new form of social-political organization began in the Persian period. In this "civic-temple-community," the landed gentry allied themselves with the Temple personnel to form a new privileged class. Although scholars have debated the details of Weinberg's model, there is general consensus that the Temple functioned as a place of power in the postexilic Judean community and was connected in some way with Persian interests. In turn, the leadership of the Temple, the priesthood, took on more of an administrative character in this period (for a more extensive discussion, see *Second Temple Studies* 1991).

The concern that Haggai, Zechariah, and Malachi devote to the Temple and its priesthood is understandable in light of Persian policy. Both the preexilic and postexilic prophets addressed the leaders of their societies; though the former leadership was concentrated in the monarchy, and the latter was to be found in the governor and in the priesthood. In addressing Zerubbabel, the Persian-appointed governor, and Joshua, the great priest, Haggai thus addresses the two major leadership roles in the Persian-period Judean community. The figures of Zerubbabel and Joshua also take center stage in Ezra 3:8, in which they wield the authority to appoint the Levites to oversee Temple rebuilding.

In Haggai's support of the ruling powers and in its attribution of eschatological significance to Zerubbabel, Paul Hanson has seen the program of an elitist party in Persian Yehud. Throughout Persian period texts, Hanson discerns the struggle between hierocratic and theocratic factions—that is, between the returnees from Babylon, who limited priesthood to the Zadokites, and those who had remained in the land, a more inclusive group who supported the rights of all descendants of Levi to serve as altar priests. In Haggai, Hanson clearly hears the program of the hierocrats, promising the population eschatological blessings if it supports the cult and its hierarchy (Hanson 1986, 262).

Hanson well recognizes that not all shared equally in the power and privilege of the reconstituted Temple and that though Zechariah favors the returnees, Third Isaiah sees the Temple as the place where various factions of the community may meld. But Hanson's stark delineation of the postexilic community into two camps—one pro-establishment and other anti-establishment—provides an overly simplistic explanation of a diverse community. More sober is the judgment of David Petersen, who claims that postexilic prophetic materials manifest a wide variety of positions on the Temple and the constituents of "Israel" (1991, 9).

Understanding the Persian setting of the book of Haggai clearly is important for an appreciation of the Temple rebuilding project itself, but the retrospective nature of the book is also intriguing. Although nothing in the book suggests a significant time lag between Haggai's supposed career and the book's composition, the fact that the book was written after the Temple was complete, after the debates over its rebuilding would have been moot, indicates another dimension to the book's argument. Its goal would have been less to convince the original audience to build than to persuade the subsequent readers of the book to think in a particular way about the past; the extraordinary lengths to which the author goes to establish that Haggai was a prophet and that the instructions to build the Temple were God's intention indicate some anxiety in the years *after* the Temple's completion. Exactly what these later debates were is difficult to ascertain, however, and without concrete historical markers, the reader is left to understand the prophet's message within its supposed time period.

THEOLOGICAL ANALYSIS

Hanson is not alone in denigrating Haggai for its concern with the Temple. Many scholars in the late-nineteenth century described Haggai as a pale imitation of the earlier classical prophets, negatively contrasting Haggai, who "only" supported the building of an edifice devoted to "ritual," with Amos, who preached passionately against those who offered their sacrifices while ignoring the poor. Such judgments arose from the understanding that "true" prophets were moral revolutionaries who stood against the ritual and institutions of their age.

Although more recent evaluations have recognized that prophets fulfilled a wide range of functions in ancient Judah—some supportive of and some challenging of institutions—Haggai's concern with the Temple continues to win it little praise. Those who find positive value in the book suggest that it can be generalized into a message about priorities, also assuming that if it were "only" about the rebuilding of the Temple it would be inferior.

When differences between the organization of the preexilic and postexilic communities are taken into account, however, prophets of the two periods may be seen as quite similar. The Temple and the sacrificial system feature prominently in Jeremiah, Ezekiel, and Isaiah, but even those preexilic books that challenge the community's treatment of others nonetheless presuppose the existence of the Temple. Only in the absence of the Temple, a situation unknown to the preexilic prophets, would the concern have arisen for the state of the Temple structure.

The centrality of the Temple in the political organization of Yehud also suggests that it took on the importance attached in the earlier preexilic period to the monarchy. Though many earlier prophets had challenged the particular policies of kings, few challenged monarchy as an institution; as the case with the Temple, monarchy was a "given," such that prophets called for its reform, and not its abolition. Haggai's support of the Temple and of the individual Zerubbabel seems little different than Isaiah's support of the role of the Temple and the ideal Davidic king. In both cases, prophets address the needs of their society and the locus of power within it.

Haggai is also seen by some as problematic for drawing a direct correlation between pleasing God and material success. Based on the Hag 1:9-11 connection of the people's suffering with their failure to build the Temple, Hanson claims that "for those who devoted themselves to the Zadokite temple program, Haggai was the bearer of lavish promises" (1986, 262). Haggai's claim may indeed be problematic, but it stands fully within the message of the preexilic prophets. Hosea and Amos also drew connections between God's favor and agricultural success, and indeed the overarching message of the prophets is that the people's behaviors bring upon them either blessing or curse.

Haggai's concern for the Temple, then, is an extension of and not a radical departure from, earlier prophecy. And the issues it raises, of God's investment in particular institutions and of the connection between earthly success and finding divine favor, are those raised not only by preexilic prophets, but also by our modern faith communities.

Recognizing that the rhetoric of the book was crafted for the sake of a community in which the Temple has already been completed also reminds the modern reader that the prophetic materials were preserved not merely as historical records of divine communication, but also as documents of persuasion. These materials seek to persuade their readers to believe something specific about God and how God works and to act in accordance with that belief.

COMMENTARY: HAGGAI

DISPUTATION OVER BUILDING (1:1-11)

After setting the prophet within a specific time frame in the Persian period, the opening unit of Haggai proclaims the divine word regarding the building of the Temple. Using classical forms of prophetic speech, the book announces that the people's lack of agricultural success is due to their failure to build Yahweh's house.

Literary Analysis

Although the opening of Haggai contains the same type of material that would be included in a prophetic superscription, it does not follow the superscription form. Rather, it reads as the beginning of a narrative, providing the setting for a recounting of what the prophet Haggai said. Employing the first of five date formulae, Hag 1:1 sets the scene in the first day of the sixth month of the second year of Darius's reign. It is unique among prophetic beginnings in indicating that the message is not to the population in general, but to two specific figures: Zerubbabel the governor and Joshua the great priest.

As in many prophetic books, the content of Haggai is marked with messenger speech (1:2, "thus says Yahweh"), but what follows is less the word of Yahweh to the leaders than it is a revelation of what the people are thinking. Yahweh's description of what the people say provides the impetus for the unit. It sets up the erroneous thesis that the rest of the unit will refute. The unit is clearly argumentative in tone, though one-sided: we hear Yahweh's statement of what the people say, not their own voice. A clear example of the multilayered nature of the "voice" of the unit is found in 1:2. Like a stack of nesting dolls, the book says that Haggai told Zerubbabel and Joshua that God said that the people said that the time had not yet come to build the Temple. Yahweh's speech in 1:4-11, though still addressed to Zerubbabel and Joshua, does not speak to them directly, but rather reports Yahweh's response to the people.

In introducing God's response to the people's claim that the Temple should not yet be rebuilt, 1:3 approximates a second beginning of the book, repeating from 1:3 that "the word of Yahweh was by the hand of Haggai the prophet" (AT). Messenger speech is used repeatedly throughout the unit, in 1:5, 7, 8, and 9, making clear that the perspective of the unit is that of Yahweh.

Yahweh's argument against the people's perspective develops in two stages, each marked by "set your hearts upon your ways" (NRSV: "consider how you have fared"). In 1:5-6, Yahweh points to the futility of the people's labors: they have worked hard yet achieved little. In 1:7-11, Yahweh explains that the people have not prospered because they have not rebuilt the Temple. The people have built their own houses (1:4, 9), though they have paid no attention to Yahweh's house (1:2, 4, 8). The drought and crop failures that the people have experienced were sent by Yahweh as punishment for their disregard of his house and of his honor (1:8). Implied in the command to build in 1:8 is the promise that the material conditions of life will improve when the people change their perspective and undertake building.

Throughout the unit, Yahweh speaks both *to* and *for* the people. Yahweh gives voice to the people's frustration in 1:6 and 1:9, though the reader never learns how the people themselves are thinking about their lack of success (Do they blame Yahweh?). The beliefs or thoughts of the people are presented not for their own sake, but as foils for Yahweh's own argument. In a tone that ranges from scolding to tantalizing, Yahweh calls the people to build the Temple.

Exegetical Analysis

The implied historical setting of the unit is clearly marked by its opening date formula: the first day of the sixth month in the second year of the Persian king Darius corresponds to August 29, 520. As discussed in the introduction, Darius took the throne of Persia late in the year 522, following Cambyses. Designating Darius as "the king" (as opposed to "the king of Persia") suggests the writer's chronological proximity and accommodation to the Persian control of Yehud.

The two recipients of the message, Zerubbabel the governor and Joshua the great priest, are also mentioned in the book of Ezra as leaders of the community. The name Zerubbabel likely is Babylonian, meaning "seed of Babylon." Haggai calls Zerubbabel the son of Shealtiel, though 1 Chr 3:19 lists him as the son of Pedaiah. Both Shealtiel and Pedaiah were sons of Jeconiah/Jehoiachin (1 Chr 3:17-18), the Judean king exiled to Babylon when Nebuchadnezzar's armies destroyed Jerusalem in 586 B.C.E. Though commentators have debated which text preserves the more accurate genealogy, of greatest importance is Zerubbabel's Davidic lineage.

Exactly what Zerubbabel's role as "governor" entailed is unclear. The term itself is ambiguous: in the Bible, the term *peḥâ* is used in texts describing Assyrian (1 Kgs 10:15; 2 Kgs 18:24), Babylonian (Jer 51:23), and Persian (Esth 3:12; Neh 2:7) contexts; and in the Persian period, *peḥâ* referred to persons of different rank (Meyers and Meyers 1987, 16). The precise administrative structure of Persian-period Yehud is also unclear. Was Yehud a smaller unit in a larger province or independent in the time of Zerubbabel? Biblical and extrabiblical texts produce a mixed picture: although Zerubbabel appears to have been granted Persian authority over the community, the testimony of the Samaritan intervention in the Temple rebuilding project (Ezra 4) suggests Samaritan oversight of Yehud (for a good discussion of these matters, see Redditt 1995, 5-10). Hence, Haggai's description of Zerubbabel as "governor" indicates that his authority was recognized by the Persian Empire, however the extent of Zerubbabel's authority remains unclear.

Just as Zerubbabel's lineage is traced back to preexilic Judah, so, too, is Joshua's. Jehozadak, his father, was the priest sent into exile by Nebuchadnezzar (1 Chr 6:15 [Heb. 5:41]). Both Joshua and Zerubbabel, then, come with preexilic pedigrees. Joshua's title as "great priest" *(hakkōhēn haggādôl)* is usually translated as "high priest." The title is used to describe preexilic leaders (2 Kgs 12:11), as is the term "chief priest" *kōhēn hār'ōš* (2 Kgs 25:18), though its usage is most prevalent in Nehemiah, Haggai, and Zechariah. Meyers and Meyers suggest that Haggai used the term to stress the administrative responsibilities of the office (1987, 181), though as in the case of the title "governor," the precise nature of Joshua's duties is not clear.

The name Haggai likely draws from the root *ḥāgag,* which means "make festival." It appears in lists of Babylonian Jews after the exile and may be an Aramaic version of the Hebrew name Haggi (Zadok 1979, 23-24). Of the three main human characters of the book, Haggai is the only one whose father's name is not specified.

The unit describes a situation in which the people have rebuilt their own homes but not yet rebuilt the Temple. The chronology of the Return given in the book of Ezra corroborates with this description. Although the altar was erected in 538 upon the initial return and the Temple foundation laid two years later, work on the Temple was not resumed until the second year of Darius (Ezra 4:24).

Underlying Haggai's critique of the people's attitudes is the recognition that the economic situation of the postexilic community was tenuous. Although most modern translations describe the people's houses as "paneled" in 1:4, the word itself may not imply luxury. The same root is used to describe work that is "finished" in 1 Kgs 6:9 and "covered" in 1 Kgs 7:7. In 1 Kgs 6:15, the root describes a ceiling and in its verbal form is translated as "roofed" in 1 Kgs 7:3. The adjective form, found here, does appear in other passages in the context of luxury, although there the paneling is specified as "with cedar" (1 Kgs 7:3; Jer 22:14). Thus, the *way* in which the houses are paneled (or roofed) may imply luxury, but not the paneling alone.

Indeed, the unit as a whole betrays the difficulties with which the postexilic community was struggling. Yahweh's argument presupposes that the people do indeed feel that they work to no avail (1:6), and 1:10-11 indicates that the land suffers from drought and crop failure. Although the prophetic rhetoric blames the people for putting their own needs ahead of rebuilding the Temple, clues in the unit indicate that they do not do so out of a selfish focus on their own luxury; rather, in a time of hardship, they see their own survival as taking precedence.

The possibility of the retrospective nature of the narrative would add another layer of "voice" to Haggai's message: this book claims that in the past God spoke to Haggai the prophet who reported what God claimed the people said. What would the function of this book have been in the years after the Temple's completion? It certainly would have underscored the centrality of the Temple because of its divine and prophetic authorization, and it would suggest that the economic well-being of the community depends upon the proper maintenance of the Temple structure.

Theological Analysis

The argument advanced in this first section of Haggai draws a direct correlation between the people's willingness to build the Temple and their material success in the land. Their reticence to build not only thwarts their wage-earning, but also affects the rain and the produce of the ground. In this way, Haggai is very similar to the book of Deuteronomy and the editorial framework of the Deuteronomistic History (Joshua, Judges, Samuel, Kings), which also promises blessings upon those who follow God's commands and curses upon those who do not.

The way in which obedience to God is identified with willingness to rebuild the Temple, however, is distinct from these other texts. If indeed the altar had already been built and sacrifices resumed, then Haggai's interest is not with the restoration of the sacrificial system. Rather, he suggests that the issue is one of God's honor (1:8). According to Haggai, by placing their own needs ahead of the Temple, even in a time of scarcity, the community has displeased God.

Appreciating the centrality that Haggai places upon the Temple edifice is difficult for many modern readers, whose own sense of faith might not be tied to institutions or particular locations. To find value in Haggai, contemporary commentators often generalize its message as one about "putting God first" or "setting priorities." Meyers and Meyers, pointing to the importance of the Temple in the governance of postexilic Yehud, suggest that for Haggai, Temple rebuilding signifies the reconstitution of the community (1987, 42)—again looking for a modern value with which Haggai can be correlated.

Without denigrating the value of these general truths drawn from the book of Haggai, it may also be important to recognize the strangeness of this book, the way in which its message might have spoken to an ancient audience in ways different than it speaks to contemporary readers. The multilayered significance of the Temple in Persian Yehud finds no ready modern counterpart. Such a recognition of the distance between Haggai's world and our own calls us to consider the historically specific nature of the Bible and how God speaks differently in different times and places.

THE COMMUNITY'S RESPONSE (1:12-15)

The narrative that begins in Hag 1:1 resumes in this section, reporting in third person narration the response of the community to the preceding argument. Although God's speech had been addressed to Zerubbabel and Joshua alone, they are joined in their response by the people, suggesting that the leaders stand as representatives of the community as a whole.

Literary Analysis

The sequence of the unit is important. First, the leaders and the people obeyed and feared God; God promised to be with them (a promise of protection, as in Jer 42:11); God stirred their spirits; and only then did they begin to work on the Temple. This sequence indicates that the building itself did not provoke God's promise to be present with the community; rather, their obedience and fear are rewarded. The people's change in attitude serves as the precondition for God stirring their spirits to act.

As in the previous one, this unit uses repetitive and verbose language. Even though Joshua and Zerubbabel have already been introduced, their credentials are described again. In 1:14, Zerubbabel's father is mentioned, though not his role as governor, and full information is given for Joshua; in 1:14 full information is given for both. In 1:13, Haggai the "messenger" speaks "with the message," and in 1:14, God stirs up the spirit of Zerubbabel *and* the spirit of Joshua *and* the spirit of the people. Yahweh is mentioned eight times and is called "their God" three times.

Exegetical Analysis

The mention of the "remnant" of the people in 1:12 and 1:14 has raised questions about whether Haggai follows Ezra and Nehemiah in recognizing subgroups within the postexilic community. Ezra, for example, makes a clear distinction between the returned exiles, sometimes called "the Gola" *(bĕnê haggôlâ or haggôlâ),* and the "people of the land." Such a distinction is not likely being made here, however, given that the "remnant of the people" seems to be treated synonymously with "the people" in 1:13 and "this people" in 1:2.

In its description of Haggai as the "messenger of Yahweh," Hag 1:13 is similar to Mal 1:1, which treats the prophet as a messenger. Though prophets are not frequently called messengers in the Bible, their characteristic use of "thus says Yahweh" casts them in the role of the ancient Near Eastern messenger.

Haggai 1:15 gives the only date formula in the book to appear at the end of a unit. The first half of the verse provides the information that this is the sixth month, twenty-three days later than the date given in 1:1; the second half of the verse further specifies that it is the second year of King Darius. Because 2:1 also begins with a date formula, most commentators understand 1:15*b* as the beginning of a new unit, such that the indication of the year belongs with the formula that begins chapter 2. The NRSV, for example, formats 1:15*b* as the beginning of chapter 2. Meyers and Meyers, however, appropriately suggest that the year belongs with both the preceding and the following date formula (1987, 36-37); and, since the entire book is set in the second year of Darius, either option renders the same date.

The importance of beginning work on the Temple is second only to the laying of the Temple foundation stone in chapter 2. As Petersen notes, the beginning of the work on 1:14 seems a fulfillment of Cyrus's instructions in 2 Chr 36:23 for the community to build Yahweh's Temple in Jerusalem; and just as in 2 Chronicles Cyrus is reported to have said "may Yahweh his God be with him" [i.e., all who return to rebuild], so, too, in Hag 1:13, Yahweh reports "I am with you" (Petersen 1984, 56-57).

Theological Analysis

The sequence of events outlined in this unit suggests that the completion of the Temple was less important than the people's obedience to the divine word as communicated through Haggai. Yahweh promised to be with the people not because of their success in building, but because they feared. As is especially clear in the book of Deuteronomy, "fear" of Yahweh is prerequisite to proper reverence and worship (Deut 4:10; 6:2, 13; 10:12, 20). The people's ability to work is not the cause of a changed relationship with God, but rather the result: God stirs their spirits to work only after they obey God and God's prophet.

Hence, though the book of Haggai places great emphasis on the rebuilding of the Temple, this unit indicates that of even greater importance is the people's proper attitude and reverence for God. The reconstructed Temple is a sign of respect for Yahweh, God of Israel.

AN ORACLE IN THE MIDST OF BUILDING THE TEMPLE (2:1-9)

This next unit shifts ahead to the twenty-first day of the seventh month, twenty-six days after the events of 1:12-15. The prophet addresses a community that has been working on the Temple (work begun in 1:14) and explains God's plans for the new edifice.

Literary Analysis

As in the beginning of chapter 1, God tells Haggai to speak to Zerubbabel and Joshua. Here, however, the "remnant of the people" is also addressed, giving them a greater role. As does 1:1-11, this unit corrects the perceptions of the people, which are presented not directly, but through the voice of the deity as delivered through the prophet. The people believe that the current Temple does not possess the same glory as the former Temple. Yahweh defends the current structure, not by arguing its magnificence, but by explaining its role in the divine plan for the cosmos. The Temple building of the present is connected with God's promises in the past (during the Exodus period, 2:5) and with the people's glorious future (2:9).

The deity's tone in correcting the people is less strident and more encouraging than in 1:1-11; here Yahweh promises "I am with you" (2:4) and "my spirit abides in your midst" (2:5), clear assurances of divine presence. Yahweh tells the people "do not fear" (2:5), and the encouragement in 2:4 to "be strong" (NRSV: "take courage") is repeated three times: once for Zerubbabel, once for Joshua, and once for the people. Apparently, the change in the people's attitudes in 1:12-15 that allowed them to begin work on the Temple has led to a new and more intimate relationship between them and Yahweh.

Yahweh's promises for the future, which begin in 1:6, are dramatic and cosmic in scope: Yahweh will shake the heavens and the earth, as well as the nations of the earth, so that the Temple will be filled with precious things. The glory (*kābôd;* NRSV: "splendor," 2:7) of the Second Temple will be greater than the glory of the First Temple, despite the people's perception of the superior glory (*kābôd,* 2:3) of the former structure.

Exegetical Analysis

As noted in the exegetical analysis of 1:12-15, many scholars maintain that 1:15*b* belongs with chapter 2. Meyers and Meyers well argue that the information appropriately belongs with chapter 1 but that the mention of the "second year" applies to both units (1987, 49). Since all of the remaining date formulae in the book are set within the second year of Darius, the placement of 1:15*b* with either chapter 1 or chapter 2 renders the same chronology.

How realistic is the address in 2:3 of those who would have seen the First Temple? Sixty-seven years would have lapsed between the Babylonian destruction of the Temple in 587 and the rebuilding project begun under Haggai's encouragement in 520. Meyers and Meyers maintain that some elderly persons, children at the time of the exile, would have been able to return to the land (1987, 49); Redditt argues that only those who had been left in Judah would fit this description, given the unlikelihood of a person in her mid- to late-seventies or eighties having been able to withstand the physical strain of the return (1995, 24). Given the argumentative nature of the book of Haggai, however, the size and constituency of this elderly population is probably less important than the rhetorical point being made: despite its modest appearance, the Second Temple will be filled with the glory of God.

This unit uses two different phrases to describe the members of the community. Haggai 2:2 speaks of "the remnant of the people" and 2:4 refers to "the people of the land." Although some commentators have inferred from the difference in terminology that Haggai's community was composed of various factions, some having returned from exile and some having remained in the land (e.g., Hanson 1975 and 1986), the parallelism between

2:2 and 2:4 suggests that the terms are being used synonymously: Yahweh both *addresses* Zerubbabel, Joshua, and the people, and *encourages* Zerubbabel, Joshua, and the people. Though Haggai uses these different descriptors for the people, the book shows no evidence of the intragroup tension that appears in the book of Ezra.

The language of "shaking" that dominates 2:6 is associated elsewhere in the Bible with theophany—the dramatic appearance of God. A form of the same root, *rā'aš*, appears in Judg 5:4 and 2 Sam 22:8 in the context of God's appearance as the Divine Warrior; and Ps 18:7, Isa 13:13, and Jer 10:10 attribute God's "shaking" of the earth to divine anger. In Hag 2:7, however, the shaking of the nations is for Judah's current benefit. Soon, God will shake the cosmos in order to restore glory to the Temple. Haggai 2:8 is best understood to mean that all gold and silver belong to Yahweh and thus are at Yahweh's disposal. Once Yahweh has acted to restore glory to the Temple, the people will live in *šālôm,* translated by the NRSV as "prosperity" but likely signifying a more inclusive sense of well-being.

Theological Analysis

Most commentators describe the future orientation of 2:6-8 as "eschatological," that is, as taking place in a future removed from the current situation. Such a description fits the unit only loosely, since, here, the splendor of the Second Temple is soon to be realized. It is perhaps more accurate to underscore that the book of Haggai sees the historical Temple rebuilding project as one step in God's larger plan to restore the glory of Judah. The historical event of Temple work leads to yet greater action on Yahweh's part.

The connection of past, present, and future is central to this unit. The same God who acted in the Exodus event is acting now in the work on the Temple and will soon act in even greater ways to restore the community. This understanding of the continuity of God's action and care is important for modern readers, who also hope that the God who acted in the past continues to work on behalf of God's people.

The unit also underscores the importance of human activity. Although God alone will shake the nations and restore the glory of the Temple, God's action is preceded by the community's resolution to work on the Temple. Important is that God's action is predicated not on the completion of the Temple, but on the people's change of heart that leads them to begin the project.

A REQUEST FOR A PRIESTLY RULING (2:10-19)

This unit, set a little more than two months after the date given in 2:1, introduces a conversation among the prophet and the priests regarding purity. The priests' ruling regarding the ability of unclean things to contaminate clean things serves to underscore the prophet's claim that an unconsecrated altar defiles the people's offerings.

Literary Analysis

The significance of the date that begins this unit is not immediately apparent, since the unit first reports what seems a general discussion over holiness and uncleanness. As the unit unfolds, however, clear attention is drawn to "this day" in 2:15 and 2:18—the day in which "a stone was placed upon a stone in Yahweh's Temple" (2:15 AT). The unit thus revolves around the important new stage of the people's work: the laying of the Temple's foundation. The importance of this date is made clear by its mention in 2:10, 18, and in the following unit at 2:20.

As in all of the units of the book, Yahweh here initiates the prophetic word. Yahweh instructs Haggai to request a ruling on holiness from the priests, and, although Haggai's compliance with Yahweh's request is not reported, it is implied from the fact that the priests reply. The questions seemed posed to the priests for rhetorical effect: one would assume that Yahweh already knows the answer to questions about holiness and perhaps that the people would as well. The real message of the unit, then, is not the ruling that the priests give, but how it provides the basis for the claim that Haggai makes in 2:14 regarding the uncleanness of the people's offerings. Haggai 2:14 is also important because, for the first time in the book, Haggai is described as speaking on his own initiative, as providing commentary on Yahweh's line of questioning.

The main point of the analogy being drawn in the discussion of the contagion of holiness is that the sanctity of the people's sacrifices is affected by what those sacrifices touch. The people's sacrifices are rendered unclean by the unconsecrated altar, whereas the holiness of the sacrifices does not render the altar holy. That the lack of a consecrated Temple is the source of the uncleanness is implied by the progression of the unit: it has moved from the priestly ruling (2:11-13) to Haggai's judgment on the people (2:14) to the significance of the laying of the Temple's foundation on "this day" (2:14-19).

In 2:15, for the third time in the book, the people are asked to consider their ways. The wording here is slightly different than before (in 1:5 and 1:7 they are instructed to "set your hearts *upon your ways*," though in 2:15 and 2:18 they are told simply to "set your hearts"; AT), but in all four cases the people are to draw conclusions from their own experience. They are reminded that before laying the Temple foundation, grain and wine were scant due to God's sending blight, mildew, and hail. On "this day," however, their fortunes have begun to improve. Although 2:19 is in the form of a question, it is rhetorical, implying that agricultural conditions are good.

Exegetical Analysis

The attention that this unit gives to the rulings of the priests is an indication of the significant role of the priesthood in post-exilic Judah. Even prior to the completion of the Temple, the priests seem a cohesive, functioning group responsible for cultic matters. Unlike much preexilic prophetic rhetoric suggesting tension between priestly and prophetic circles, Haggai appears to accept the authority of the priests in his community.

The ruling that the priests are asked to make involves what is holy and what is unclean. As Petersen points out, these two terms are not the most usual pairing (1984, 74). The opposite of "holy" *(qōdeš)* is "profane" *(ḥōl)*, and the opposite of "unclean" *(ṭāmēʾ)* is "clean" *(ṭāhôr)*. By asking the priests to rule on what is holy and what is unclean, the two extremes of the holiness continuum, Yahweh makes the case most dramatically that positive states of being are not contagious, but negative states are. The case of uncleanness chosen, that of touching a dead body, is also an extreme case, since contact with a corpse is treated by Num 19:11-13 as one of the most defiling acts possible; if a person is not cleansed on the third and seventh days after contact with a corpse, that person is cut off from the community. By their ruling, the priests declare that something cannot become holy by touching something else holy, but that uncleanness is easily transferable.

The readiness with which the priests answer Yahweh's queries and the way in which they form the basis for the lesson Haggai makes suggest that the rulings are not contentious ones. They seem readily accepted by the community, and they fit well with the purity guidelines outlined in the book of Leviticus.

In drawing an analogy from the priestly rulings to the state of the community, Haggai clearly indicates that, up to this point, the people's offerings have been unclean because they have been contaminated by something unclean. That is, the offerings are problematic not in themselves, but because of what they have touched. Petersen convincingly argues that Haggai understands uncleanness to have been transmitted by an unconsecrated altar (1984, 84-85). In order to underscore just how crucial the laying of the Temple's foundation is, Haggai explains that the sacrifices that the people have made on the altar since their return to the land are unclean because the entire Temple structure has not been reconsecrated.

The significance of laying the Temple foundation deposit, in distinction from the more general Temple work that the people began in 1:12, is made clear both by the attention given "this day" in 2:10-19 and also by parallels in ancient Near Eastern Temple ceremonies. Petersen has demonstrated the strong similarities between

2:15-19 and the Mesopotamian *kalû* ritual (1984, 9-90). In both cases, the laying of the Temple foundation was marked by a grand ceremony, readings, and sacrifices; and the event was understood to bestow upon the community agricultural and other blessings. In Haggai, Yahweh's rewards seem to begin immediately: crops appear to be flourishing, and Yahweh promises future blessings (2:19).

Theological Analysis

The premise on which Haggai bases his judgment of the people is foreign to many readers: the communal and emotional weight of the purity system is far removed from the daily lives of most Christians and many contemporary Jews. Nonetheless, the general idea that individual actions, even well-intentioned ones, can be tainted by participation in a flawed system is familiar to many of us. Even on the level of interpersonal reconciliation, addressing one minor problem without paying attention to larger issues is doomed to failure.

As in earlier units, Haggai clearly argues that a functional altar and a functional priesthood are not sufficient: the Temple as a whole must be restored and filled with glory. The ceremonial rededication of the Temple is fundamental for Haggai because it marks a recognition that worship goes beyond sacrifice to the recognition of the glory of God.

This unit, as others in Haggai, promises that if the community properly honors God, it will be rewarded with abundant crops. In drawing such a direct correlation between faithfulness and prosperity, Haggai sets the grounds for a theological quandary: is all misfortune to be attributed to divine displeasure? As explored in our discussion on Habakkuk, the Bible provides various answers to that question—ranging from an apparent affirmation in the book of Deuteronomy to a direct challenge in the book of Ecclesiastes. Haggai raises but does not address the question of theodicy. Rather, the book remains focused on its attempt to persuade the community that honoring God brings rewards.

ORACLE REGARDING ZERUBBABEL (2:20-23)

Set on the same day as the previous unit, this final section of Haggai records yet another divine promise—this time regarding Zerubbabel, the governor of Judah and the descendant of David. Zerubbabel is granted an exalted, if undefined, role in God's restoration of the community.

Literary Analysis

Like the previous unit, this oracle is set on the twenty-fourth day of the ninth month, the day of the Temple rededication ceremony. In the context of that momentous day, promises are given to Zerubbabel, the governor of the community. Although the divine word is described as coming to Haggai, the promise is punctuated by reminders that it is ultimately from God. Yahweh speaks in first person, and messenger speech appears three times in the final verse.

As in 2:7, Yahweh promises to "shake" the heavens and the earth. But though the earlier shaking was to restore precious things to the Temple as a way to reestablish its glory, this shaking will topple other kingdoms. Once their might, described as military power, is destroyed, then Yahweh will inaugurate a new role for Zerubbabel.

Zerubbabel is the exclusive recipient of this message. Yahweh instructs Haggai to speak to Zerubbabel in 2:21, and Yahweh's words directly address Zerubbabel in 2:23. In the first of these two verses, Zerubbabel is described only as governor, not with his father's name; in the second, "governor" is dropped, and he is described both as "son of Shealtiel" and also as "my servant." Two additional descriptors of Zerubbabel are given in the final verse: Yahweh will set him like a "signet ring," and he is "chosen" by God.

As seen in the commentary to 2:7, "shaking" is elsewhere associated with theophany: God's appearance on earth rattles its very foundations and denotes God's intention to intervene in human affairs for the sake of righting wrongs. That "shaking" is here used in connection with Zerubbabel indicates that his role is as equally important and cosmic as the returning of glory to the Temple, though in the temporal flow of the book the restoration of the Temple's glory is prerequisite to the new role that Zerubbabel will play.

Exegetical Analysis

Exactly what role the book of Haggai envisions for Zerubbabel is greatly debated. Although Zerubbabel's Davidic lineage is never explicitly mentioned in Haggai itself, his genealogy is made clear in 1 Chr 3 and, later, in 1 Esd 5:5. Does Haggai envision the restoration of the Davidic monarchy under Zerubbabel?

Redditt (1995, 32-33) argues that Haggai does indeed announce the reestablishment of the Davidic kingdom. In a bold anti-imperial move, Haggai foresees a reversal of Judah's economic and political futures. Instead of Judah paying tribute into Persians coffers, riches will flow from the nations to Jerusalem. Redditt sees the description of Zerubbabel as "like a signet ring" in 2:23 as a direct contradiction of Jeremiah, which claims that none of Jehoaikin/Jeconiah's offspring will ever rule Judah: "even if King Coniah son of Jehoiakim of Judah were the signet ring on my right hand, even from there I would tear you off" (Jer 22:24).

On the contrary, Meyers and Meyers maintain that Haggai consciously avoids making monarchical claims for Zerubbabel: the titles of "servant" and "signet ring" give him a role subordinate to Yahweh (1987, 68-70). Claiming for Zerubbabel a role other than king in Yahweh's future, the book of Haggai stresses the importance of Jerusalem over that of the monarchy (Meyers and Meyers 1987, 82-83).

Petersen takes somewhat of a middle position. He emphasizes the Davidic nature of the language used to describe Zerubbabel's role ("servant," "signet ring," and "chosen"), but he claims that the author of Haggai was sufficiently savvy to recognize the political impossibility of independent rule for Judah in the Persian context. Haggai does claim a place for a Davidide in the community's future but does not explicate the precise character of that role (Petersen 1984, 104-6).

All three positions appropriately recognize that Zerubbabel is being marked for a unique role in the new era that will follow Yahweh's overthrow of kingdoms. Here, Zerubbabel is no longer called "governor," and Joshua fades from view. Noteworthy, however, is that Zerubbabel's Davidic lineage is never explicitly mentioned and the explicit monarchic/messianic language of "anointed one" is not used. Haggai, it seems, leaves intentionally ambiguous what Zerubbabel's role will be—a position that would appease both those yearning for the reestablishment of independent rule and those who accepted the subordination of nationalistic claims to the realities of Persian control.

Meyers and Meyers' claim that "the naming of an historical personage to figure in God's eschatological purpose is unique in Hebrew prophecy" (1987, 68) is difficult to support. Clearly, other prophetic books use exalted language to describe the future role of the Davidic king: the description of Hezekiah in Isa 9 is much bolder than that of Zerubbabel in Hag 2. The term "eschatological" is a slippery one. It refers to an understanding of the unfolding of the future but in itself does not indicate *how* that future will unfold. In the case of Haggai, there is no indication of when and how these new events will begin—whether through God's stirring up of human powers or through an apocalyptic intervention. The book of Haggai may be read as continuous with classical prophecy as anticipating God's ultimate control over rulers and kingdoms.

Theological Analysis

The ambiguity of Haggai's vision of Zerubbabel's future role renders likewise ambiguous the theological claim of the book's conclusion. Does Haggai value political autonomy for the community, or does monarchy take a subordinate role to the Temple, as Meyers and Meyers claim?

The primary role that the Temple plays in the book of Haggai, as well as the even greater importance that the book places on the Temple rededication ceremony, suggests that whatever role Zerubbabel is to play will be possible only after the reestablishment of the Temple as the center of the community. Haggai's Temple focus itself, however, carries political weight. Part of the administrative structure for Persian administration of Yehud, the Temple was not only devoted to worship.

On the one hand, Haggai's support of the Temple may have advanced Persian interests, providing a theological rationale for an institution valuable to imperial aims. Haggai's particular understanding of the Temple, on the other hand, implicitly critiques Persian control. By stressing the importance of the Temple's glory *(kābôd)* and by linking its completion with a cosmic shaking that will topple kingdoms, Haggai stresses the sovereignty of God over all human institutions. The ultimate power is not Darius the king, whose control is acknowledged in the date formulae that punctuate the book, but in the God whose Temple Haggai places at the center of the community.

INTRODUCTION:
ZECHARIAH

Zechariah is a complex book. It is filled with puzzling images, and its various parts fit uneasily together.

Since at least the eighteenth century, scholars have noted a major disjunction between chapters 1–8 and 9–14. In the earlier chapters, the prophet's own personality is evident, as he enters into dialogue with a divine messenger. The bulk of these chapters is devoted to a series of visions, many of which involve the Jerusalem Temple and the leadership of the postexilic community. In chapters 9–14, however, the prophet remains invisible, and visions disappear. Attention turns to nations other than Judah and to criticism of the leaders of the community.

Unevenness also characterizes the material *within* each of these two major sections of the book. In chapters 2, 4, and 6, oracles interrupt the visions. In chapter 1, characters shift within the space of a few verses, and in chapter 3, two crowns are described but only one wearer. New headings mark both chapters 9 and 12.

Such observations about the diverse elements of Zechariah have convinced most scholars that the final form of the book is a result of redaction. At least since the eighteenth century, scholars have distinguished 1–8 as "First Zechariah" and 9–14 as "Second Zechariah" or "Deutero-Zechariah." Most agree as well that 1–8 begins and ends with the work of redactors and that chapter 3, which speaks of the high priest Joshua, has undergone change over time.

Evidence for the redaction of the book is found further in Zechariah's similarity with the book of Haggai. The two share both the style and the content of date formula, set within the reign of the Persian king Darius. And Meyers and Meyers have outlined at length the similarities in vocabulary and theme between the two books. They deem Haggai and Zech 1–8 a "composite work" (1987, xliv-xlviii).

Scholars have not reached consensus, however, on when and how these redactions took place. In the eighteenth century, many Christian scholars argued that Second Zechariah was the earlier composition, later added to the work of the Persian period prophet. Their argument relied in part on a desire to support the veracity of Matt 27:9, which attributes the mention of thirty pieces of silver in Zech 11:12-13 to the prophet Jeremiah. Most contemporary scholars, however, understand Deutero-Zechariah as a later composition, primarily because of its similarity to later apocalyptic literature (see below).

Although scholars recognize that Zechariah was composed from discrete parts, greater attention has recently turned to understanding—and valuing—the books as they now stand. For example, Haggai and Zechariah may have had a joined redactional history, but in their final forms, the books complement but differ from each other. Haggai devotes much more attention to Zerubbabel the governor than does Zechariah, while Zechariah envisions a larger role for Joshua the high priest. Haggai is more critical in tone; Zechariah, more comforting of the community. In terms of style, the visions in Zech 1–8 and the words against the nations in Zech 9–14 set Yahweh's work within a global— even cosmic—scale, while Haggai focuses on the drought and construction work of the postexilic community.

The visionary, cosmic scope of Zechariah often earns it the label "apocalyptic." The term is often loosely used to refer to futuristic visions, though it has no agreed-upon definition. Scholars usually reserve the noun "apocalypse" for a particular style of literature, characterized by features such as the periodization of history, accounts of otherworldly journeys, and, particularly, the belief that the future will be known only by the revelation of divine secrets. Some scholars also speak of "apocalyptic eschatology," arguing that even material without the formal features of an apocalypse may share the conviction that God's future salvation will require a radical disjunction with the established course of human history.

First Zechariah uses the style and symbols of apocalyptic also found in books such as Daniel and Revelation; visions are replete with horses and colors, and they are interpreted by a divine figure. Although employing fewer symbolic visions, Second Zechariah's depiction of a future conflict between God and the nations fits the definition of apocalyptic eschatology: it portrays God's reestablishment of justice as requiring bold, divine intervention. Some interpreters have suggested that the book as a whole provides evidence of developing apocalypticism in the Persian period, though others argue that the visions of Zech 1–8 are extensions of classical prophecy, more akin to the visions in Amos 7–9 than to those in Daniel.

Paul Hanson (1975) discerns within Second Zechariah a major step in the "dawn of apocalyptic." As discussed in the introductions to Haggai and Malachi, Hanson traces within postexilic Yehud tension between a hierocratic party, with its focus on the Aaronide/Zadokite Temple establishment, and a theocratic party, with its passions directed toward a more inclusive vision of community. Hanson identifies First Zechariah as the purview of the hierocrats: by bolstering the high priest Joshua with ecstatic visions, the Temple establishment attempted to further its ideological hold on Yehud. In Second Zechariah, Hanson sees the work of theocratic visionaries who drew from ancient prophetic and legal forms (1975, summary 399-400). It was these visionaries to whom Hanson attributes the growth of apocalyptic eschatology. Despairing that any true challenge to unjust powers could be brought about by human hands, the visionaries reframed ancient images to express their belief that God would intervene in the course of human history to right wrongs.

As many have noted, Hanson's demonstration that apocalyptic style and eschatology have precedents within Israelite tradition and need not be attributed to foreign influence is highly valuable.

The discussions that follow evaluate Hanson's claims further, as well as other schemes proposed for understanding First and Second Zechariah, and even the wisdom of distinguishing between "apocalyptic" and "prophetic."

This treatment of the book of Zechariah recognizes the unity of the final collection as well as the distinctiveness of chapters 1–8 and 9–14. The commentary will separate the book into First and Second Zechariah, and it will also consider the ways in which these sections work together in the book as a whole.

INTRODUCTION: ZECHARIAH 1–8

LITERARY ANALYSIS

Although Zech 1–8 belongs to larger literary units (perhaps joined at one time with the book of Haggai and now part of the book of Zechariah as a whole), these chapters also form a discrete literary unit. After a date formula that sets the activity of the prophet within the second year of King Darius, the book opens with an appeal to the audience not to be like their "fathers" (NRSV: "ancestors").

A series of visions, with occasional oracles interspersed, runs throughout the first six chapters. Some scholars have seen a precise formal structure in the presentation of the visions, suggesting that they form a chiastic structure, though such a scheme appears somewhat forced. All speak to the reconstitution of the community and the Temple.

The final two chapters present a series of seven oracles, all of which begin with some variation of "the word of Yahweh came to Zechariah" and "thus says Yahweh of hosts."

The question about fasting, which begins in the first unit, is not answered directly until 8:18-19. Intervening are four oracles that underscore the ways in which the rebuilding of the Temple not only ends the punishment of the exile, but also inaugurates a new glorious future for Yehud. The final oracle expands the future promises voiced in 8:1-8, and it also returns to the vocabulary and theme of 7:1-7: in both the first and final units, people "entreat the favor of Yahweh" and recognize the special status of those living in Jerusalem.

An outline of First Zechariah follows. Chapter and verse divisions follow the English translation, which, for chapter 2, is different from those in the Hebrew text. In English, chapter 1 has twenty-one verses, while in Hebrew, chapter 1 ends with verse 17.

1:1-6	Connecting Zechariah's work with the past	
1:7-6:15	Visions, with oracles interspersed	
	1:7-17	First vision: Man on a horse
	1:18-21 (Heb. 2:1-4)	Second vision: Four horns
	2:1-5 (Heb. 2:5-9)	Third vision: Measuring line
	2:6-13 (Heb. 2:10-17)	Oracle to the exiles
	3:1-10	Fourth vision: The Adversary
	4:1-14	Fifth vision: Lampstand, olive trees, and Zerubbabel
	5:1-4	Sixth vision: Flying scroll
	5:5-11	Seventh vision: Flying ephah
	6:1-8	Eighth vision: Four chariots
	6:9-15	Oracle regarding Joshua
7:1-8:23	Conclusion, relating the present, past, and future	
	7:1-7	Question regarding fasting
	7:8-14	Past unfaithfulness
	8:1-8	Zion's future
	8:9-13	The present situation
	8:14-17	Past contrasted with the present
	8:18-19	Answer regarding fasting
	8:20-23	Zion's future

The visions that constitute the main body of the work are its most striking stylistic feature. The prophet sees everyday objects and creatures, such as a measuring line and horses, much like earlier prophets such as Amos. He also sees more mystical images, such as a flying scroll and a heavenly Adversary who condemns Joshua the high priest, much like in the book of Daniel. The visions are interpreted for the prophet by a *malʾāk*, a messenger. Most English Bibles translate *malʾāk* as "angel," though it is the same term translated throughout the book of Malachi as "messenger." This messenger clearly does have access to God, speaking to and interpreting for the deity.

In addition to the striking visual element of the visions, a dialogic style is also evident in First Zechariah. Within the visions themselves, the prophet, God, the messenger, and occasionally another figure speak back and forth, most often marked by the Hebrew verb *ʿānāh*, "answered." The word *ʿānāh* appears fourteen times in Zech 1–8, often in successive verses as in 1:11, 12, and 13. Because the NRSV uses a variety of verbs to translate *ʿānāh*, the repetition is not as obvious in the NRSV as in the Hebrew text. The related word *ʾāmar*, "say" or "speak," appears more than sixty times in the course of First Zechariah, taking as its subject both God and other characters. Hence, although First Zechariah is a visual collection, it is also filled with conversation.

The past is a frequent motif in the collection. The phrase "former prophets" appears both in the Introduction (1:4) and twice in the Conclusion (7:7, 12). The proclamation of the earlier prophets is summarized as one of calling people to repentance, and it is evoked as a spur to the present generation not to follow the bad paths of their ancestors.

SOCIAL AND HISTORICAL ANALYSIS

As discussed in the general introduction to the book of Zechariah, the book is widely understood to be composed of two major sections: First Zechariah, chapters 1–8, and Second Zechariah, chapters 9–14. First Zechariah is explicitly set in the Persian period. The date formulae that punctuate 1:1, 1:7, and 7:1 are set within the reign of the Persian king Darius. The first date, within the eighth month of Darius's second year, sets the book a month or so prior to the last date mentioned in the book of Haggai. Zechariah 1:7 moves forward three months, and 7:1 sets Zechariah in the fourth year of Darius. This last date corresponds to the year 518 B.C.E., several years before the completion of the Second Temple.

The date of First Zechariah's composition (as distinguished from the date of its literary setting) is also generally understood to be within the Persian period. The material manifests no clues that it was composed significantly later than the setting it describes. As Persian-period text, Zechariah reflects many of the same concerns of the books of Haggai and Malachi. Like Haggai, it places great importance on the rebuilding of the Temple, and like Malachi, it understands the Temple as central to the Yehud (the name given the community in the postexilic period).

Zechariah also reflects concern, in retrospect, with the Babylonian exile. Zechariah 1:21 (Heb. 2:4) refers to the "scattering" that Judah has undergone, and in 6:10, the members of the community are called "the exile." In the vision of the woman in the ephah in 5:5-11, the woman (called Wickedness) is sent to the land of Shinar (Babylon). The brief genealogy in 1:1 identifies Zechariah as the *grandson* of Iddo, though Ezra 5:1 and 6:14 call Zechariah the *son* of Iddo; and Neh 12:16 lists Zechariah son of Iddo as among the priestly families who returned from exile with Zerubbabel and Joshua.

The connections between Zech 1–8 and the book of Haggai have been noted above. The two works bear a similar use of date formula, both hope for the building of the Temple in Jerusalem, and both use such phrases as "do not fear" (Zech 8:13, 15; Hag 2:5) and "people of the land" (Zech 7:5; Hag 2:4) (for a chart of similarities, see Meyers and Meyers 1987, xlix). Both First Zechariah and Haggai import much significance to the laying of the Temple foundation (Hag 2:15-19; Zech 4:8-10). These similarities suggest a common redactional history for the two works.

In its focus on the role of Joshua the high priest, reaching its culmination in the vision of Joshua's purification (3:1-10), First Zechariah points to the centrality of Temple leadership in Persian-period Yehud. As discussed in the introduction to Haggai, the Temple and the priests played an important administrative as well as religious role in the community. But although Haggai saw a joint role for the governor and the priest, Zechariah (at least in its final form) prioritizes the role of high priest over that of governor. Many understand Zech 6 to have been altered at some point in its history: the presence of two crowns suggests that at one point the oracle spoke of both Zerubbabel and Joshua, though the text now only mentions Joshua. Zechariah 6, then, reflects the declining importance of civil authority and the increased stature of the high priest, a situation that was modified to some degree by Nehemiah's return as governor, but that persisted into the Roman period.

The attention that First Zechariah pays to the "former prophets" and to an encapsulation of their message raises the possibility that some form of written collection of prophets had begun by the Persian period. Of course, the proclamation of the prophets may have been remembered through the oral transmission of their sayings, but it is possible that the words of the prophets were taking on written form and that a preliminary canon was in the making. Meyers and Meyers, for example, suggest that Zechariah's reference to earlier prophecy "constitutes an overt example of inner biblical exegesis" (1987, 102).

THEOLOGICAL ANALYSIS

The primary message of First Zechariah is that of Yahweh's care for Jerusalem and Yahweh's intention to restore Jerusalem. The collection makes clear that Judah's suffering was punishment for its own failings, and it repeatedly urges the present community to learn from the mistakes of its ancestors. But it also announces that the time of suffering has ended: God is about to choose Jerusalem once again. Very soon, Yahweh will be the only protection that Jerusalem needs. The city will not need walls, because God will encircle it with walls of fire (2:4-5; Heb. 2:8-9). Following the perspective of the Deuteronomy, Zechariah claims that the punishment of God is not permanent.

The building of the Second Temple is treated as a sign of

God's returned favor to Jerusalem. Unlike Haggai, which argues the people into taking up the work of the Temple themselves, Zechariah stresses the divine role in Temple construction. "My house shall be built in it," Yahweh claims in 1:16, but *who* will build the house is not specified. Zechariah 6:15 envisions that those outside of Judah will aid the rebuilding project, but nowhere does First Zechariah call the people to build. Haggai attributes the ruined Temple to the failure of the people to prioritize its reconstruction; Zechariah sees the absence of a Temple as punishment for the people's sin. The issue is not laziness or misguided priorities, but guilt. Hence, for Zechariah, the announcement that Yahweh's intentions toward Judah have changed serves as the signal that the Temple will soon be restored.

Zechariah may be seen as an important step in the development of ideas that become increasingly important in the late Persian, Hellenistic, and Roman eras. As noted above, the visions point the way toward a full-blown apocalyptic style. Although earlier prophets such as Amos also saw visions, the presence of a divine interpreter for the visions of Zechariah marks an important step on the way to books such as Daniel.

In addition, the role that Zech 3 grants to the Adversary may be seen as part of the development of the understanding of Satan as a cosmic foe to God. In the Hebrew Bible, only Num 22:22, 32; Job 1-2; 1 Chr 21:1; and Zech 3:1-12 describe a *śāṭān* as a heavenly being who stands in opposition to a human figure. In Zechariah (as in Numbers and Job) *śāṭān* is a title (the "Adversary") rather than a proper name; but like these other texts, Zechariah attributes evil to a power other than Yahweh.

COMMENTARY: ZECHARIAH 1–8

CONNECTING ZECHARIAH'S WORK WITH THE PAST (1:1-6)

After situating the prophet within his historical period, the book opens with a speech of Yahweh. The deity warns the current community not to be like its ancestors, who refused to obey and heed the words of the prophets.

Literary Analysis

The book of Zechariah opens with the type of material common to a prophetic superscription. It gives the date (the eighth month of the second year of the Persian king Darius), a formula for a prophetic collection ("the word of Yahweh was to . . ."), the name of the prophet (Zechariah), and a short genealogy (son of Berechiah son of Iddo); it also explicitly calls Zechariah a prophet. Zechariah 1:1 is not properly a superscription, however, since it does not stand alone as a description of the collection, but rather is integrated into the narrative of the book by the final word, "saying." Zechariah thus opens in a very similar way to the book of Jonah, which also indicates that the word of Yahweh came to the prophet, "saying . . ." (Jonah 1:1).

After a declarative statement ("Yahweh was angry with your fathers"; NRSV: "ancestors"), Yahweh instructs the prophet to speak to the people. Although the verb translated in the NRSV as "*say* to them" is technically in past tense ("you said"), it functions here as an imperative ("you will say to them"). The primary message that the prophet is to deliver is found in 1:3*b*: "Return to me . . . and I will return to you." Zechariah 1:3 overlaps with Mal 3:7, both in phraseology and in theme: "Ever since the days of your ancestors you have turned aside from my statutes and have not kept them. Return to me, and I will return to you, says Yahweh of hosts. But you say, 'How shall we return?'" (Mal 3:7).

The rest of the unit serves to underscore this call to return by encouraging the present generation to avoid the experience of their "fathers" (NRSV: "ancestors"). Because their fathers did not listen to the prophets through whom Yahweh spoke, they suffered and only subsequently repented. Zechariah 1:1-6 suggests that the same fate awaits the people of the current generation if they do not heed the voice of the prophets of their own day. In the past and presumably in the present, Yahweh deals with people according to their deeds and according to divine plans. Throughout, this unit is concerned with the past. The term "fathers" appears in 1:2, 4, and 5; and 1:4 mentions the "earlier" or "former" prophets, those who spoke in Israel's past.

Like the book of Haggai, this unit employs frequent messenger speech and other indicators that the material is to be understood as the word of Yahweh. "Thus says Yahweh" punctuates 1:3 and 4; "says Yahweh" appears in 1:3; and "utterance of Yahweh" is found in 1:3 and 4. Zechariah 1:3 employs all three phrases.

In terms of larger structural units, this unit forms an *inclusio* (or envelope pattern) with chapters 7–8. The closing chapters of First Zechariah also concern the proclamation of earlier prophets (7:8-14) and the apostasy of earlier generations (8:14-17).

Exegetical Analysis

The date formula that opens the book is set within the second year of the Persian king Darius, the same year that features prominently in the book of Haggai. The month given is the eighth, one month earlier than the last date given in Haggai (2:20). The date corresponds with October or November 520, shortly before the laying of the Temple foundation.

The clear correspondence between Zech 1:1 and the book of Haggai is likely the work of a redactor who shaped the two collections to be read in conjunction with each other. Indeed, Zech 1:1-6 is likely an editorial addition, made in conjunction with Zech 7–8. The two bookends of the collection grant it cohesiveness, in that they frame the collection in terms of Israel's past. This redaction was likely independent from the one that joined Second Zechariah to First Zechariah, since chapters 1, 7, and 8 share little with Zech 9–14.

The name Zechariah (along with its variant, Zechariyahu) is a common name in the Hebrew Bible, meaning "Yah(weh) has remembered." The particular man identified here is also mentioned in Neh 12:16 and in Ezra 5:1 and 6:14, where he is paired with Haggai. In Neh 12, Zechariah is listed within a priestly genealogy.

Zechariah 1:1 gives two generations of Zechariah's ancestry. The name of his father, Berechiah, is shared by other persons in the Bible (1 Chr 3:20; 9:16; 15:23; Neh 3:4, 30; 6:18); and in Isa 8:2, a priest named Zechariah is listed as son of Jeberechiah, a closely related name. The name of Zechariah's grandfather, Iddo, is shared by other figures in 1 Chr 6:21 (Heb. 6:6) and 2 Chr 12:15; 13:22.

Problematic is that when the prophet Zechariah is identified in Ezra 5:1 and 6:14, he is called the son of Iddo, as opposed to his grandson. This discrepancy may arise from a general usage of "son of" to include broader genealogical information. But it may also reflect some confusion as to the nature of Zechariah's precise heritage. Sweeney suggests that the introduction of Berechiah into Zechariah's lineage was intended to portray Zechariah as a fulfillment of the prophecies of Isa 8:2 (2000, 563).

As suggested in the introduction, the mention in 1:4 of the "former prophets" and the summaries of earlier prophetic teaching raise the possibility that, by the Persian period, some prophetic traditions were in written form and perhaps were being collected into a preliminary canon. Zechariah provides few clues, however, about which prophetic works form this proto-canon, since the proclamations of diverse prophets have been harmonized into a single message: "Return from your evil ways and from your evil deeds" (1:4). That prophets are reported as relaying Yahweh's "words and statutes" (two terms more commonly associated with Pentateuchal and, more specifically, Deuteronomic teachings) suggests that, already, prophets were understood as supporting the injunctions of the Torah—a perspective shared by the Deuteronomistic History: "Yet Yahweh warned Israel and Judah by every prophet and every seer, saying, 'Turn from your evil ways and keep my commandments and my statutes, in accordance with all the law that I commanded your ancestors and that I sent to you by my servants the prophets'" (2 Kgs 17:13). The language used in Zech 1:1-6 is also similar to that used in the books of Ezekiel and Jeremiah:

> Say to them, As I live, says the Lord GOD, I have no pleasure in the death of the wicked, but that the wicked turn from their ways and live; turn back, turn back from your evil ways; for why will you die, O house of Israel? (Ezek 33:11)

> From the day that your ancestors came out of the land of Egypt until this day, I have persistently sent all my servants the prophets to them, day after day. (Jer 7:25)

> Yet I persistently sent to you all my servants the prophets, saying, "I beg you not to do this abominable thing that I hate!" (Jer 44:4)

Theological Analysis

The introduction to First Zechariah, which, in the book's final form, also serves as the introduction to the book as a whole, invokes the experience of the people's ancestors as instructive for their own lives. The people are encouraged to behave differently from their ancestors, who only repented after Yahweh's words "overtook" them.

The history of the ancestors may have been known to the generation of Zechariah by the written word. If, as suggested above, the prophetic materials had taken some written form by the Persian period, the community here is encouraged to glean from texts instruction about how Yahweh behaves and what human attitudes and actions avoid God's wrath.

Contemporary faith communities that turn to the Bible for guidance in the present find in Zech 1:1-6 a kindred spirit. For both ancient and contemporary communities, the written words of the past provide insight into who God is and how God works in the world. The *way* in which Zech 1 reapplies earlier prophecy, however, serves as a reminder that Scripture does not present a singular meaning; it must be interpreted. Zechariah 1 summarizes the words of very different prophetic voices into a unified call to repentance, apparently ignoring the frequent prophetic announcements of inevitable destruction and their promises of hope.

Zechariah might be accused of flattening out the diverse words of the prophets, but this specific summary of the prophetic message may also be understood as a contextual application of prophetic texts: driven by his own sense of his community's need to repent, the author found in the words of earlier writers support of his conviction. Other writers, in other times and places, have prioritized other aspects of the prophetic legacy. Later in the Hellenistic period, for example, Sirach summarized the work of the prophets (or at least that of the twelve minor prophets) this way: "they comforted the people of Jacob and delivered them with confident hope" (Sir 49:10).

In the present as well, Scripture is understood in light of readers' convictions and needs. No one reading exhausts the meaning of the text, and readers do well to articulate clearly the interests and values that guide their own particular understandings of the materials they have inherited from their ancestors in faith.

FIRST VISION: MAN ON A HORSE (1:7-17)

Set within the Persian period, the first vision of the book of Zechariah establishes a pattern for visions to follow. The prophet sees a vision, which is in turn interpreted by a divine messenger. Here, from a vision of horses and riders, comes Yahweh's announcement that Jerusalem will again be chosen for divine favor.

Literary Analysis

A new unit opens in 1:7 with the appearance of a new date formula: Yahweh's word came to Zechariah again on the twenty-fourth day of the eleventh month, three months later than the initial date given in 1:1. The month is given its name as well: Shebat. Except for the difference in the dates, 1:7 repeats 1:1, again naming Zechariah and a two-generation genealogy.

In Hebrew, both 1:1 and 1:7 end with "saying," a word that usually functions to begin a quotation. When 1:7 is read this way, however, confusion arises about the speakers in the unit. "Saying" at the end of 1:7 implies that what follows is Yahweh's voice, though 1:8 begins with "I saw," and in 1:9, the same "I" seems to be identified with the prophet. To resolve this difficulty, the NRSV emends the end of 1:7 to read "and Zechariah said." The *TANAKH*, NKJV, and NIV omit the word completely, while the NJB translates it "as follows." Although the use of this traditional marker of prophetic speech to introduce a vision is odd, it fits well the final form of the book of Zechariah, which presents the receiving of visions as prophetic activity.

Numerous characters appear in the unit, many of whom arrive on the scene without introduction. The prophet initially sees an unidentified man on a horse, behind whom are three additional horses. The prophet does not understand the vision and asks for clarification from a figure he addresses as "my lord," apparently a title of respect, who is then called "the messenger who was speaking with me." This messenger *(mal'āk),* translated as an "angel" by most translations, has not appeared earlier in the book. The descriptor "who was speaking with me" might suggest that the two already have conversed, though if the "man" is also understood as a divine figure, the phrase may serve to distinguish the "messenger who spoke with me" from the messenger on the horse. The messenger promises to respond (1:9), but the man on the horse actually answers the question (1:10), and then "they" (1:11)—apparently the horses or perhaps their riders—speak to the messenger. That is, in 1:6-11, the prophet asks a question of the angel; it is answered by the man on the horse, and further explanation comes from the horses.

In 1:12-17, the voice of Yahweh joins the conversation. Here, the messenger asks a question of Yahweh, Yahweh speaks comforting words to the messenger, and then the messenger gives to the prophet a message of Yahweh to deliver to the people. The section ends with speech uttered by Yahweh.

The entire process of the vision, then, is that other voices mediate to the prophet Yahweh's word. Unlike the visions of Amos 7–9, which are explained to the prophet directly by Yahweh, the vision of Zech 1:7-17 is explained by a messenger as well as by a figure within the vision itself. As a result of the explanation, the prophet is given by the messenger a message to proclaim, though the book does not narrate the prophet's deliverance of that message.

Despite the strong visual content of the unit, it is primarily devoted to conversation. The word "answered" (ʿānāh) appears in the Hebrew text of 1:11, 12, 13; and forms of the word "say" (ʾāmar) appear in 1:6, 7, 8, 10, 11, 12, 14, 16, and 17. Also repeated is the word "compassion" (root: rāḥam): in 1:12, the messenger asks how long until Yahweh will withhold compassion (NRSV: "mercy"); and in 1:16, Yahweh announces, "I have returned in compassion." Both 1:13 and 1:17 describe Yahweh as "comforting" (root: nāḥam).

Exegetical Analysis

The word malʾāk is better translated "messenger" than "angel," in order to reflect that the same word is used elsewhere to describe human figures, including prophets and priests (see the book of Malachi). Nonetheless, the messenger in Zech 1:7-17 is clearly presented as an intermediary for God, one who has insight into what Yahweh is doing and who can ask God questions. The figure in Zechariah functions in much the same way Gabriel functions in Dan 8: he also has the appearance of a "man" (Dan 8:15) and interprets what Daniel sees. Interestingly, however, the term "messenger" appears in the book of Daniel only in the narrative Aramaic sections of the book (Dan 3:28; 6:22) and is not used to describe the interpreter of the visions in Dan 9–12.

The appearance in Zech 1–8 of an interpreter of visions is often seen as evidence that First Zechariah marks a development toward apocalyptic thought. This unit clearly uses the apocalyptic style of vision and interpreter, though recent study of apocalyptic has argued that apocalyptic style and apocalyptic eschatology do not always coincide. In this vision, the messenger announces not a disruption in how Yahweh will act with humans, but rather that Yahweh has already returned to Jerusalem in compassion. Although the full effects of that returning are yet to be realized (the building of the Temple and the city's overflowing with prosperity), these turns of fate are presented as those within the parameters of existing structures.

Much discussion has involved the meaning of the images in the vision, including the color of the horses. The fact that both the initial horse and one of the other three are called "red" has led some to emend the text, and the term translated as "sorrel" in the NRSV is often understood as "dappled," since it likely refers to a mixture of red and white and since, in the eighth vision (6:1-8), one of the horse colors given is "dappled." A determination of the symbolic significance of the specific color terms is not possible, but their rhetorical effect is nonetheless important: these terms, whatever their precise meaning, "give color" to the vision, inviting the reader to understand it as something not intellectually crafted by the prophet, but *experienced* through his senses.

As Meyers and Meyers well underscore (1987, 113), mules

rather than horses were used for everyday transportation in ancient Israel. Horses were used almost exclusively by the military and by royalty and were famed for their speed. Many have suggested that this vision draws from the image of the mounted messengers of the Persian Empire, famed for their ability to disseminate information rapidly. The image of the horses is also used in later apocalyptic writings—most famously in the book of Revelation.

The claim in 1:12 that Yahweh has been angry with Jerusalem for seventy years is likely dependent on Jer 29:10, which claims that the exile will last seventy years. Daniel 9 also draws from and modifies Jeremiah's number to describe how long his later community must suffer. The span between the beginning of the exile in 587 and the chronological setting of Zech 1:7 (520) is approximately though not exactly seventy years. That the angel refers back to the words of Jeremiah may be further indication that a written version of prophetic materials existed in the Persian period.

Like the book of Haggai, Zech 1:16 claims that the building of the Temple is vitally important to Yahweh. Different from Haggai, however, Zechariah does not directly call the people to build. The verb in 1:16 is passive: the Temple *will be* built, though precisely who will build is not stated. Indeed, the unit as a whole portrays the delay in building the Temple as not the fault of the people, but an indicator of God's displeasure.

Though not marked in the translational footnotes to the NRSV, 1:16 also contains an example of a *qere/kethib* reading. While what is written *(kethib)* in the consonantal text of the Hebrew is the noun form of the verb "wait, hope" *(qāwāh)*, the scribes who transmitted the text judged that the word should read *(qere)* as "(measuring) line" *(qāw)*. All major English translations read in this way.

Theological Analysis

In matters of interpretation, the style of this vision is often given more attention than its message. The theological perspective advanced here, however, deserves attention.

The assertion of the horses that the earth is at peace (1:11) might be heard as good news. Zechariah 1:15 suggests otherwise, however, given that Yahweh criticizes the nations for being at ease. The tranquility of the earth is not good if Judah remains without mercy. The absence of conflict is not itself a value. Rather, true peace is possible only when the suffering are comforted and justice is done.

Zechariah 1:14-17 introduces to the book a tension between Judah and the nations, blaming not just the Babylonians, but the "nations" as a whole for the devastation that has befallen Judah. Although 1:6 suggests that the exile is God's punishment on the ancestors for failing to heed Yahweh's words, 1:15 claims that God was only "a little angry." The true cause of Jerusalem's desolation is the nations: they "helped to evil" (NRSV: "they made the disaster worse"). When 1:1-6 and 1:7-17 are read together, as in their current final form, Zechariah presents two reasons for the exile: it is God's just punishment and also the unjust oppression of the nations. This dual message is underscored in 1:15, in which forms of the word "anger" describe Yahweh's attitudes toward both Judah and the nations.

The proclamation that the messenger gives to the prophet to proclaim is that God is jealous for Jerusalem. Although "jealousy" is often seen as a negative emotion, denoting one party's attention to own or control another, in the Old Testament it also is given positive weight, denoting God's passionate commitment to the people. The claim in 1:17 that Yahweh will again choose Jerusalem echoes the language of covenant, especially as articulated in Deuteronomy (e.g., Deut 7:6-7). This unit suggests that God has returned to comfort Jerusalem less because of a change on the part of the people than because of God's passionate love.

In this unit, Yahweh is willing to stand with those in Jerusalem against their adversaries, not because of their goodness, but because of divine compassion. Readers who readily identify themselves with Jerusalem likely find comfort in this image of God as one who protects. And yet, faithful reading questions such an easy identification of oneself with the object of divine favor. Might the reader also bear some resemblance to the "nations," the ones who have worked against God's purposes and deserve punishment? Indeed, any reading strategy that simply replaces "me" for a character in the text is problematic in this way. How do we know with whom to identify?

An alternative reading strategy is to focus on what texts tell us about the character of God. In Zech 1, God is gracious but also protective of those whom God loves.

SECOND VISION: FOUR HORNS (1:18-21 [HEB. 2:1-4])

In a second vision, the prophet sees four horns and then four blacksmiths. The interpreting messenger, along with Yahweh, explains that those who rose up against Judah will be struck down.

Literary Analysis

Hebrew manuscripts and modern English Bibles start chapter 2 at different places. In Hebrew, the chapter opens with the second vision, while in English, the second vision is the end of chapter 1, leaving the first chapter with seventeen verses in Hebrew and twenty-one in English. Throughout chapter 2, then, the number of the verse in Hebrew is four higher than in English.

Using slightly different language than the opening of 1:7, Zech 1:18 (Heb. 2:1) reports that the prophet "looked up and saw" four horns. As previously, the prophet asks the messenger for explanation, though in this unit the answer comes immediately and directly from the messenger. In 1:20 (Heb. 2:3), another vision is added to the first. Here, Yahweh is the agent of seeing, showing the prophet four smiths. When the prophet seeks explanation, "he" responds (lit., "he said, saying," 1:21 [Heb. 2:4]). Although some have suggested that "he" refers back to the messenger, the antecedent of "he" grammatically would be Yahweh, who interacts with the prophet directly in the second part of this vision.

This short unit employs two primary images. The first is of horns, typically used in apocalyptic literature to symbolize the *heads* of nations, but here referring to nations, given the explanation in 1:21 (Heb. 2:4) that they scattered Judah, Israel, and Jerusalem. Although some interpretations attempt to assign an identity to each horn, the number four may also represent "totality of military control," since various ancient Near Eastern rulers spoke of themselves as rulers of the "four corners of the earth." The imagery may be of a horned headdress of a warrior.

The translation of the second image is more disputed. The NRSV translates it "blacksmiths," while the NIV and NASB translate it "craftsmen." The root *ḥārāš* usually means "plow" or "engrave." In Isa 40:19 and 41:7, the noun form refers to one who works in metal, and in Isa 54:16 more specifically to one who forges weapons. In passages such as Isa 44:11 and Jer 10:3, it refers to skilled workers of any type.

These two images are brought together in 1:21 (Heb. 2:4). The smiths have come to strike down the horns. The verse uses the term "horn" in two ways: they (the smiths) have come to strike down the *horns* of the nations who lifted up a *horn* against the land of Judah. The double use of "horn," in the plural and in the singular, indicates that the word denotes an agent of dominion.

Exegetical Analysis

In its discussion of "scattering," the unit reflects the effects—and the trauma—of ancient warfare. Various ancient Near Eastern empires, especially the Assyrian and Babylonian empires, dispersed those conquered in war to new territories as a means of sealing their control over the land and of minimizing the possibility of resistance. The Assyrian policy of dividing a conquered nation into smaller groups for relocation to various locations was extremely effective; after the Assyrian defeat of Israel in 722 or 721, the northern kingdom never again regained a national identity. The Babylonian policy of exiling subject peoples in larger groups did allow the preservation of group identity, such that the Judeans taken in exile to Babylon in 597 and 587 survived as a unit sufficiently distinct to be recognized by the subsequent Persian government as the ones who belonged to the land of

Judah. But although the biblical text speaks of the new Persian policy of home rule as the "return" or "restoration" of Judah, the process of diaspora ("scattering") that began in the Assyrian period was not reversed. By the Persian period, former Judeans lived in various parts of the ancient Near East—in Egypt, Babylonia, and elsewhere. In referring to the scattering of "Judah, Israel, and Jerusalem," Zech 1:19 (Heb. 2:2) evokes not only the Babylonian exile, but also other dispersions. Indeed, this "scattering," which Zechariah decries, has indeed been a long-standing reality of Judaism.

The use of these three place names (Judah, Israel, and Jerusalem) is noteworthy. As noted, the mention of Israel indicates that the writer is concerned with the return of those scattered by the Assyrians in 722 or 721, a concern also expressed in Zech 8:13 and quite explicitly in chapter 11. Despite the apparent regard for Israel, however, the unit soon narrows its focus solely to Judah: although the horns are described as scattering all three locales in 1:19 (Heb. 2:2), the same horns are attributed with scattering only Judah in 1:21 (Heb. 2:4). In this way, the unit is consistent with the larger book of Zechariah, which, despite occasional professions of concern about Israel, remains focused on Judah. Elsewhere in the book, Judah is at times treated as independent of Jerusalem, likely signifying all of Judah other than Jerusalem (see chs. 12 and 14). Here, however, the final reference to Judah likely encompasses Jerusalem.

Though later apocalyptic literature employs images as symbolic code, such that each image finds a concrete correspondence, Zechariah's images appear to function on the level of theme. For example, the horns of Dan 8 are decoded in Dan 11 as particular rulers, while Zech 1:21 (Heb. 2:3) uses "horns" to represent power more generally. Such a difference may be one of style and perspective, but it may also be an indicator that apocalyptic vocabulary and imagery developed over time. Zechariah, building on the vision traditions of Amos and Jeremiah and Isaiah, may have placed new importance of the role of visions and introduced the imagery of horns, while later works such as

Daniel built upon Zechariah's visions to make even more pointed claims about the military powers of their own times. The number four, central to this unit, is also important in Daniel's visions as well as in the book of Revelation.

Theological Analysis

For the writer of First Zechariah, diaspora is not positive. The scattering of the people is treated as a past insult, for which instigators will be punished. Long-standing resentment against the military policies of the Assyrians, Babylonians, and perhaps also the Persians is here given voice. In this vision, however, Judah remains scattered. The time in which those scattered will be returned to the land is not described. Here, diaspora is lamented but not reversed

Various aspects of this unit stress Yahweh's total control of the world and its rulers. In the second half of the unit, Yahweh alone introduces the smiths and announces that they will punish the nations. Although the book of Zechariah draws no sharp distinction between Yahweh and the messenger, this announcement of the impending punishment of imperial powers gains additional weight by being spoken directly by Yahweh. The number four, the number of the horns and the smiths, also underscores God's worldwide control. Yahweh—not Assyrian or Babylonian monarchs—is ruler of the four corners of the earth.

This unit builds upon and extends the previous one to suggest that the nations are primarily responsible for the exile. Zechariah 1:1-6 suggests that exile was due in part to the ancestor's refusal to heed the words of the former prophets; in 1:15-17, the nations are accused of exploiting God's punishment of Judah for their own gain; and in the current unit, the nations are to be punished for their scattering of God's people. Each of the units of the book encountered so far provides theological explanations for the exile; but while they differ in the specific assignment of blame, they join in stressing Yahweh's compassion for those who suffer the effects of global politics.

THIRD VISION: MEASURING LINE (2:1-5 [HEB. 2:5-9])

The prophet's third vision, that of a man with a measuring line in his hand, signifies the enormousness of the restored Jerusalem. The oppressing nations having been destroyed, Jerusalem will again prosper.

Literary Analysis

The first three visions in the book of Zechariah follow a similar pattern (the prophet sees something and asks for explanation), but they differ in stylistic details. In this unit, after seeing a man with a measuring line in his hand, the prophet does not ask about *what* he sees, but rather *where* the man is going; he asks for explanation directly from the man in the vision and not from "the messenger who talked with me." The man answers the prophet's question, but the meaning of the vision is expanded further when the messenger is instructed by a second messenger to address the man in the vision, telling him that the measuring line he carries is unnecessary: Jerusalem will soon spill beyond measurable limits.

The expanse that Jerusalem will enjoy is described in several ways. The city, which, like most major sites in the ancient Near East, was walled for protection through most of its history, will spread out as an unwalled village. Further, it will not need the protection of walls, because Yahweh himself will wall the city with fire.

Exegetical Analysis

This unit shares much with Ezek 40–48, which also describes a prophetic vision in which a man sets out to measure walls—the man in Ezekiel using a measuring reed and the one in Zechariah a measuring cord. The second messenger's challenge to the measuring, however, distinguishes the two visions. For Ezekiel, the measuring of the walls of the Temple is presented positively, part of a program for rebuilding; for Zechariah, measuring contradicts the purposes Yahweh has for the city of Jerusalem. In almost direct contrast to Ezek 43:4-5, in which the glory of Yahweh enters the Temple through a gate in its walls, Zechariah depicts Yahweh's glory residing in the entire unwalled city of Jerusalem.

The similarity in style but distinction in content between the visions of Zechariah and of Ezekiel raise the possibility that this vision is a challenge to Ezekiel's program for the restored community. Although Paul Hanson has argued that both Zech 1–8 and Ezekiel are products of the hierocratic faction, the former promulgating the latter (Hanson 1979, 245-59), the differences between the two are important. As a whole, the book of Zechariah does support the rebuilding of the Temple, but it is not the pro-establishment, accommodationist document that Hanson portrays. In this unit, Yahweh is concerned with the city as a whole and with those scattered.

If Zechariah literally intended that Jerusalem remain unwalled, then it also stands in opposition with the later rebuilding project undertaken during the time of Nehemiah. According to the books of Ezra and Nehemiah, Nehemiah's primary mission was to repair the walls of the city, both to end the city's disgrace (Neh 2:17) and perhaps, too, as a sign of the city's political autonomy (as suggested by the opposition to the wall, Neh 6:6).

Theological Analysis

The image of an ancient city without walls is a bold, if not utopian, vision. As the book of Nehemiah makes clear, walls not only help defend a city against outside attack, but also grant it status. By claiming that Jerusalem's only defense will be Yahweh, Zechariah places radical trust in divine protection.

Because this picture of Jerusalem is portrayed as revealed in a vision and is described in the future tense, the question remains how soon Zechariah anticipated the fulfillment of this promise. Does the vision argue against any human attempts to protect the city; or is its purview a perfect future, fully at the discretion of God? Is it an apocalyptic vision, one that will require the disruption of all human institutions and patterns; or is it a statement against the kind of program envisioned by Ezekiel?

Those difficult questions remain unanswered in this unit, but the larger book of Zechariah does provide some clues. At least in the final form of the book, Zechariah is presented as supportive of the Temple rebuilding project, certainly not as anti-Temple. Rather, the clear message of this unit and others in Zechariah is that whatever rebuilding is done is the purview of Yahweh. Although Temple rebuilding may require human participation, Jerusalem's ultimate security comes not from human structures, but from God alone.

ORACLE TO THE EXILES (2:6-13 [HEB. 2:10-17])

This unit is the first of two prose oracles included within the visions. Here and in 6:9-15, images give way to divine speech. To indicate this disruption, the NRSV provides the heading "Interlude."

Literary Analysis

This unit fits uneasily into its current literary context. Not only is it a prose oracle in the midst of a series of visions, but also, in addressing those still in exile in Babylon, it breaks with the chronological and spatial orientation of the book, which has been set by its earlier date formulae in the Persian period, after the Return. For these reasons, the unit is often treated as the product of redaction.

In its final form, however, the unit both continues and expands the concern with exile that dominated the prior unit. Here, one who has already returned calls for yet others to return from exile; clearly Zechariah does not see the first wave of returnees to the land as sufficient. "Zion" is used to describe both the city of Jerusalem (2:10 [Heb. 2:14]) and also the exiles who dwell in Babylon (2:7, Heb. 2:11). Zion is properly read as a vocative: "Escape, Zion!"

The unit opens with an interjection, *hôy*. The term is used frequently in the prophetic literature, often carrying the nuance of "woe," but also capable of expressing a variety of sentiments. The NRSV translation "Up! Up!" is an attempt to avoid the funerary associations of *hôy*, which also opens 2:7 (Heb. 2:11).

The unit flows as a series of instructions, in 2:6, 7, 10, and 13 (Heb. 2:10, 11, 14, and 17). The first three are imperatives, and the last another interjection: "hush, shh." In 2:6 (Heb. 2:10) the imperative is masculine plural, while in 2:7 and 10 (Heb. 2:11 and 14), the imperatives are feminine singular. This form of the imperative indicates that "Zion" in 2:7 (Heb. 2:11) should be understood as the one addressed ("Escape, O Zion"), as does the feminine singular form used for "the one who inhabits Daughter Babylon."

The unit uses covenantal language to underscore the bonds between Yahweh and Zion. Zechariah 2:11 (Heb. 2:15) uses the language of "shall be my people," part of the covenant formulary; and 2:12 (Heb. 2:16) repeats the promise of 1:17 that Yahweh "will again choose Jerusalem."

As in the previous unit, the nations will be punished for their treatment of Judah, disgracefully plundered by their own slaves. Yahweh's jealousy for Judah will lead to its vindication. The harsh language of 2:9 (Heb. 2:13) and the image of Yahweh as a Warrior rousing himself from the heavens to march on behalf of the people are threatening and ominous and will return later in the book, most dramatically in Zech 14. The second half of this unit, however, also includes the nations in God's coming redemption. In a striking statement, Zech 2:11 (Heb. 2:15) not only claims that many nations shall be joined to Yahweh, but also uses traditional covenant language to describe their inclusion: they (the nations) will be Yahweh's people. Some, such as Ollenberger, consider the statements of inclusion to be a later expansion of the oracle, since the end of the unit returns to Yahweh's special care for Jerusalem (1996, 759-62). As the unit stands, however, it holds in creative tension Yahweh's care for Judah and for the nations.

Like previous ones, this unit uses language much like that of the book of Jeremiah. Zechariah 1:12 refers to the "seventy years" of Judah's exile outlined in Jer 25:11-12; Zech 2:6 (Heb.

2:10) calls Babylon "the land of the north," as does Jer 6:22 and 31:8; and Zech 2:13 (Heb. 2:17) depicts Yahweh roaring from his holy dwelling, as does Jer 25:30. In many ways, Jeremiah is seen to be one of the "former prophets" from whose teachings Zechariah attempts to glean new meanings for a later time (Zech 1:4).

Exegetical Analysis

Several confusing phrases and difficult translations mark this unit. In 2:8 (Heb. 2:12) the phrase "after his glory [he] sent me" is treated as parenthetical in the NRSV, though other English translations attempt to integrate it into the sentence. The RSV, for example, reads "after his glory sent me to the nations who plundered you." The NRSV is a reasonable conclusion, given that "glory" is repeated here from 2:5 (Heb. 2:9) and that the credentials of the prophet ("me") are also a concern in 2:9 (Heb. 2:13). Indeed, this latter phrase ("you will know that Yahweh has sent me") appears twice in the unit, in 2:9 and 11 (Heb. 2:13 and 15).

The traditional translation of 2:8 (Heb. 2:12), "the one who touches you touches the apple of my eye," is so popular that the phrase "apple of the eye" has become idiomatic in English to refer to one especially favored. The meaning of the word *bābâ*, however, is disputed, since in the entire Old Testament it appears only here. Based on the similarity of the word with the Aramaic word for "gate," some translations read "pupil of his eye," as in the *TANAKH*: "one who touches you touches the pupil of his own eye." Petersen has argued that the violent connotations of the verb, much stronger than "touch," give the verse a threatening tone: the one who strikes Zion's eye will be held accountable for striking the eye of God (1984, 177). Many commentators suggest that the original text read "the apple of my eye" but was altered by later scribes to avoid anthropomorphism; Zechariah, however, elsewhere describes the eyes of Yahweh (4:10).

Theological Analysis

The tension in this unit between the inclusion of all nations in God's plan and the special concern that God shows to Israel renders it a complex message for contemporary readers who value an inclusive vision of God's care and concern. On the one hand, the unit does extend the covenant promises of Exodus to "many nations." On the other hand, it repeatedly makes the point that Judah enjoys special favor: many nations might belong to God, but Judah is as dear to Yahweh as his own eye, and Yahweh will inherit Judah as his own portion. The oracle, at least a few verses, advocates the inclusion of the nations but not their equality with Judah.

Modern readers who are clear about their own commitment to theological formulations that prioritize equality of those included in the community, then, are challenged to recognize both the promise and the limitations of Zechariah's understanding of Yahweh's treatment of the nations.

FOURTH VISION: THE ADVERSARY (3:1-10)

As visions resume after the oracle ending chapter 2, the prophet now sees Joshua, the high priest. Joshua is first accused by a heavenly Adversary but then purified, and the coming of a Branch from the line of David is promised as the beginning of an age of peace.

Literary Analysis

This unit returns the reader to the vision sequence that was interrupted by the previous prose oracle. The unit starts, as does 1:20 (Heb. 2:3), with "he showed me," though, unlike 1:20, Zech 3:1 does not give Yahweh as the subject of the verb. Indeed, "he" may be understood either as Yahweh or as the messenger who will appear later in the unit.

Among the cast that animates this scene, several are returning characters. Yahweh appears, as does the messenger, though the latter is not described here as "the messenger who spoke with me." New characters also emerge. The high priest Joshua, known from the book of Haggai but not yet mentioned in the book of Zechariah, takes center stage. The unit also introduces the Accuser, in Hebrew, the *śāṭān,* who accuses (from the same root *śṭn*) Joshua. That the term *śāṭān* is to be understood as a title and not a name is made clear by the definite article that precedes it, even though the NRSV translates "Satan." In 3:4, the messenger speaks to other characters who are also present and who change Joshua's clothes. Zechariah 3:8 speaks of Joshua's "colleagues" as well, though does not make clear if they are seen in the context of the vision. In 3:7, the messenger addresses Joshua in the characteristic style of the prophet—"Thus says Yahweh," appropriately enough called messenger speech—underscoring the commonalities between not only God and the messenger, but also the messenger and the prophet.

The scene is set within the court of Yahweh, imaged as a king with courtiers standing before him. Indeed, many of these characters are described as "standing." Joshua *stands* before the messenger (3:1, 3); the Accuser *stands* to his right (3:1); others are *standing* before the angel (3:4); the messenger of Yahweh *stands* by (3:5); and Joshua is given control over the Temple and access to Yahweh's heavenly courts among those who *stand* there (3:7).

Here, in Yahweh's court, Joshua is put on trial and ultimately vindicated. Joshua's dignity is challenged not only by the Accuser, but also by his filthy clothing; once Yahweh rebukes the Accuser, Joshua is then cleansed and promised both earthly and heavenly powers. The charges of the Accuser are never spelled out and never directly addressed; rather, he is implicitly refuted and effectively silenced by the cleansing and reclothing ceremony. In the NRSV translation of 3:6, Joshua is "assured" by the messenger, though the translation "admonish" (NKJV, NASB) is closer to the meaning of the Hebrew word and also more appropriate to the literary context of the verse. Only if Joshua keeps Yahweh's requirements will he be rewarded.

After Joshua is vindicated and promised great things, the unit then announces to Joshua and to his "colleagues" the coming of a new figure, someone called "my servant, Branch," who also features prominently in chapter 6. Zechariah 3:9 also introduces a new object: a stone with seven facets, which Yahweh will engrave. That image is not explained, and neither the prophet nor the messenger ask for clarification; but the image is directly followed by promises that the guilt of the land will be instantly removed and that each person will sit under a vine and fig tree, a biblical image of peace (Isa 36:16; Mic 4:4; see also 1 Kgs 4:25; 18:31). The number seven, used here to describe the facets on the stone, becomes important in the following unit.

Exegetical Analysis

In a helpful study of this unit, VanderKam (1991) well argues that the imagery of Joshua's clothing draws from the description of Aaron's garments in Exod 28. Not only does Joshua wear the turban that marks Aaron's office, but also the stones mentioned in 3:9 refer to the precious stones that adorned the high priest's ephod and the breastplate. In depicting Joshua's investiture after the manner of Aaron's, Zechariah thus grants control over the Temple to Joshua and signals that atonement for sins, the purview of Temple worship, is thereby restored. VanderKam's study well explains not only the imagery of the unit, but also the connection between the vision of the stones and the removal of guilt. He argues further that this unit, different from Zech 6, focuses on the high priest alone, granting him prerogatives enjoyed earlier only by prophets: the high priest, along with the prophets, has access to the Divine Court. Ollenberger's observation of the connection between this unit and the royal commissioning of 1 Kgs 2:3 augments the sense that in Zech 3 the priest is given exalted prerogatives. Like Joshua, Solomon is charged to "keep the charge of Yahweh your God, walking in his ways" (Ollenberger 1996, 765).

In pointing to the coming of the Branch, however, the unit indicates that power will soon be shared. The imagery of the Branch draws from Jer 33:15, which speaks of a Branch that will spring from David, and Jeremiah may use the same Davidic "tree" imagery developed in Isa 7–9. Jeremiah 33 provides an even further parallel with Zech 3: Jer 33:17-18 speaks not only of perpetual monarchy, but also of perpetual priesthood, just as Zechariah treats Joshua's restoration as the prelude to the restoration of the royal line.

Although later Jewish and Christian tradition would describe Satan as a malevolent power independent of Yahweh, Zech 3 describes the Accuser *(śāṭān)* as one within the heavenly court; he enjoys an adversarial relationship with humans, but he remains under Yahweh's control. This image of courtiers who surround the divine throne is also found in other ancient Near Eastern literature, especially from Ugarit, as well as in the opening of the book of Job. In Job the *śāṭān* is described as one of the sons of God who reports on what he has seen on the earth, implying that overseeing humans is the role of these heavenly messengers. Indeed, although "angels" and "Satan" become opponents in later literature, here in Zechariah, the *mal'āk* and the *śāṭān* are both portrayed as members of the divine court. Zechariah is different from Job, however, in that Joshua's tribulations are not caused by the Accuser, as Job's are. Rather, the Accuser raises the concerns likely shared by members of Zechariah's own community. Community disputes are seen as replicated in the heavenly court, and their resolution in heaven may be implied to silence their earthly counterparts.

The description of Joshua as "a brand plucked from the fire" likely refers to the fact that he was saved from exile. As in earlier units, the exile powerfully shapes Zechariah's message.

This unit, which many scholars consider a later addition to First Zechariah, serves in its final form to establish firmly the role of the high priest in the leadership of the postexilic community. The coming of the Branch, a Davidic figure, will supplement but not replace the role of Joshua in the community.

Theological Analysis

Joshua's need for cleansing is less as an indicator of his sinfulness than of Yahweh's desire to restore the reputation of the priesthood in the eyes of the community. The exile might be seen to have soiled the priesthood and to have rendered its leaders unfit for service, but the vision underscores that Yahweh considers Joshua as one saved from extinction for a purpose. Joshua's new clothes are the effect, and not the cause, of his restoration. Even though the land will be cleared of guilt at the coming of the Branch, Joshua is already fit for leadership.

Although many later Christian interpreters interpreted the promise of the coming Branch as a messianic prediction fulfilled in the person of Jesus, the meaning of the unit in its own historical context is theologically important. In the face of the trauma of exile, God promises good news to the postexilic community: it will be restored and led by a new type of leadership, one shared by religious and Davidic personnel. In response to a new set of historical realities, God creates a new type of community and provides it with the appropriate leadership for the present. Clearly in this unit, tradition is honored, but also modified when necessary. Ways in which God has worked in the community in the past are celebrated, but God is also shown to respond to new needs and new crises by raising up new kinds of leaders.

This unit does not advance the concept of a cosmic Satan, as do later Jewish and Christian writings; and unlike Job, it does not suggest that human suffering derives from heavenly disputes. Rather, this vision, like others in First Zechariah, perceives a heavenly dimension to the flesh-and-blood disputes of the community. Such a perspective runs the risk of making human disputes into God's disputes and human adversaries into devils, but it also affirms that what happens on earth matters to God and that, at least sometimes, God takes sides in human disputes.

FIFTH VISION: LAMPSTAND, OLIVE TREES, AND ZERUBBABEL (4:1-14)

This unit returns to the style of the first three visions. "The messenger that talked with me" returns, absent since 2:3 (Heb. 2:7); and the prophet resumes dialogue with the messenger.

Through a vision of Temple furnishings, the prophet learns the role of Zerubbabel the governor in Yahweh's plan for the community.

Literary Analysis

The messenger awakens the prophet, "as a man is awakened from his sleep" (AT). Because of this language, some interpreters have suggested that Zechariah's visions are described as dreams, in keeping with the mention in 1:8 that the first vision came "at night." Such an understanding, however, is misguided. Not only is this the only vision to employ the language of waking, but also it makes clear that the vision comes only *after* the prophet is wakened. The setting of the first vision at night may be due to the distinctive nature of that unit.

The unit is structured into three distinct parts, each with complex imagery. In 4:1-3, the prophet sees a golden lampstand topped by a bowl, upon which are seven lamps, each with seven lips or spouts. On either side of the bowl is an olive tree. A second section is found in 4:4-10a, which connects the vision to Zerubbabel, who is contrasted with a mountain and credited with bringing out a "head stone" and laying the foundation of the Temple. A final section, 4:10b-14, returns to the initial vision. The number seven is explained, and the prophet asks about the olive trees; but, before the messenger can answer, the prophet asks yet another question about new imagery—that of branches and pipes. The unit closes affirming that two anointed ones (lit., "sons of oil") stand by Yahweh, though the description of what pours through the pipes is not clear.

Although this unit may be a composite of different materials, in its final form, it presents a multifaceted image, one primarily devoted to Temple furnishings. The meaning of each symbol may be translated into its concrete equivalent, but the cumulative force of the unit is expansive and evocative. Zechariah's vision presents the reader with familiar objects, rearranged in unfamiliar ways. It exalts Zerubbabel for his role in Temple building, and, in its current placement within First Zechariah, it is complementary to the previous unit. While chapter 3 stresses Yahweh's plans for Joshua, chapter 4 stresses the role of Zerubbabel and shows the two as complementary "sons of oil."

Exegetical Analysis

Much of the unit is difficult to translate, and the components of the vision are difficult to integrate into a coherent image. The lampstand first described, for example, fits none of the descriptions of lampstands in other biblical texts. Meyers and Meyers suggest that it marks the conflation of two traditions, an attempt to integrate the descriptions of the menorah in Exodus and in 1 Kings (1987, 232-33). They well argue that the menorah described here is not a whole lamp, but a cylindrical stand on which a lamp sits. The "bowl" described may indeed be a bowl-style oil lamp. Lamps with seven "lips," or pinched spouts, were not common in the ancient world but were used in cultic contexts (Meyers and Meyers 1987, 237). Petersen provides drawings of a seven-spouted lamp on a stand, found at the ancient site of Dan (1984, 222).

The oracle concerning Zerubbabel clearly interrupts the vision. Indeed, if one jumps from 4:5 to 4:10b, the unit reads more coherently than in its current form. In a unit devoted to the equality of the two olive trees, the "sons of oil" Joshua and Zerubbabel, the addition stands out in privileging Zerubbabel and granting him the most credit for Temple rebuilding. On the one hand, then, the insertion stands in tension with the egalitarian theme of the unit. If on the other hand, however, the oracle regarding Joshua in chapter 3 was itself an addition to the unit, the addition of the oracle regarding Zerubbabel in chapter 4 serves to balance the relative importance of the two figures. In the final form of First Zechariah, both Joshua and Zerubbabel are addressed with oracular speech.

In 4:7, Zerubbabel is contrasted with "you, O great mountain," which will become as a level plain before him. Petersen maintains that the mountain symbolizes a human adversary, perhaps the high priest Joshua (1984, 239), while Ollenberger suggests that the mountain is the rubble of the first Temple (1996, 770). Positing a symbolic meaning of the verse, however, is unnecessary, since it may serve as hyperbole: even a great mountain will be as a level plain before the glory of Zerubbabel.

The inserted oracle regarding Zerubbabel also indicates that he will bring out a "top stone" (4:7). Many interpreters agree that the imagery here derives from ancient Temple foundation ceremonies. In ancient Near Eastern Temple reconstruction projects such as in Warka, a prominent stone from the original structure was symbolically built into the new Temple. These ceremonies, called *kalû* after the singers who were part of the ritual, sought to ensure continuity between the old and the new structures. Both Haggai's and Zechariah's concerns with the laying of the Temple foundation suggest that a similar ritual might have been used in the postexilic rebuilding of the Temple. Documents reporting on ancient Near Eastern Temple rebuilding projects also indicate that one or more metal blocks were used in construction, primarily for ceremonial purposes; such may be the meaning of "the tin stone" mentioned in 4:10, translated in the NRSV as "plummet."

When in 4:10*b* the unit returns to the initial vision, it immediately explains the number seven (it does so without indicating who is speaking, a further suggestion that 4:6-10*b* is an interruption). The seven lamps with seven wicks represent the seven eyes of Yahweh, a powerful symbol for God's all-encompassing purview. A similar verse appears in 2 Chr 16:9: "For the eyes of Yahweh range throughout the entire earth, to strengthen those whose heart is true to him." In 2 Chronicles, as well as in books such as Ezekiel, God's eyes anthropomorphically indicate divine omniscience.

The precise meaning of 4:12 is difficult to determine. First, the word translated as "branches" in the NRSV literally means "something flowing" and is translated in the NAB as "tufts"; it is not the same Hebrew word translated as "Branch" in 3:8. Second, the NRSV, along with most translations, reads "pour out the oil" as a correction to the Hebrew. Since the MT reads "pour out the gold," the emendation is based on the logic that gold does not flow and that the pipes mentioned at the end of the verse are themselves gold. The NIV and NASB translations attempt to honor the Hebrew wording by translating "golden oil," and Meyers and Meyers similarly argue that the "gold" must indeed be oil (1987, 256-57). Such precision, however, seems unwarranted in a vision that endeavors to communicate the impression of sacred objects rather than to depict a realistic scene. The golden pipes portrayed at the end of 4:12 have not been mentioned previously, and how they connect to the olive trees and to the lampstand is not clear. The image may be understood to depict gold as flowing from the trees to the lampstand and serving as fuel for the lamp.

The phrase "sons of oil" in 4:14 is usually understood to refer to the sacred roles of Joshua and Zerubbabel in the reconstituted community. It is translated in the NRSV as "anointed ones"; but although anointing in ancient Israel was done with oil, the phrase may be stressing their role as the "fuel" of the restored Temple and its worship. If "these" in 4:14 refers to the "these branches" in 4:12, the unit, interestingly, describes Joshua and Zerubbabel not as the olive trees themselves, but rather as the branches of the olive trees. The import of this distinction is not clear, though it indicates that they are but an "arm" of something larger than themselves—perhaps the priesthood and the monarchy.

Theological Analysis

In various ways, this unit focuses attention on the Temple. The imagery of the menorah, drawn eclectically from several texts, and the explicit statement of Zerubbabel's role in laying the Temple foundation highlight the importance of the Temple in Zechariah's vision of the restored community. In Zechariah's understanding, the restoration of the Temple is central to Yahweh's presence with the postexilic community. Hanson has criticized this aspect of Zechariah as evidence of the book's hierocratic program, but the focus on the Temple also underscores the sovereignty of God within the community. The Temple will not be merely a channel for Persian control of Judah, but even more a holy site.

Similarly, although the unit exalts Zerubbabel, it subordinates him to Yahweh's purposes: "Not by might, nor by power, but by my spirit, says Yahweh" (4:6). It is unwise to make too much of the designation of Zerubbabel and Joshua as the branches of the olive trees and not the trees themselves, but 4:13 may make the leaders the instruments for larger concerns.

The anthropomorphism of the "eyes of Yahweh" in 4:10*b* makes, in its own way, a statement about the omniscience of God. God surveys the entire earth. The complex and extravagant imagery of the unit, indeed, makes its own theological statement: divine revelation is not always clear and decisive, but is sometimes evocative and enigmatic, engaging the imagination as well as the intellect.

SIXTH VISION: FLYING SCROLL (5:1-4)

The vision of a flying scroll highlights the importance of Torah to the postexilic community. Just as chapter 4 underscores the role of the Temple, so chapter 5 underscores the importance of the written word.

Literary Analysis

This unit uses much of the language and style of earlier ones: the prophet "lifts up" his eye and "sees," as in 1:18 (Heb. 2:1) and 2:1 (Heb. 2:5). Someone interrogates the prophet about what he sees and interprets for him the vision; and although the "he" who speaks is not identified, his role is identical to that of the messenger who appears in other units.

The scroll seen by the prophet is described only by its movement (it flies) and by its size (the equivalent of 33 feet by 15 feet). The meaning of the scroll is described immediately by the messenger: it represents the curse that awaits those who steal and swear (falsely). The scroll will enter the houses of both and consume them.

In 5:3, the imagery suggested by the NRSV, NIV, NASB and other translations is that of a scroll with writing on both sides. The translation of Meyers and Meyers, however, is closer to the Hebrew: "every thief according to it has been acquitted, and every perjurer according to it has been acquitted." In light of this translation, the description of the scroll is not about its appearance, but about the importance of its content (Meyers and Meyers 1987, 277).

Exegetical Analysis

The central role of the scroll in this unit highlights not only the technology of writing in the ancient world, but also the theological importance of written materials in the postexilic period. Although the unit does not specify the contents of the scroll, it is clear that the scroll conveys norms and controls for the community. The scroll condemns theft and false swearing, here in a hyper-literal way: it consumes the wrongdoer's house.

Some have suggested that the scroll is that of the Torah, which forbids theft (Exod 20:15; Lev 19:11; Deut 5:19) and swearing falsely (Lev 19:12; Deut 6:13), and indeed the codification of legal materials was an important part of the postexilic community. The exaggerated size of the scroll in this vision, as well as its extreme mobility, suggests in a concrete way the importance and universality of the law. No one can hide from its purview, and for those who violate Torah, it serves as a curse.

This unit moves away from the focus on the Temple and its leadership that occupies the fourth and fifth visions, but it joins those units in establishing the basis for life and leadership in the community. Yehud is centered on the Temple and Torah and is led by a priest and a descendant of David.

Theological Analysis

This unit underscores that Zechariah's vision addresses not only the form of leadership that is to govern the postexilic community, but also the norms by which the community will live. Every individual is held accountable to a document, the Torah.

Although the Protestant focus on the Bible as the "only rule of faith and practice" reflects a much later concept, it finds some commonalities in Zechariah's vision. Zechariah offers an early reflection on what it means to live in relation to a book. Although Zechariah implies that the scroll's judgment on certain wrongdoers is clear, modern-day readers of the Bible also know how contested the relation between scripture and contemporary ethics can be. In Zechariah's vision, the scroll itself consumes those who steal and swear falsely—cases on which the Torah is consistent—that is, the punishment is clear and the results divinely executed. Zechariah, however, gives little instruction about other cases—especially ones in which the Torah disagrees—and little guidance on how humans are to enforce the regulations of the Bible.

SEVENTH VISION: FLYING EPHAH (5:5-11)

The vision of a woman trapped in a basket stresses the error of goddess worship. Winged figures transport the basket to Babylon, where such worship belongs.

Literary Analysis

Using a variation of the recurrent vocabulary of First Zechariah, the messenger commands the prophet to "lift up" his eyes and "see" a new vision. After the prophet asks what the object is, the messenger explains that it is an ephah. An ephah is a unit of dry measurement, about six gallons. The ephah is described in 5:8 as a container that can be covered; the NRSV calls it a "basket" and the NIV a "measuring basket" (5:6).

The messenger explains the meaning of the basket in 5:6, though the translation of the verse differs in English Bibles. The Hebrew reads "their eyes," which is reflected in the KJV and ASV, as well as in the NASB translation of "their appearance." The NRSV, RSV, and NAB follow the reading of the Septuagint and the Syriac of "their iniquity." The difference between these two words in Hebrew is slight: the difference between ʿênām and ʿăwōnām. As suggested below, retaining the Hebrew reading of "eyes" fits well into the symbolism of the book and links this vision with the two preceding ones.

Several females are mentioned in the unit. A woman, who is identified as Wickedness or the Wicked One, is sitting in the ephah; and two female figures with wings transport the ephah away from the prophet. These latter women are responsible for the changing spatial location of the ephah: it is first put into a liminal space, suspended between earth and heaven, and then moved to the land of Shinar, another name for Babylonia. Although some previous units have also presented action, such as the changing of Joshua's clothes in the fourth vision, this one contains more movement than most, and much of the meaning of the unit is contained in the changing locales of the ephah.

Exegetical Analysis

Often this unit is understood to envision the transference of Judah's guilt, symbolized by a woman, to Babylon. The symbolic use of a female character to denote Wickedness would not be unique in the Bible, nor in the prophetic literature in which sinful nations are often personified as women. Michael Floyd (1996) convincingly argues, however, that the Hebrew reading of "their eyes" should be retained and that this unit is not about the removal of guilt. Rather, he argues, the unit mocks one possible direction of the postexilic community: the worship of a female deity outside of the Temple. Extending the concepts of the fourth vision, in which the Temple is marked as the center of Judah's life, and of the fifth vision, which highlights the role of Torah, this vision argues that worship of a female deity is not viable: she remains in limbo between earth and heaven, and she belongs in Babylonia, not in Judah.

In support of Floyd's reading, the vision of the flying ephah uses much of the same vocabulary of the previous two visions: it "goes out" (5:3, 5), it is in "all the land" (4:14; 5:3, 6), and it bears "eyes" (4:10; 5:6). The woman, then, stands as the antithesis of the lampstand and scroll: in direct contrast to the earlier visions, she represents worship that is not centered on the Temple and the Torah and that includes a female deity. As such, she is named Wickedness and evicted from the land; worship of a female deity finds no place in the postexilic community.

Why the two winged creatures are described as women is not clear. The image may draw from ancient Near Eastern iconography (see Petersen 1984, 260), or be suggested by the association of the stork with maternal characteristics (see Meyers and Meyers 1984, 307). The wings of the women underscore their ability to move; "wings" can symbolize a place of refuge (Ps 17:8; Ruth 2:12) and along with the "wind" can also indicate mobility (2 Sam 22:11 // Ps 18:10).

Theological Analysis

Much of the Hebrew Bible warns against goddess worship. The worship of the Canaanite deity Asherah, along with her male consort Baal, is derided repeatedly in the Deuteronomistic History and in prophetic books such as Hosea. Although it is not clear that Asherah worship continued in the postexilic period, the returnees from Babylon would have been very familiar with the worship of Ishtar, an important feminine deity of Mesopotamia. Zechariah, like other prophetic voices, insists that such worship is unacceptable for the Judean community, though Zechariah is distinctive in seeing it as acceptable elsewhere.

The denigration of the worship of a female deity and the personification of Wickedness as feminine raises questions for some modern-day readers about whether Zechariah advances a demeaning view of women. A mixed answer to such a question seems in order. On the one hand, Zechariah's primary concern appears to be with the exclusive worship of Yahweh; all other deities, male and female, are to be shunned, such that the writer's challenge to goddess worship could be seen as simply addressing the particular form of idolatry then in competition with Yahwism.

On the other hand, Zechariah follows the dominant ideology

of the Bible in referring to Yahweh as male and in singling out goddess worship as particularly problematic. That is, Zechariah does nothing to challenge the androcentrism and patriarchy of the Bible. In using this image, the writer does not create, but certainly perpetuates, the view of the danger of worshiping female images.

In either case, Zechariah does not attempt to be evenhanded or inclusive of diverse religious traditions. It is clear and passionate about single-minded worship of Yahweh.

EIGHTH VISION: FOUR CHARIOTS (6:1-8)

This eighth and final vision of First Zechariah returns to the imagery and vocabulary of the first vision, again speaking of colored horses and their riders. The conclusion drawn from the vision, however, is a positive one: God's spirit is now at rest.

Literary Analysis

This unit employs much of the same structure and style as the previous ones. The prophet again lifts up his eyes and sees the vision, inquires of the messenger "who spoke with me" about its meaning, and receives the interpretation. Like the previous vision, this one is not static but involves movement (6:7-8). Language of "going out" (6:1, 5), "winds" (6:5), and "all the earth" (6:5) returns from the seventh vision.

More important, this vision returns to the imagery and vocabulary of the first vision. Both portray colored horses (1:8; 6:7) who patrol the earth, and both end with a statement about the earth at rest. In its reemployment of the imagery, however, the final vision expands beyond the first. While in the first vision a man rode a red horse and was followed by red, sorrel, and white horses, here *chariots* are pulled by red, black, white, and spotted horses; and while the man of the initial vision is found among the myrtles, here the chariots emerge from between two mountains. The four chariots are described as representing the four winds of heaven and are sent to specific quadrants of the earth:

the black to the north, the white to the west, and the dappled to the south (suggesting that the red horse goes to the east).

The conclusion of this vision takes on a nuance different from the first as well. Although the report that the earth was "at peace" in 1:11 evoked the messenger's protest, the "resting" of God's spirit in the north in 6:8 is presented positively. The initial vision of the horses in 1:7-17 concluded with a promise that the Temple would be built and Zion again would be comforted and chosen. That promise, in many ways, was actualized in the subsequent visions:

> in the second (1:18-21; Heb. 2:1-4), Judah was saved from the terror of other nations (cf. 1:15);
> in the third (2:1-5; Heb. 2:5-9), Judah could not be measured with a line (the same term used in 1:16);
> in the interlude of 2:6-13 (Heb. 2:10-17), Judah was chosen (cf. 1:17);
> in the fourth (3:1-10), the Temple foundation was set (cf. 1:16);
> in the fifth (4:1-14), the foundation was also described, as is the community's leadership (cf. 1:16).

The way in which the sixth and seventh visions "fulfill" the promises of the first is less direct, though in establishing Torah and exclusive worship of Yahweh as the charter of the community, they highlight how Yahweh is "jealous" for Jerusalem (compare 1:14) and how Yahweh has chosen Judah for a unique relationship (compare 1:17).

When in the eighth vision the horses again patrol the earth, they find a situation changed from their initial mission in the first vision. With the intervening visions having "actualized" God's fulfillment of the promises made in 1:7-17, they now find that God's spirit is at rest.

Exegetical Analysis

As noted in the exegetical analysis of the first vision, the translation of the colors of the horses is often debated. The first three colors are straightforward (red, black, and white), though the fourth is less so. In Hebrew, the fourth chariot is described as pulled by horses that are *běruddîm* and *ʾămuṣṣîm*. The root of the first word, *brd,* is used in Gen 31 to describe the patterned sheep over which Jacob and Laban compete and elsewhere to describe hail; for this reason, it is often translated as "dappled" or "spotted." The NRSV rendering of "dappled gray" is an attempt to retain a continuity of color description, though the Hebrew word carries no connotation of color. The root of the second word, *ʾms,* means "strong" and is lost in the NRSV, though retained in the NASB, NIV, and other translations. As before, the function of these color terms is to underscore the book's claim that these visions were divinely given—only received by the prophet rather than generated by him.

In 6:5, the chariots are identified in the NRSV as the four "winds" of heaven (as in 2:6 [Heb. 2:10]). Importantly, however, the Hebrew word *(rûaḥ)* can be translated as either "wind" or "spirit" and is the same word used in 6:8 to describe the spirit of Yahweh. The double meaning of *rûaḥ* serves as the basis for understanding the meaning of this unit: the spreading out of the four chariots over the face of the earth signifies that Yahweh's spirit now rests over all the earth. Especially, Yahweh's spirit rests "in the north country," likely a reference to Babylon, as in 2:6 (Heb. 2:10). Although Meyers and Meyers contend that "the north" refers to Judah's current occupiers, the Persians (1987, 331), the passage is likely better understood as indicating that Yahweh's spirit is now pacified against Babylon. Having already acted against Babylon (in 2:6-13 [Heb. 2:10-17]) and having banished goddess worship to Babylon (5:5-11), Yahweh's work with Babylon is now complete.

Theological Analysis

As in the previous visions of Zechariah, this unit gives theological ideas a concrete, visual form. Chariots, known in the ancient Near East as the transportation of kings and military conquerors, represent the spirit of God: Yahweh's sovereignty spreads out to the four corners of the earth—everywhere. Yahweh's sovereignty even extends to those who humbled Judah, the Babylonians. And with God's subduing of Babylon complete, God's spirit is calmed.

Much like the vision in Ezek 1, Zechariah demonstrates the omnipresence and omnipotence of God in visual form. And in returning to and expanding the imagery of the first vision, this final vision underscores that God fulfills God's intentions. What Yahweh set out to do in chapter 1—to comfort Jerusalem and punish her enemies—is now accomplished. In Zechariah, Yahweh is compassionate to the people and keeps promises.

ORACLE REGARDING JOSHUA (6:9-15)

The visions of First Zechariah completed, the collection now turns to more standard prophetic oracles. Yahweh instructs the prophet to collect gold from the exiles (four of whom are named), to make crowns, and to set at least one of them upon the head of Joshua the high priest. Joshua is then instructed regarding one called "Branch."

Literary Analysis

The unit begins with the formula that opens many prophetic proclamations, "the word of Yahweh came to me" (as in Jer 1:4, 11, 13; 2:1; Ezek 6:1; 7:1), and prophetic messenger speech ("thus says Yahweh") punctuates 6:12. Gone is the interpreting messenger, and the word of Yahweh comes directly to the prophet. Gone is the visionary, metaphorical language, and God's speech to the prophet becomes clear and direct.

As in the fourth vision, Yahweh speaks of one named Branch. Interestingly, the designation is explained here, though not in the previous occurrence: the man is called Branch because he will "branch out of his place."

The identity of Branch is not easily determined; he is clearly a royal figure. Although the translation of *hôd* in 6:13 is more accurately "majesty" than the "royal honor" of NRSV, the language of "ruling" and "sitting upon his throne" does indeed bear royal connotations. But should Branch be understood as Zerubbabel or as a future Davidic ruler? This conundrum will be treated further under the exegetical analysis, but its literary effect is to blur the distinction between the two—and between the present and the future.

Exegetical Analysis

Several elements of this passage trouble interpreters. First, the prophet is instructed to make "crowns"—clearly plural in Hebrew despite its rendering in the NRSV as singular—even though only one wearer is mentioned. To solve this puzzle, some interpreters have speculated that Zech 6:9-15 at some point was altered from its original version. Some suggest that the passage originally described the coronation of Zerubbabel as Davidic king, but that it was changed to refer to Joshua after the Persians dashed Zerubbabel's messianic pretensions. The plural of "crowns" would have been a redactor's attempt to obscure the messianic claims of the original oracle.

Positing such a history of the text is highly speculative, and, given the book's ongoing concern for the dual roles of priest and Davidic heir, there is no reason to believe that the oracle was ever only about Zerubabbel. If two crowns are imagined, the designation of one crown for the Davidide and one crown for the high priest, "with peaceful understanding between the two of them" (6:13), would fit well into the larger context of the book. As in the fifth vision, the high priest and the Davidic heir rule jointly as the "two anointed ones" (4:14).

A second related question arises about the identity of Branch: is this a designation for Zerubbabel or for a future Davidic ruler? On the one hand, the resonances with the fourth vision suggest a future orientation: in 3:8-10, Branch is yet to come, as seen in the use of future (imperfect) verb tenses and of prophetic eschatological language ("on that day," "vine and fig tree"). On the other hand, this unit also uses much of the same language for Branch that was used for Zerubbabel in the fifth vision. Zerubbabel is to complete the building of the Temple (4:9), as is Branch (6:12); and the work of both Zerubbabel and Branch will validate the words of the prophet: "You shall know that Yahweh of hosts has sent me to you" (4:9; 6:15). Within the unit itself, two contrary clues also appear. On the one hand, that Joshua is introduced to Branch as "here is the man" (6:12) suggests that Branch is already on the scene; on the other hand, that the crown is deposited in the Temple and not placed on anyone's head suggests that Zerubbabel is not yet crowned as ruler.

Given the tensions within the unit, it is not surprising that many scholars posit that it has undergone a complex history of redaction—as the text was edited over time to reflect new sensibilities. In its final form, however, the passage seems to integrate the description of Branch in the fourth vision and the description of Zerubbabel in the fifth, suggesting that Zerubbabel will soon become Branch. Although the time is not yet come for his coronation, the historical Zerubbabel is the one who will fulfill the promises of Branch: he is both the one who will build the Temple (4:9; 6:13) and the one whose rule will mark the beginning of a new day of peace and prosperity (3:10; 6:15).

In addition to articulating the writer's vision of the future, this passage also provides a brief glimpse into the makeup of the post-exilic community. It gives the names of four members of the community, called Heldai, Tobijah, Jedaiah, and Josiah son of Zephaniah in 6:10, but Helem, Tobiah, Jedaiah, and Hen son of Zephaniah in 6:14 (in Hebrew Bible and reflected in NASB). Since nothing is known of these men, most scholars assume that both lists refer to the same people. The men are also called *haggôlâ*, translated in NRSV as "the exiles" but more accurately rendered "the exile." Such a designation fits the usage of the book of Ezra, which also confines the bounds of the postexilic community to those who have returned from captivity in Babylon.

Theological Analysis

In reporting God's command to make crowns for both the high priest and the Davidic heir, the author of Zechariah clearly affirms the conviction that dual leadership of the community is God's will. In the contemporary setting of the United States, such a vision would, on the surface, seem to favor the pairing of religious and secular rule and to question the separation of church and state.

As noted in the theological discussion on chapter 3, however, the sociohistorical situation in which the author of Zechariah wrote was vastly different from that of contemporary democratic states. Postexilic Yehud lived under Persian rule, and its priesthood was by no means removed from the administrative workings of the empire. In claiming that a Davidic heir would again participate in the leadership of the community, the author voiced the conviction that God's past promises to provide a Davidic leader were not nullified by contemporary politics. The priesthood, which had taken on greater importance during the crisis of the exile and during the rule of the Persians, would continue; but so too would the promise of the Davidic covenant. In the time of new things, God's earlier promises remain in effect.

In suggesting that the historical Zerubbabel shares function if not identity with the Branch, the author of First Zechariah also underscores that a holy future is not removed from the agency of historical individuals. Although God is the ultimate agent planning and carrying out Judah's restoration and return to glory, the role of individuals—Zerubbabel and the four exiles here named—play an important role. God's action does not preclude, but rather works in tandem with, human effort.

QUESTION REGARDING FASTING (7:1-7)

The conclusion of First Zechariah is a series of seven oracles that runs from 7:1 to 8:23. The question about fasting, introduced here in this first unit, is not answered directly until 8:18-19. Intervening are four oracles that underscore the ways in which the rebuilding of the Temple not only ends the punishment of the exile, but also inaugurates a new glorious future for Yehud.

Literary Analysis

This unit begins with a date formula, the first since chapter 1 to do so. It is set a year and ten months after the date listed in 1:7—that is, in 518 B.C.E.

The "word of Yahweh [that] came to Zechariah" on this date is explained as in response to an inquiry by a delegation from Bethel. Obviously recognizing the authority of the Jerusalemite priests and prophets, Bethel sent two named and other unnamed men to ask if mourning for the fall of Jerusalem should continue now that the Temple was being rebuilt.

Although the Bethel delegation posed the question to the priests and prophets, Yahweh responds through Zechariah, and rather than speaking only to the Bethelites, Zechariah speaks to all "the people of the land" and the priests. A direct answer to the inquiry is not yet given (it will come later, in 8:18-19), but the prophet poses three apparently rhetorical questions, all of which suggest that Yahweh is not interested in the people's fasts and mourning.

The final question, "Were these not the words that Yahweh proclaimed by the former prophets?" (7:7), may be understood in at least two ways. It may refer only to the question at hand regarding fasting, indicating that since the fall of Jerusalem was due to divine intention, Yahweh does not approve of mourning the event. "These words," however, may also point forward into the next oracle, referring to the summary of the preaching of the former prophets quoted in 7:9-10.

Exegetical Analysis

If this unit is historically accurate, then it provides valuable information about the workings of postexilic Yehud. It not only gives the names of individual Yehudites, but also provides a brief glimpse into Judahite communities outside of Jerusalem.

Bethel, mentioned in 7:1-3, remained an important religious center throughout much of Jewish history. Already during the period of the judges, it was one of the religious centers visited by

Samuel (along with Mizpah and Gilgal; 1 Sam 7:16). After the dissolution of the United Monarchy, it was one of the two worship centers established in the northern kingdom (1 Kgs 12:29). After the fall of Samaria in 722 or 721, priests from Samaria came to Bethel to teach people how to worship (2 Kgs 17:28).

Archaeological investigations at Bethel (= Beitin) suggest that the city was not destroyed by the Babylonians when Judah fell to Nebuchadnezzar's armies in 587 or 586. Rather, the site enjoyed continuous occupation through the neo-Babylonian period ("the exile"), and archaeological as well as literary evidence suggest the likelihood that sacrificial worship continued there throughout the period. Precise dates for the destruction or abandonment of the site are not known, though a general mid-sixth-century time frame is usually suggested.

In the Persian period, Bethel belonged to the northernmost of the five administrative districts into which Yehud was divided, the one headquartered in Mizpah (Blenkinsopp 1998, 29). Jeremiah 40–41 indicates that Mizpah was established as an important administrative center already in the neo-Babylonian period: those who were left in the land after the fall of Jerusalem were overseen at Mizpah by a local governor named Gedaliah. Joseph Blenkinsopp has argued that, after Gedaliah's assassination (Jer 41), Bethel replaced Mizpah as a center of worship and that it continued to function as a major worship site during the Persian period.

If Blenkinsopp's theory is correct, it suggests that Bethel was a worship center competing with Jerusalem in the Persian period. Even if Blenkinsopp's theory is not correct, at the very least, Bethel represented a center of power removed from the Jerusalemite hierarchy. Its experience was not that of exile, but of continued worship and life in the land of Israel.

This history of Bethel resonates in interesting ways with Zech 7:1-3, which is most commonly understood as depicting a delegation from Bethel coming to Jerusalem to inquire about cultic matters. The translation of 7:2, however, is troublesome. A singular verb ("sent") is followed by a series of nouns: Bethel,

Sharezer, and Regemmelech. The NRSV understands the first as the subject of the verb and the remaining nouns as objects ("Bethel had sent Sharezer and Regemmelech"); to avoid the apparent awkwardness of a city functioning as the subject of a verb, it has added *"people of* Bethel." Other translations understand all of the nouns to constitute the subject, with no object (TANAKH: "Bethel-sharezer and Regem-melech and his men sent to entreat").

Blenkinsopp, however, has argued that Bethel should be understood as the object of the sentence—that is, as the destination of the delegation and not its origin: "Sareser, Regemmelech and his men had sent to Bethel" (1998, 32). Noting that there was a "house of Yahweh" (7:3*a*) at Bethel but not yet at Jerusalem, Blenkinsopp interprets this verse as indicating that a delegation from Jerusalem asked cultic advice from the priests and prophets at Bethel, an action criticized by Zechariah (1998, 33).

Blenkinsopp's reading of the Hebrew is tenable and is supported by other ancient Versions. Moreover, a temple to Yahweh was in operation at Bethel, as Jer 41:5 suggests. The unit as a whole, however, is better understood in the more traditional way, as Bethelites sending to Jerusalem. Such an image clearly privileges Jerusalem over Bethel, claiming that those outside Jerusalem recognized its authority in matters of sacrifice.

Indeed, a case may be made for understanding the entire unit of 7:1-7 as Zechariah's polemic against worship practices at Bethel.

1. Zechariah's response comes to "all the people of the land." Although in Hag 2:4 the phrase refers to the exiles, in other postexilic literature it refers to those who remained in the land and did not go to Babylon (Ezra 4:4; 9:11; 10:2, 11; Neh 9:24; 10:30).

2. Although the original question regards fasting in the fifth month, Zechariah's response also mentions the seventh month. Jerusalem fell in the fifth month of 586 (2 Kgs 25:8). The seventh month likely refers to the time of the murder of Gedaliah (2 Kgs

25:25) and the concurrent slaughter of Judeans, Babylonian soldiers, and pilgrims (Jer 41). Such events would have been more likely observed by those in Bethel and Mizpah than by those in Jerusalem.

3. Zechariah's charge that the people's fasting is their own idea, not Yahweh's, may reflect the prophet's more general disapproval of the worship practices at Bethel. Although the writer imputes to the Bethelites sorrow over the destruction of the Jerusalemite Temple, the words of the prophet appear to deny the validity of the fasting that has continued "these seventy years" (7:5; see also Zech 1:12).

If this unit does indeed reflect conflict between Bethel and Jerusalem in the Persian period, then it also demonstrates the writer's pro-Jerusalem perspective. Depicting the Bethelites as petitioning ritual advice from Jerusalem (assuming the traditional translation, not that of Blenkinsopp), the writer of Zech 7 expresses a clear ideology against those who remained in the land. Noteworthy in this regard is the clear articulation of Yahweh's jealousy for Jerusalem that returns in Zech 8.

The unit may also reflect other historical dynamics of the period. Fasting in the fifth month, known in the Jewish calendar as Av, became obligatory by the end of the first century C.E. According to Jewish tradition, both the First and Second Temples were destroyed on the Ninth of Av. Zechariah 7:1-3 indicates that the fasting in the fifth month had begun already in the Persian period. Moreover, as noted in the discussion of Zech 1, the collection's reference to "the former prophets" (1:4; 7:7) suggests the beginning stages of the formulation of Scripture. The writer of Zechariah not only accepts the words of the prophets as authoritative but also presupposes that his audience accepts those words as authoritative; for a rhetorical question to be effective, the reader must assent to the premise of the question.

Theological Analysis

Because Zechariah's response regarding fasting comes in the form of rhetorical questions rather than directly, discerning the theological logic that underlies the questions is difficult. The first rhetorical question could be understood as challenging the legitimacy of fasting altogether. By asking, "Was it for me that you fasted?" Yahweh may imply that fasting merits no divine concern. Indeed, a long tradition of Christian interpretation has understood the prophets of Israel as challenging the legitimacy of ritual and advancing instead a theology devoted to social justice.

Such an understanding, however, does not take into account the ways in which the prophets presuppose Temple worship and use hyperbolic language to chasten the people's intentions. In the case of Zech 7:1-7, it also fails to explain the second of the rhetorical questions, "Do you not eat and drink only for yourselves?" If the question is understood as a negative judgment on the people, then the basis of that judgment is unclear: what would it mean to eat and drink for reasons other than oneself?

The third of the questions in this unit may help explain the other two. It implies that the destruction of Jerusalem was God's intention, a perspective that is articulated in 1:1-6 and reiterated in 8:8-14. Because God intended Jerusalem's fall, mourning and fasting its fate met a human need and not a divine need. The questions may not necessarily criticize the Bethelites for lamenting the fall of the Temple, but they do underscore that mourning is for humans, not for God. In this way, the closing verses of the unit remind readers that mourning rituals address human grief and problems. They are not divine in and of themselves, but serve the function of helping humans deal with trauma and loss.

Moreover, the possibility that this unit reflects tension within postexilic Yehud raises the possibility that the concern of the writer is more with the legitimacy of worship at Bethel than of fasting as a religious practice. Readers do well to remember that the Bible does not express atemporal, purely theological concerns.

In stressing that Jerusalem was the only legitimate place of worship in Yehud, the writer of Zech 7 expresses the belief that Yahweh's choice of Jerusalem as a holy city had not been disrupted by the Babylonian exile. That perspective was theological but also had profound implications for the workings of the post-exilic community. In the past as in the present, reflections about God and about worship are intricately interrelated with political and social struggles.

PAST UNFAITHFULNESS (7:8-14)

This unit is linked with the previous one through the evoking of the preaching of the previous prophets. The word of Yahweh that came to Zechariah summarizes the preaching of the former prophets, the same former prophets described at the close of the previous unit (7:7) and mentioned again in 7:12.

Literary Analysis

The resonances between 7:8-12 and other prophetic literature are many. Zechariah 7:8-10 uses standard prophetic vocabulary for describing social justice: justice *(mišpāṭ)*; truth *(ʾemet)*; loyalty or kindness *(ḥesed)*; compassion *(raḥămîm)*. It also calls for special treatment of the standard list of the disenfranchised: the orphan, the widow, and the poor. Just how characteristic of prophetic discourse this vocabulary is can be seen by comparing other prophetic passages (vocabulary shared with Zech 7:9-10 is italicized):

Isaiah 1:17 Learn to do good; seek *justice,* rescue the oppressed, defend the *orphan,* plead for the *widow.*

Isaiah 10:2 To turn aside the needy from *justice* and to rob the *poor* of my people of their right, that *widows* may be your spoil, and that you may make the *orphans* your prey!

Jeremiah 5:28 They have grown fat and sleek. They know no limits in deeds of wickedness; they do not judge with *justice* the cause of the *orphan,* to make it prosper, and they do not defend the rights of the needy.

Jeremiah 22:3 Thus says the LORD: Act with *justice* and righteousness, and deliver from the hand of the oppressor anyone who has been robbed. And do no wrong or violence to the alien, the *orphan,* and the *widow,* or shed innocent blood in this place.

Micah 6:8 He has told you, O mortal, what is good; and what does the LORD require of you but to do *justice,* and to love *kindness,* and to walk humbly with your God?

Malachi 3:5 Then I will draw near to you for *judgment;* I will be swift to bear witness against the sorcerers, against the adulterers, against those who swear falsely, against those who oppress the hired workers in their wages, the *widow* and the *orphan,* against those who thrust aside the alien, and do not fear me, says the LORD of hosts.

In terms of vocabulary, Zech 7:11 also resonates with Isa 6:10. Both passages refer to the "stopping" of "ears," although in Isaiah the deity is the one responsible for the people's deafness, and in Zechariah, they stop their own ears. Jeremiah 23:19 also shares vocabulary with Zech 7:14: "Look, the storm [whirlwind] of the LORD! Wrath has gone forth, a whirling tempest; it will burst upon the head of the wicked."

In terms of theme, the entire unit summarizes the teaching of the prophets, especially that of Jeremiah. Because the people did not heed the voice of Yahweh, Yahweh was angry and scattered them.

Exegetical Analysis

The strong resonances between this unit and other prophetic books strengthen the likelihood, mentioned before, that portions of the prophetic material had been committed to writing by the Persian period. The writer of Zechariah is familiar not only with the general themes of the prophetic books, but also with their distinctive vocabulary. Of course, general vocabulary would have been common from oral transmission of the teachings of the prophets, but the close overlap between Zechariah and other prophetic books is better explained by literary dependence.

The way in which Zechariah draws from earlier prophets to bolster its own argument points a shift in prophecy by the Persian period. Although Zechariah does claim to reveal new divine speech, it also discerns revelation in the words of the past. As in the anonymous material attached to earlier prophets' names (often called "deutero-prophetic" literature; examples include Isa 40–55 and Isa 56–66), prophecy becomes at least in part an exegetical enterprise. God's will is known not only by the word sent to contemporary spokespersons, but also by meditating on and interpreting the words entrusted to earlier prophets.

This "exegetical turn" in prophecy by the Persian period provides further insight into the composition of the prophetic books. Prophetic scholars have long argued that the prophetic books as we now have them have been shaped by multiple and complex redactions; a prophetic book does not give us a pure sense of what God said only to one prophet, but rather provides witness to how generations of readers and editors updated and clarified that message for their own time. Zechariah 7 supports such an understanding, because it clearly shows a writer explaining how the words of past prophets bear upon a later community. That is, Zech 7 provides a glimpse into the understanding of the prophetic past that also finds expression in the redactional process.

In light of the tension between Bethel and Jerusalem reflected in the previous unit, it is possible that this word of Zechariah was directed not only to the Jerusalemite community but also to the Bethelites and other "people of the land." The closing claim of the unit that the wrath of God left the land desolate, so that "no one went to and fro" (7:14), certainly challenges the claim of those of Bethel to be a remnant of Yahweh's people. In articulating a theory of "the empty land," the writer of Zech 7 directly challenges the legitimacy of those who had not been exiled.

Theological Analysis

The particular way in which Zech 7 summarizes the teaching of the former prophets provides insight into its writer's distinctive theology. Given the wide range of topics and sayings covered by the prophetic corpus, defining "the" message of the prophets is, clearly, a subjective judgment.

The writer has chosen to highlight one aspect of prophetic teaching: that the exile is God's punishment for the people's failure to heed the call to social justice. Missing from Zechariah is the perspective of Ezekiel that improper worship contributed to God's punishment or even Jeremiah's claim that both social injustice and improper worship led to the fall of Jerusalem.

Zechariah's focus on the care of the widow, orphan, and the poor challenges the claim that the postexilic community was concerned only with the sacrificial cult. Zechariah does, indeed, call for the rebuilding of the Temple and for the reestablishment of Temple worship, but this passage indicates that such concerns do not overshadow the call for just dealings in the community. In invoking the former prophets as calling for fair treatment of the poor, this author stresses that proper worship and social justice are not mutually exclusive.

By claiming, unlike Isa 6:10, that the people stopped their own ears, Zechariah also assumes that human beings have the ability—and the responsibility—to respond to God. Although the claim in 7:13 is harsh ("Just as, when I called, they would not hear, so, when they called, I would not hear."), it underscores that worship requires not only praise, but also service to others.

The theology of "the empty land," expressed in 7:14, bears both ancient and contemporary dynamics. As Robert Carroll (1992) has poignantly shown, the depiction of the land of Israel as "without inhabitants" was an important ideological underpinning not only of the initial settlement of the land under Joshua, but also of the Return. One can call Judah "empty" prior to the Return of the exiles only if those who remained in the land are ignored. One of the great scandals of the Bible is that it does not trace the story of all of the descendants of Jacob. The stories of those scattered by the Assyrians, of those who remained in the land after the Babylonian destruction of Jerusalem, and of those who chose to remain in Babylon are stories lost to readers of the Bible.

This same "empty land" theology was shared by other settlers in later periods. The Europeans who settled the "new world" and the Jews who returned to an "empty" Palestine in the mid-twentieth century both spoke of themselves as pioneers, staking out a homeland in a land wanted by no one else. The voices of Native Americans and of Palestinians have reminded us of the tragic effect of that rhetoric on their own claims to land and dignity.

Perhaps one of the greatest challenges of the modern era is to learn to speak the truth of multiple and competing claims to land. Perhaps the first step is to hear the tensions even in our sacred texts—such as that between Bethel and Jerusalem in Zech 7.

ZION'S FUTURE (8:1-8)

This oracle announces the return of Yahweh to Jerusalem. As in 1:14, Yahweh is "jealous" for Jerusalem and is about to restore peace to its streets.

Literary Analysis

In its variation of the standard phrase used in 7:1 to 8:23, this unit includes no object: the unit opens with "the word of Yahweh was, saying" (the NRSV has added "to me"). "Thus says Yahweh," the other phrase shared with the surrounding units, immediately follows in 1:2 and appears four more times in the unit (8:3, 4, 6, and 7).

In contrast to the faithlessness of previous generations that was explored in the preceding unit, this unit tells of the glory that Jerusalem is about to experience. As in 1:14-17, Yahweh announces divine jealousy for Jerusalem and anger against those who seek its harm. Indeed, many similarities exist between 8:1-8 and 1:13-17. Both announce that Yahweh's anger has turned from *against* Jerusalem to anger *for* Jerusalem, and both promise a hopeful future. Both also end with the reaffirmation of earlier promises of divine favor: just as 1:17 uses the traditional language of "choosing" Jerusalem, so, too, this unit ends with an affirmation of the Mosaic covenant—"they shall be my people and I will be their God" (compare the covenant formula in Exod 6:7). Similar themes are also developed in 2:10-12.

The unit is filled with poetic images. Zion and Jerusalem are used interchangeably, much like the synonymous parallelism of Hebrew poetry. And like the poetic speech of other prophets, Zechariah gives new names to Jerusalem, calling it "Faithful City" and "Holy Mountain" (see, too, Mal 1:2-5, which calls Edom "The Wicked Country" and "The People with Whom Yahweh Is Angry Forever").

The image of Jerusalem's future is one of peace and harmony, one balanced in age and gender. Old men and old women, living long, sit in the streets; young girls and young boys play in the streets. This image is one not only of the absence of violence and war, but also of abundant population, expanded not only by growth within the current population, but also by the return of yet other exiles. Zechariah 8:7-8 speaks of ones returning from east and west—from the rising of the sun to its setting.

Repetition of key words marks this unit. In 8:2, a form of the word "jealous" appears three times. The Hebrew word *'emet,* usually translated as "truth" but rendered in the NRSV as "faithfulness," appears several times in this unit and in the one that follows it (Zech 8:3, 8, 16, 19).

Exegetical Analysis

The pro-Jerusalem perspective of this unit is clear. The future of the community clearly is synonymous with the future of Jerusalem. In apparent disregard of those who worship at Bethel or elsewhere in the land, Yahweh is jealous for Jerusalem alone.

The word translated as "streets" in NRSV is literally "open places" *(rehōbôt).* It refers not to strips of land dedicated to transportation, as the modern English word "street" would imply, but rather to areas not occupied by houses. Other biblical usages of *reḥōbôt* suggest that these "open places" were public plazas or squares, common space (Gen 19:2; Prov 1:20; 7:12; Isa 59:14; Amos 5:16). Several biblical passages describe the distress of cities as manifested in the public square. Jeremiah 49:26 and 50:30 describe the destruction of the nations as "young men fall in her squares," and in portraying the fall of Jerusalem, Lam 2:11 bemoans, "infants and babes faint in the streets of the city." In envisioning both the old and the young as thriving in the public spaces of Jerusalem, Zech 8 radically reverses these images: the population of Jerusalem not only escapes destruction, but also thrives—the elderly live to great age and the children play.

Recognizing the idealism of the vision of Zech 8 is enhanced by considering the demographics of postexilic Yehud. The average life expectancy during this period was probably forty years, and the population of Jerusalem may have been between 750 and 1500 inhabitants (Kessler 2001, 147). Hence, the image of a city filled with people, and particularly with the aged, denotes the belief that the future will be very different from the present.

As Meyers and Meyers have argued, the vision of occupants enjoying leisure also provides a striking contrast with the reality of the need for work in the ancient world (1987, 415). In few societies are the elderly relieved of the responsibility for productive labor. Even more strikingly, the passage envisions children playing in the squares. Although the notion of children at play is not surprising for modern readers, it is a relatively new concept in human culture. In agrarian economies, children are also workers, able to produce more than they consume by the age of seven. Childhood as a time of innocence, nonproductive work, and development arose only during the nineteenth century.

Several relatively rare words appear in the unit. The word used for "play" (*śāḥaq*) is more literally "laugh" and is the same root used in the pun on Isaac's name in Gen 21. The verb is used for a contest between the men of David and those of Saul in 2 Sam 2:14, for the dancing of David in front of the ark of the covenant in 2 Sam 6:21, and for mocking in Job 30:1. In Job 41:5 (Heb. 40:29), it seems to describe playing with a pet. The

Hebrew word here translated as "girls" is rare in the Hebrew Bible *(yĕlādôt)*. The root appears elsewhere only in Gen 34:4, referring to a woman being taken as a wife, and in Joel 3:3, describing young females being sold as prostitutes. Other Hebrew words are translated in the NRSV as "girl," the most frequent *(naᶜărâ)* often referring to females of marriageable age (Deut 22:15; 1 Kgs 1:3; Esth 2:4).

In sum, the Hebrew Bible, like most literature prior to the eighteenth century, gives little attention to childhood and its delights. That Zech 8 includes children in its vision of an idyllic future is striking.

In Zech 8:6, as later in 8:12, Zechariah calls the community the "remnant of this people." The same language is used in Hag 1:12, 14; and 2:2. Although Zechariah does not provide independent evidence for tension between groups in the community, we have noted elsewhere (as in Zech 7) that the book does recognize that not all were returnees.

The language of "remnant" suggests that the writer assumes that the returnees comprise the true community. In this way, Zechariah shares with other exilic and postexilic biblical literature in the "myth of the empty land," the term used by R. Carroll (1992) and H. Barstad (1996) to denote an ideology that promoted the idea that the land to which the exiles returned was uninhabited. Blenkinsopp (2002) helpfully surveys the political interests served by such a myth as well as the archaeological and literary evidence of those who remained in Judah after the Babylonian invasions of 587 or 586 (the possibility for a continuous occupation of Bethel was mentioned in the discussion of Zech 7). That the writer envisions the population as growing through immigration and not through inclusion of diverse groups is underscored in the final verses of the unit: they will come from the directions of the rising and setting sun, denoting the two geographical extremes of dispersion.

Theological Analysis

In Jewish and Christian theological reflection, the value of idyllic visions of the future have been variously assessed. Do promises of a better future fail to take seriously contemporary human pain, weakening one's resolve to change the present? Or, by bearing witness to an alternate reality, do such visions evoke faithfulness to something bigger and more true than the current situation; do they resist current structures by changing one's allegiances?

Debate between these two positions is heated, but in Zech 8, the gap between the future and the present is bridged by the message of the collection as a whole. First Zechariah makes clear that the current, historical event of rebuilding the Temple is itself inaugurating a new era. The coming of an idyllic future is envisioned not as a radical disruption of current events, but as an unfolding of them. The current work of Zerubbabel, Joshua, and the remnant of the people is part of God's plan for a new Jerusalem. Indeed, 8:4 makes clear that the future of Jerusalem is understood as a return to its past: the aged will "again" sit in the open places of the city.

Nowhere does First Zechariah underplay the importance of human participation in God's plan for the future. Although the people's salvation (8:7) is God's doing, they are called to build the Temple and to respond to God's call through the prophets.

THE PRESENT SITUATION (8:9-13)

In this oracle, Yahweh encourages the people to be strong. Before the Temple foundation was laid, God thwarted the people's success; now in light of the people's rebuilding efforts, they will be rewarded.

Literary Analysis

The future promise articulated in the previous unit leads here to encouragement for the present. Those who hear the prophet's words are exhorted to be strong. In an *inclusio* (where a unit begins and ends with similar vocabulary or theme), both 8:9 and 8:13 admonish the people to strengthen their hands. The call of 8:13, "do not fear," also appears in Hag 2:5.

Between these two bookends of encouragement, the prophet employs juxtaposition to underscore a change in God's intentions. *Before*, neither human nor animal received reward for work; *now*, in contrast to former days, the vine will produce and the skies give dew. *Before*, the people were a curse; *now*, they will be a blessing.

The frequent use of temporal terminology underscores the past-present-future scheme of the larger section of which this unit is a part. "These days" (NRSV: "recently"; 8:9), "before those days" (8:10), "now" (8:11), and "former days" (8:11) all highlight that Yahweh's plans for Yehud have changed. In effect, this unit explains the logic that unites the two previous units: the disjunction between Yehud's past and its future is due to the present work of Zechariah's community. In the past, there was no safety from the foe (8:10); in the future, the old and young will sit in Jerusalem's streets (8:1-8) and the people will thrive (8:12).

Exegetical Analysis

In 8:9, mention is made of "prophets" who were present when the foundation of the Temple was laid. This plural reference is intriguing, since it clearly recognizes multiple prophetic voices in sixth-century Yehud. One possibility is that two prophets are indicated—Zechariah and Haggai. The editorial frameworks of the books set them in the same time period and attribute a similar message to the prophets for whom they are named. In Ezra 5:1 and 6:14, Haggai and Zechariah are together mentioned as encouraging the Temple rebuilding project. Neither Haggai nor Zechariah, however, mentions the other prophet, and thus 8:9 may be the only corroboration within the prophetic books of their contemporaneous careers. Unfortunately, the verse provides little data. Although it certainly fits the thesis that Haggai is inferred, it does not provide independent evidence for that thesis.

The Hebrew of 8:11 is more intriguing than the NRSV translation would suggest. The MT literally reads, "Now I am not to the remnant of this people as in the former days," while an additional verb has been supplied by the NRSV ("I will not deal with the remnant of this people as in the former days") and other translations (NAB and NKJV) add "treat." The Hebrew implies that God, and not only God's dealing with people, changes.

As in the previous unit, the community of Yehud is here described as the "remnant of the people." As noted above, such language advances the ideology that only those who have returned from exile belong on the land. Zechariah 8:12 underscores that Yahweh will cause the "remnant" to "possess" the produce of the land.

By referring both to the house of Israel and to the house of Judah, Zech 8:13 expresses the hope that the restoration of the nation will be total. While some biblical literature uses the term "Israel" to refer to the postexilic community (Neh 10:33; 11:20; Mal 2:11), other passages continue to speak of both Israel and Judah long after the fall of the northern kingdom (Jer 50:33; 51:5; Ezek 37). By speaking of both "houses," Zechariah foresees a turn of fortune both for those exiled from Judah and also for those dispersed by the Assyrians in 722 or 721. This theme will feature prominently in Zech 10.

Such as previous passages in First Zechariah, this unit underscores the importance that the writer places on the laying of the foundation of the Temple. As in 4:9, Zech 8:9 marks time from the foundation laying; the beginning of the Temple project began a new relationship between God and people, and its completion will bring a yet greater future.

Theological Analysis

Throughout this unit, the writer is adamant that, until the people began the Temple project, Yahweh was against them. Yahweh allowed neither humans nor animals to enjoy the benefit of their labors ("wages"), and Yahweh set the members of the community against one another (8:10). When Yahweh's intentions toward the people turned, the earth again produced food. Clearly, total control over humans, animals, and agricultural produce is attributed to Yahweh, though human action spurs Yahweh's choices.

The God described by Zech 8 is not an unchangeable, static deity. Rather, Yahweh changes his mind in response to human attitudes and behaviors. Although some find the notion of a deity who changes as unsettling, too unstable to trust, the Hebrew Bible's affirmation that Yahweh repents and changes may be seen as good news. The fate of humans is not sealed or beyond their control. Rather, the Yahweh who intends harm can be persuaded to intend good.

In First Zechariah, the human action that changes Yahweh is the laying of the Temple's foundation. When the people choose to prioritize restoring the community with the Temple at its center, their ignoble past is transformed into a glorious future.

PAST CONTRASTED WITH THE PRESENT (8:14-17)

This short unit, the beginning of which is signaled by "Thus says Yahweh," synthesizes the themes that have been developed so far in chapter 8. It contrasts the disaster provoked by the ancestors with the good that Yahweh now intends for the people.

Literary Analysis

The speech of Yahweh outlines the behavior expected of the people. The list of behaviors summarizes not only 8:7-14, but also the general themes of the "former prophets." It is especially close in wording, for example, to Amos 5:15: "Hate evil and love good, and establish justice in the gate; it may be that Yahweh, the God of hosts, will be gracious to the remnant of Joseph."

The unit also returns to vocabulary already used in the larger unit of 7:1–8:23. Like 8:13, Zech 8:15 instructs the people not to be afraid, and like Zech 7:9; 8:3; and 8:8, Zech 8:16 draws heavily on the term 'emet ("truth"). Its poetic character is enhanced by repetition of the phrase "man against his neighbor" in the middle of 8:16 and in the beginning of 8:17.

Exegetical Analysis

While the previous unit set in parallel "house of Judah" and "house of Israel," Zech 8:15 speaks of "Jerusalem and the house of Judah." These terms might be seen as synonymous, but other indications in the book of Zechariah suggest that the authors often use "Judah" to refer to all Yehud *other than* Jerusalem. In Zech 12, for example, the fates of Judah and Jerusalem are clearly distinguished.

The call for "justice in the gates" in 8:16 reflects one aspect of the sociology of ancient Near Eastern cities. Because most ancient cities were walled, the gates that controlled entry and exit to the city became places of public gathering and more specifically of communal decision making. In Ruth 4, business is transacted in the city gate; and in Prov 22:22 and Job 29:7-9, justice is determined there. In Deut 2 and 22, communal punishment is executed at the gate. The prophets regularly lambast the failure of the people to carry out justice in the gate (Isa 29:21; Amos 5:10, 12, 15).

In its injunctions to treat the neighbor justly, Zechariah echoes the teaching of the prophets and of the Pentateuch. The community is called to care in taking oaths (Lev 5:4; see, too, Sir 23:11) and to render just judgments.

Theological Analysis

In its reiteration of earlier units, Zech 8:14-17 emphasizes the importance of fair treatment of the neighbor. Decisions regarding the neighbor must meet the criteria of truth, justice, and peace. As noted earlier, Zechariah recognizes no distinction between morality and ritual: the same voice that supports the rebuilding of the Temple calls for truth and justice in human interactions.

In keeping with the rhetoric of other prophets (Hos 9:15; Amos 5:21; 6:8; Mal 1:2-5), the unit also attributes to Yahweh the strong emotion of hate. Although some interpreters have attempted to soften the impact of such language, suggesting that "hate" in the Bible merely means "love less," the intensity of the word is likely intended. Zechariah, like other prophets, insists

that Yahweh is a God of intense commitment, passionately advo-
cating the cause of the downtrodden.

ANSWER REGARDING FASTING (8:18-19)

This unit offers the answer to the inquiry regarding fasting
that was posed in 7:3. Given that the Temple has been rebuilt,
mourning is no longer necessary.

Literary Analysis

The book finally returns to the question posed by the delegation from Bethel in chapter 7: should they continue to fast in the
fifth month? The initial response to the question, offered in 7:4-
7, speaks of the fasts of the fifth and seventh months. This unit,
however, speaks of fasting in additional months—the fourth,
fifth, seventh, and tenth. Interesting is that each subsequent
response to the original inquiry expands the months of fasting.
Zechariah 7 and 8 explicitly overturn the practice of fasting in
these months, but these chapters in effect call attention to those
fasts. The author appears to recognize more fast days than the
Bethelites who originally asked the question. In two short verses,
the prophet reports that "the word of Yahweh came to me" and
that the days of fasting should be converted to festivals of rejoic-
ing. The closing verses repeat vocabulary from earlier units: the
people are called to love truth (ʾemet; see 7:9; 8:3, 8, 16) and
peace (šālôm; see 8:10, 12, 16).

Exegetical Analysis

Four fasts are mentioned in this unit. The fast of the fifth
month is corroborated elsewhere; as noted in the discussion of
7:1-7, the Ninth of Av was considered a mandatory observance
by the end of the first century C.E. The fast of the seventh month,
also mentioned in 7:1-7, may be in commemoration of the assassination of Gedaliah, as recorded in 2 Kgs 25:25.

Less clear are the significance and origins of the fasts of the fourth and tenth months. They are mentioned neither in chapter 7 nor in any other extant literature. The books of 2 Kings and Jeremiah correlate these months with important events related to the fall of Jerusalem: the walls of Jerusalem were breached in the fourth month (Jer 39:2), and Nebuchadnezzar's siege of the city began in the tenth month (Jer 39:1; 2 Kgs 25:1). Although it is reasonable to assume that Zechariah refers to fasts commemorating these tragic events surrounding the fall of the Temple, no evidence for such observances exists outside of the book of Zechariah.

Theological Analysis

In its response to the Bethelites, Zechariah actually shows just how traumatic the fall of the Temple was. Even though the delegation from Bethel only asked about the fast of the fifth month, when the Temple actually fell, each response intensifies the significance of the Temple's destruction. Zechariah—not the Bethelites—refers to fasts that mourn a whole series of events surrounding the Temple's fall: the beginning of the siege of the city, the breaching of the wall, the actual fall of the Temple, and the murder of Gedaliah.

Zechariah consistently reflects an ideology in which the Temple remains the center of the community. The fall of the Temple marks sacred seasons; the rebuilding of the Temple marks a new era. In our own time it is common to speak of the First and Second Temples, though Zechariah sees the Temple building project not as creating a new Temple, but as restoring what has been lost.

This passage bears witness both to the need and to the difficulty of coming to terms with past trauma. The writer affirms that mourning for the past cannot continue indefinitely and that in light of new events, a community must move forward; what had been occasion for mourning might become, in another era, an occasion for celebration. And yet the writer demonstrates that grief continues to shape the imagination. Even while calling for the end to fasts, the writer renews the memory of all that Judah has suffered.

Zion's Future (8:20-23)

This last unit of First Zechariah expands on the future glory of Jerusalem that was described in 8:1-8. Not only will the inhabitants of Jerusalem enjoy leisure and long life (8:4-5), but also others will come and swell Jerusalem's ranks. While those "others" in 8:7 were exiled Judeans, here they are from other nations.

Literary Analysis

The word "entreat" *(ḥālāh)* appears twice in this unit (8:21, 22), both times in the context of describing those who will come to Jerusalem to entreat Yahweh's favor. This turn of events is exactly what did happen in 7:2, in which a delegation from Bethel came to "entreat" the favor of Yahweh. This *inclusio* structure suggests that the writer understood the Bethelites' recognition of the authority of the Jerusalemite community as the beginning of a larger influx of people recognizing Jerusalem's importance.

The ending of the unit is highly poetic and hyperbolic. "Ten men" is likely symbolic of "significant unit," and those men are described as not merely asking to be included in the Jerusalemite community, but "taking a firm hold" of a Jew (the same root for "making strong" the hands in Zech 8:9 and 13).

Exegetical Analysis

In its description of all people streaming to Jerusalem, Zechariah speaks both of "many cities" and "many nations." The cities may refer either to Yehudite cities or to those of the nations. The former option, however, fits the description of those from Bethel coming to Jerusalem for instruction in proper worship; it provides an inclusive vision of both those within the province and beyond it as recognizing Jerusalem's importance.

In its description of "the nations" flocking to Jerusalem, the unit shares much with Isa 2 and Mic 4:1-4. In all three passages, the writers envision those of "many nations" coming to Jerusalem and asking to be instructed in the worship of Yahweh. Those who study the compositional history of prophetic books have suggested that both Isa 2 and Mic 4 are later additions to their respective books. In such an understanding, the composition of Zech 8 may be roughly contemporaneous with the parallel passages from Isaiah and Micah. A good case could be made for Zechariah's dependence on these passages, however, since the writer both presupposes and goes beyond them when describing the nations "taking hold" of a Jew.

Although the term "Jew" in the NRSV is relatively rare, used in the Old Testament only in Esther and Zech 8:23, the Hebrew word from which it is translated, *yĕhûdî*, is more common and has a wider range of meanings. It and its plural form are used to refer to "Judahites" or "Judeans" in Isa 36:11 and Jer 32:12, and it functions as a name in Jer 36. The term appears often in Nehemiah and Esther. The designation is noteworthy, referring to the community as "Judean" (or "Yehudite," after the name of the Persian province) even after the exile, as in Nehemiah, and showing one step in the development of the term "Jew" that functions prominently in subsequent literature.

Theological Analysis

Passages such as Zech 8:20-23 are often understood to be radically inclusive, welcoming all people, regardless of ethnicity, into the fold of Yahweh. This passage does, indeed, expand the community far beyond its current configuration and welcomes those of other nations. At the same time, the invitation to inclusion comes with particular terms. Other nations are envisioned as worshiping Yehud's God; their hope lies in recognizing the supremacy of Jerusalem.

Such an understanding of the future indicates that Zechariah does not share the modern view of inclusion as the equal sharing of and respect for all traditions. Rather, the book, from start to finish, claims the radical particularly of Israel's faith. Modern readers do well to reflect upon the value and the weaknesses of such a vision of the future. Can we appropriate Zechariah's vision for our own time in ways that affirm the inclusiveness of Yahweh without demanding that it be on our own terms?

The closing of First Zechariah underscores the theme that has been developed throughout these chapters. The building of the Temple in Jerusalem is presented by this writer as God's intention for the community. The people's willingness to begin the project is rewarded in the present and promises great things for their future.

INTRODUCTION: ZECHARIAH 9–14

In crossing the boundary between Zech 8 and 9, the reader enters a different world. Gone are the interpreting messenger, Zerubbabel, and Joshua. Gone is the exclusive focus on Jerusalem. New vocabulary and a new style dominate the scene, and the label "oracle" *(maśśāʾ)* delineates new units at 9:1 and 12:1. Numerous place names are used, including that of Greece (9:13), and militaristic language abounds. For these and other reasons, for several hundred years, biblical scholars have maintained that Zech 9–14 was not written by the same author as Zech 1–8 and have labeled the book's latter portion "Second Zechariah."

This designation might imply that the collection bears some sort of unity in terms of theme, authorial voice, or structure. Such is not the case. These chapters are complex and uneven, ranging from the symbolic and formulaic to the historically specific and at times reading as little more than a haphazard collection of pieces of prophetic tradition strung together by catchwords. Some have suggested the presence of more than two collections, speaking of Third Zechariah or of even more diverse authorship.

Given these features of the book, the diversity of theories about the date of the collection is not surprising. In the seventeenth and eighteen centuries, many interpreters maintained that much of Second Zechariah is preexilic, partially based on the fact that Matt 27:9 quotes Zech 11:12-13 but attributes it to

Jeremiah. The two major positions today advance dates in (1) the Hellenistic period, based primarily on the reference to Greece in 9:13, or (2) the Persian period, some time after the composition of Zech 1–8 and the completion of the Second Temple.

Meyers and Meyers (1993), as well as Petersen (1995), set Second Zechariah in the mid-fifth century, in the context of the Persian-Greek wars. Such a date makes the best sense of these difficult chapters; as explored in the commentary, the unit appears to reflect the ongoing dynamics of Persian rule of Yehud.

These two parts of Zechariah have been edited into a single book, with some continuity of theme, vocabulary, and perspective. Second Zechariah shares with First Zechariah the primary concern with the restoration of Jerusalem, the belief that nations that oppose Jerusalem will be punished, and hints of tension between Jerusalem and the rest of Yehud.

Nonetheless, the tone of 9–14 differs sufficiently from 1–8 to lead to the conclusion that Second Zechariah is a discrete collection —if not from a different hand, then at least utilizing a different style. These chapters extend, elaborate, and redirect the content of First Zechariah.

Second Zechariah is often deemed "apocalyptic" or "proto-apocalyptic" literature, based on the conviction that its hopes for the future break with human history in ways that First Zechariah does not. As discussed more fully in the exegetical analysis of Zech 14, the distinction between "prophetic" and "apocalyptic" is difficult to make. For example, Zech 1–8 unpacks the cosmological significance of the historical building of the Temple, whereas Zech 9–14 (and especially chapter 14) focuses more directly on the nature of that future.

Both sections and the book as a whole, however, remain fully within the stream of prophetic discourse. Like other prophetic books, Zechariah claims to discern Yahweh's intention for humanity and to demonstrate God's care and demand for human accountability.

Delineating the units of Second Zechariah is difficult, though the following structure is utilized here:

9:1-8	Yahweh against the nations
9:9-17	Yahweh to save Jerusalem
10:1-12	Yahweh against the shepherds
11:1-17	Shepherds of the community
12:1-9	The protection of Judah and Jerusalem
12:10-14	The pierced one
13:1-9	The end of idolatry and prophecy
14:1-21	The final supremacy of Jerusalem

COMMENTARY: ZECHARIAH 9–14

YAHWEH AGAINST THE NATIONS (9:1-8)

This new section of Zechariah, introduced with the label "oracle," directs attention to other nations. Yahweh vents anger against Syrian and Phoenician cities, announcing their pending destruction.

Literary Analysis

The unit opens with a standard label for prophetic collections: "oracle" *(maśśā²)*. The term, which also appears in Nah 1:1 and Mal 1:1, may designate not simply this unit, but also the larger collection of 9:1–11:17, since *maśśā²* also begins collections that start at Zech 12:1 and Mal 1:1. The second phrase, "word of Yahweh," often serves as a label for prophetic collections (as in Hos 1:1; Joel 1:1; Mic 1:1; Zeph 1:1; and Zech 12:1) and is used frequently in First Zechariah with forms of the verb "to be" (1:7; 4:6; 6:9; 7:8).

Attention turns immediately to expressing God's opposition to various cities outside of Judah. In harsh, violent language, the verses make clear that these cities are soon to receive God's judgment. Although First Zechariah envisions the nations as joining, even capitulating to, Jerusalem, the nations here receive much harsher treatment.

All of their fates are not the same, however. As Meyers and Meyers have highlighted, the Syrian cities (Hadrach, Damascus, and Hamath) are placed under Yahweh's control though not destroyed; the Phoenician cities (Tyre and Sidon) lose their wealth; and the Philistine cities (Ashkelon, Gaza, Ekron, Ashdod) suffer political crisis (1993, 162-67).

The unit's closing focus on the Temple and its protection explains why God is against these cities. They are oppressors of God's people, and their subjugation ensures Jerusalem's safety. That the ultimate concern of the unit is with the well-being of Judah is also made clear by the end of 9:7: the territory of the Philistines will be appropriated by Judah, just as the territory of the Jebusites was.

This material best fits the genre Oracle against the Nations, a form also used in Amos 1–2, Isa 13–23, and elsewhere. Indeed, this unit is much like Amos 1–2, not only in listing Gaza, Ekron, Ashkelon, and Tyre as cities to be destroyed, but also in leveling the threat of fire "eating" the city (Amos 1:4, 7, 10, 12, 14; 2:2, 5; 5:6). Zephaniah 2:4-7 also lambasts the Philistine cities and declares that they "shall become the possession of the remnant of the house of Judah" (Zeph 2:7; cf. Zech 9:7).

Distinguishing Hebrew prose from poetry is often difficult, but clearly this unit employs, or at least imitates, poetic parallelism. Synonymous parallelism, in which two lines express the same idea, is used in 9:7a // 9:7b and in 9:3b // 9:3c. More frequently, a subsequent line extends the first in a similar cadence, in a style called synthetic parallelism. The first three lines of Zech 9:5, for example, build a list of Philistine cities to be destroyed, the verbs of each line carrying over to the next:

Ashkelon will see and fear

And Gaza will writhe greatly

And Ekron because her hope is put to shame. (AT)

Exegetical Analysis

In compiling the list of cities described in 9:1-8, at least one translation issue arises. The MT of 9:1 reads "because the eye of [the] human belongs to Yahweh." The NRSV translates "capital of Aram," based on an emendation of the Hebrew letter *d* to an *r* (visually similar and often confused in ancient manuscripts). Such an emendation is not necessary, since the MT fits the contextual sense of the verse: Yahweh can issue a word against these foreign cities because all things belong to Yahweh.

The governing logic behind the long list of cities is unclear. Various scholars have attempted a sociopolitical explanation of the list, correlating it with the campaigns of Alexander the Great or with neo-Assyrian conquests. Meyers and Meyers have suggested that the cities serve to demarcate the boundaries of "ideal" Israel. Since the Syrian cities are beyond the ideal borders of Israel, they are merely controlled by Yahweh; since the Phoenician cities might be understood as traditional Israelite territory (land allotted to Asher, Josh 19:28-30), they are plundered; and since the Philistine cities are integrally related to Israel, they will suffer political loss and be incorporated into Judahite territory (Meyers and Meyers 1993, 162-67).

Other, more literary, factors should also be considered as underlying this list. Given the unit's similarities with Amos, Zephaniah, and other Oracles against the Nations, some of the list may be stereotypical. Indeed, the mention of a nation's "pride" (9:6) is a traditional element in the OAN (see Isa 10:12; 13:19; 16:6; Jer 48:29; 49:16; 51:41), as is the threat against its "wise" ones (9:2). Jeremiah 50:35 and 51:57 speak of Yahweh confounding the nations' wise ones, and in Obad 8 Yahweh claims to destroy the wise out of Edom.

Whatever the origin of the list of cities, its effect is a subversive one. In a time in which others hold political control over Yehud (either Persians or Hellenists), the claim that Yahweh will reconfigure national boundaries challenges those who wield control. This writer envisions a new time, in which Yehud will thrive at the expense of its political enemies.

Theological Analysis

Formulating a judgment about whether the Oracles against the Nations in general and this passage in particular are xenophobic is complicated by our ignorance about the function they played in the ancient world and the political situations in which they were articulated. Certainly, in times of national security and prosperity, such sentiments regarding international neighbors sound nationalistic and isolationist. Such passages would resonate differently, however, in times of colonial rule and defeat. For example, cries of Black Africans under apartheid against those international players who had benefited from their oppression might be understood as an expression of righteous indignation, whereas the voice of a white, middle-class American railing against Mexicans might not.

In either the Persian or Hellenistic periods, the two time frames most likely for the composition of Second Zechariah, the situation of Yehud/Judah would have been that of a colonized power. Controlled by others, with no political autonomy, Yehud would have been at the mercy of others. Articulating the hope that Yahweh's promises of care for Judah were still valid and that God might act to stop the oppression of the people was a bold political and theological move.

Appropriating Second Zechariah's message for today might mean holding fast to the belief that God sees the oppression of the people and will act to overturn it. This passage can serve as a voice of hope to the downtrodden. It, of course, may also serve the interests of militaristic nationalism, and thus the ethical responsibility of the reader to seek for interpretations that make for peace becomes essential.

YAHWEH TO SAVE JERUSALEM (9:9-17)

This unit opens with imperatives: Zion and Jerusalem, treated in parallelism, are told to "shout" and "rejoice." The good news for Judah that ends the previous unit now is more fully explored. Jerusalem should rejoice because a king is coming and because Yahweh is about to act as a mighty warrior on behalf of the people.

Literary Analysis

Three subunits make up the larger passage:

9-10	Description of the coming king
11-13	Implications for Judah and Ephraim
14-16	Yahweh as a saving warrior

In its effort to depict Yahweh as Judah's savior, the unit develops numerous images of the deity. In 9:9-10, Yahweh's military might is highlighted. The Hebrew of 9:10 begins "I will cut off" (as opposed to the NRSV: "he will cut off"), attributing the end of war to Yahweh's actions. As explored further below, the subunit of 9:9-10 also blurs the identities of Yahweh and the king, depicting the deity as one who rules.

The second and third subunits develop the image of Yahweh the Divine Warrior. Yahweh will abolish chariot, war horse, and battle bow (9:10); wield the covenant people as a bow, an arrow, and a sword (9:13); and appear with arrow and trumpet, marching forth (9:14). Slingers will be trod down (9:15). As discussed in the treatment of Nah 1 and Hab 3, the Divine Warrior imagery functioned in different ways in different periods of Israel's history. Here in Zech 9, fewer mythological images are invoked than in Habakkuk, though clearly the goal of Yahweh's march is to vindicate his people. The precise translation of 9:15 is unclear, the NRSV supplying the word "blood" in keeping with some Greek manuscripts and in keeping with the imagery of blood dashed against the sacrificial altar at the end of the verse. Similar imagery is found in Isa 49:26, in which Yahweh forces Judah's oppressors to drink their own blood like wine. Although the promise of peace in 9:10 and the claim of Yahweh's goodness and beauty in 9:17 seem ironic in such a bellicose unit, the interweaving of war and peace is common to Divine Warrior literature and stands as the core message of this unit: Yahweh's victory over the nations will put an end to war and usher in an era of peace for Judah.

The final subunit (9:14-17) adds yet a third image of Yahweh.

Judah is a flock of which Yahweh is the shepherd. Judah also shines like jewels in a crown, perhaps the crown of King Yahweh.

Poetic parallelism is employed throughout this unit. The words for animals in the last line of 9:9 are clearly treated as synonyms, since one person can ride only one animal. Zechariah 9:10 opens with a parallel phrase regarding Ephraim and Jerusalem, and, in 9:17b and c, young men and young women are treated in parallel. The end of the unit introduces a metaphor that will figure prominently in chapter 10. In 9:16, the people are called Yahweh's "flock."

Exegetical Analysis

The identity of the king described in 9:9-10 is difficult to determine for several reasons. First, on the syntactical level, the mention of the king in third person is soon followed by Yahweh's speech in first person. This aspect of the unit is obscured in the NRSV translation, which translates 9:10 as "he will cut off the chariot," although the MT reads "*I* will cut off." The third-person masculine forms that follow in 9:10, then, may be understood to refer back either to the king or to Yahweh. Second, the larger literary context of the book itself points in two different directions. In First Zechariah, the only "king" named is Darius, king of Persia, although the role of a future Davidide is made clear in chapter 6. In Second Zechariah, the only other mention of a king appears in chapter 14, in which Yahweh is called king (14:9, 16, 17). Third, this unit may allude to other biblical literature that speaks of a king in specific ways. As Petersen (1995, 57-58) has well noted, this unit overlaps in significant ways with Zeph 3:14-20, which also calls Daughter Zion to rejoice and depicts Yahweh as a warrior about to save the people. In Zeph 3, the king is Yahweh (3:14).

One additional factor in identifying the king is understanding the connotations of the animals on which he rides. Three different animals are mentioned in Hebrew: the king rides upon a donkey *(ḥămôr)*, which is treated in synonymous parallelism with a "male ass" *(ᶜayir)*, the son of "she-asses" *(ᵓatōnôt)*. All three are common animals in the Bible, used for riding and as pack animals. Some have suggested that riding such animals bears royal connotations, given that the first two are mentioned in the blessing of Judah as a ruler in Gen 49:10-11 and that 1 Kgs 1:33-44 describes Solomon's royal procession as taking place on David's mule. The word used in 1 Kings for "mule" *(pirdâ)*, however, is yet a different one than those used in Zech 9:9.

In response to these contrary clues, interpreters have understood Zech 9:9 in various ways, seeing the king as (1) Yahweh, as in Zeph 3 and Zech 14, described in the anthropomorphic language of riding an animal; (2) a future Davidic king, as in Zech 6, whose reign is inaugurated by Yahweh's mighty deeds; or (3) Darius, as in Zech 1:1, in whom the inhabitants of Yehud find hope.

Any solution to this puzzle must recognize the importance that the unit places on Yahweh's saving deeds. It is *Yahweh* who cuts off the chariot from Judah (9:10), sets prisoners free (9:11), protects the people (9:15), and saves them (9:16). Even if the king is a human figure, the power through which he reigns is that of Yahweh alone. Indeed, Zech 9:9-10 may be intentionally ambiguous, blurring the distinction between Yahweh and Yahweh's agents.

In the second subunit, the referents of pronouns are often implied rather than explained. In 9:11, for example, "you" is likely Jerusalem, since it is feminine singular, as are the imperatives addressed to Jerusalem // Zion in 9:9. "Them" in 9:14 seems to refer back to the "sons of Zion" in 9:13 and accounts for the masculine plural forms that predominate in the unit beginning at 9:13 (in contrast to the earlier second-person feminine singular forms). Throughout, Yahweh promises to advocate for Judah over against Greece.

Attempts to date Zechariah have focused great attention on 9:13, which describes the "sons of Greece" as enemies of Zion. Many interpreters have found here an indication that the collection was written in the Hellenistic era, when Alexander the Great and his later successors ruled Judah. The Greeks were of concern to Yehud long before 333, however, and several scholars have convincingly argued that this reference reflects the military clashes between Greece and Persia in the early fifth century B.C.E. The military threat from Greece provoked military buildup by the Persians throughout the ancient world, including in Yehud, dampening hopes for Judahite autonomy (Meyers and Meyers 1993, 148; Petersen 1995, 63). In such a scenario, Judean antagonism toward the "sons of Greece" fits well into the Persian period, as does the promise in 9:10 that Yahweh's dominion will be from "the River to the ends of the earth," since Yehud belonged to the province called "Beyond the River."

Although the mention of the "blood of the covenant" in 9:11 is very specific, alluding to the ritual binding the Mosaic covenant in Exod 24:8, the connotation of the "prisoners" in 9:11-12 is more ambiguous. Are the prisoners understood as those in the dispersion who are now enabled to return to Yehud or are those now in Yehud described as prisoners? That the prisoners are to be freed from "the pit that has no water" provides little additional information; a similar description is given to the pit into which Joseph was thrown by his brothers in Gen 37:24.

The explicit mention of Ephraim in 9:10 and 9:13 does, however, indicate a specific concern with exiles. Indeed, it suggests the hope for the return not only of those dispersed by the Babylonians in 587, but also of those scattered by the Assyrians in 722 or 721—a hope further explored in Zech 10. The hope that those scattered so long ago—close to three hundred years from the time of the author of Second Zechariah—suggests that this writer sees far beyond the current circumstances of the day to a bigger, bolder claim in Yahweh's ability to return Israel to the glory it once enjoyed.

Theological Analysis

In depicting Yahweh as executing a "war to end all war," this unit clearly raises important questions about violence in the Bible. Like the descriptions of the Divine Warrior in Nahum and in Habakkuk, Zech 9 portrays Yahweh as exulting in the overthrow of Judah's enemies.

When compared to Nahum, however, the description in Zech 9 makes the suffering of the enemy much less explicit. Unlike Nahum, which through vivid imagery paints a striking picture of dead bodies, raped women, and infants dashed to the ground, Zechariah focuses more on the victory of Yahweh and less on the delight of the reader in imagining the suffering of the enemy. And, yet, readers do well to be suspicious of "polite" depictions of war. Even though the agent of the destruction is God, this unit clearly calls for the death and the suffering of others.

In the political context in which Zech 9 likely was written, in the midst of wars between the Persians and the Greeks, it clearly articulates a voice of resistance. Although in the current climate Yehud may be at the mercy of powers larger than it is, the unit affirms that God the Warrior is far greater than any human army and that war will not last forever.

The use of Zech 9:9 in the New Testament suggests how this multivalent image of a future king could be interpreted in later generations. Matthew 21 clearly read Zech 9 as messianic, to the point that the writer described Jesus as riding on two animals to demonstrate his fulfillment of this "prophecy." John 12 also applies Zech 9:9 to Jesus, though, apparently more accurately understanding poetic parallelism, it depicts Jesus as riding only one animal.

Both Zechariah and Matthew recognize that riding on a donkey constitutes a claim to royalty. Absalom, Mephibosheth, and Solomon all ride donkeys in asserting royal ambitions (2 Sam 18:9; 19:27; and 1 Kgs 1:32-40). Matthew's application of Zechariah's message to Jesus' triumphal entry fits with the Gospel writer's larger goal of showing Jesus as "filling up" the promises of Scripture.

The New Testament usage of Zech 9 does not, however, exhaust the passage's meaning for Christians. This passage tells much about God—about God's faithfulness to "the blood of the covenant" and God's power over all earthly rulers—and continues to inspire hope for faithful readers.

YAHWEH AGAINST THE SHEPHERDS (10:1-12)

The unit opens on an adversarial note. The power of Yahweh to send rain is contrasted negatively with the power of other forces, and the dire fate of the "shepherds" is contrasted negatively with the hopeful future that Yahweh's flock soon will enjoy. The unit progressively focuses more fully on promises of return and joy for Judah and for Ephraim and only at its end acknowledges that their good news is bad news for Assyria and Egypt.

Literary Analysis

This unit opens with a second-person masculine plural address ("*you* ask rain"), but soon turns to the first-person speech of Yahweh. Although third-person description occasionally appears, the unit is predominantly presented as the direct speech of the deity.

The metaphor of shepherd and flock, which begins in 9:16, is here fully employed. Based on 10:2, the "shepherds" of 10:3 appear to be leaders, an inference that the NRSV makes explicit by its translation of 10:3*b*, although the Hebrew literally reads "shepherds" and "he-goats." The people, called the "house of Judah," are considered the flock. The people are portrayed as wandering aimlessly, without one to guide them.

In a striking change of imagery, Yahweh will transform these sheep into an array of powerful figures. In 10:3-5, the people are depicted as a war horse, a cornerstone, a tent peg, a battle bow, a taskmaster (the same word used in 9:8 for "oppressor"), and warriors. All but the second and third images fit well into a military context: the people will become Yahweh's weapons of war. The cornerstone and tent peg do not clearly derive from the practice of war; rather, they employ imagery from architecture to depict those who give structure and stability. These warriors will fight on foot, yet overcome those who ride horses.

The root for the word "warrior," *gbr*, appears in various forms in this unit. It is used in verbal forms in 10:6 and 10:12 in the sense of "strengthen, make strong," and it appears in noun form ("warriors") in both 10:5 and 10:7. The effect of this repetition is to intensify the militaristic flavor of the depictions of Judah. Judah will be empowered to fight alongside the Divine Warrior.

The theme of "return" dominates 10:6-12 and particularly 10:9-12. Those once dispersed from Judah and from Ephraim by Yahweh will be brought back to fill the land. While the promise of return from Egypt may have historical dimensions (see the exegetical analysis below), it also creates literary allusions to the period of bondage in Egypt. As in the biblical accounts of the Exodus, the people will again pass safely through dangerous seas (10:11).

The promise that those of the northern kingdom will also return draws from the language of earlier prophets as well. As in the oracles of Isaiah, the "pride of Assyria" will be humbled (Zech 10:11; Isa 10:12). The pairing of Egypt and Assyria as places to which the northern tribes were sent also appears in Isa 11:11, 15-16; and 27:13; Mic 7:12 names both as locales of Ephraim's dispersion; and Hos 11:11 tells of Ephraim's return from Egypt and Assyria.

Exegetical Analysis

Although the "shepherds" of this unit are clearly leaders of some description, further identification is difficult. Sweeney argues that Persian overlords of Yehud are described here (2000, 669), since "shepherd" is a common ancient Near Eastern metaphor for kings and since the parallel term "he-goats" (NRSV: "leaders") is a synonym for kings in Isa 14:9. Petersen, on the contrary, maintains that the term refers to leaders within the community itself (1995, 73). Noting that the criticism of the shepherds directly follows that of teraphim and diviners, Meyers and Meyers suggest that the shepherds are those who (falsely) claim to speak for Yahweh (1993, 187).

The identification is complicated, as elsewhere in Second Zechariah, by the fact that the language draws heavily on earlier prophetic literature. Zechariah 10, for example, duplicates much of Jer 2. Both Jer 23:2 and Zech 10:3 employ a common dual use of "attend to" (*pqd*). The word describes both Yahweh's negative attitude toward the shepherds ("punish") and Yahweh's positive attitude toward the people ("care for"). In addition, both Jer 23 and Zech 10 are concerned with the return of the flock to its land and with their multiplying in numbers. In Jer 23, the promise of future faithful shepherds is followed by the promise of a Davidic heir called Branch, a name that features prominently in Zech 3:8 and 6:12. Ezekiel 34 also calls the leaders of the community "shepherds" and promises the return of the scattered sheep to their land.

In sum, these literary allusions encourage the reader to understand "shepherds" in the same way as Jeremiah and Ezekiel do, as local leaders of Yehud, even though Second Zechariah may have been applying traditional language to a new set of leaders. Nothing within the unit makes a definitive identification possible.

The "teraphim," "diviners," and "dreamers" of 10:2 denote improper means of discerning the divine will. The teraphim are best understood as household gods, as in Gen 31, and Michal's dressing of teraphim in 1 Sam 19:13 suggests that they were images of people, likely family ancestors. Second Kings 23:24 labels the teraphim as idolatrous. Divination is forbidden by Deut 18:10, which identifies it as the worship practice of foreign nations. Most pointedly, Jer 14:14 discusses divination in the context of false prophecy, and Jer 27:9 and 29:8 pair "diviners" and "dreamers" as those who lead the people astray. In a similar way, Jer 10 may suggest that those (falsely) claiming to speak for Yahweh have been faithless shepherds of Yahweh's flock.

In addressing and envisioning the return of the "house of Joseph" (10:6) and "Ephraim" (10:7), Second Zechariah extends the hope of return to include those exiled from the northern tribes when the Assyrians destroyed Israel in 722 or 721. As discussed above, the expectation of the return of both the northern and southern tribes is shared by other biblical literature, such as Micah. The three-hundred-year gap between the fall of the

North in 722 or 721 and the likely composition of Second Zechariah circa 450 witnesses to the power that the image of the ideal united Israel continued to hold for the Judahites. Moreover, the remote historical possibility of such a return may suggest that Second Zechariah goes much farther than First Zechariah in anticipating a radical restructuring of current reality. Although the two collections do share in their hope for a return to Israel's illustrious past, Second Zechariah's vision requires much more dramatic acts on Yahweh's part.

The description of a return from Egypt (10:10) may allude to the exodus, but the specific reference in the era of Second Zechariah may be to Judean exiles who fled to Egypt after the Babylonian destruction of Jerusalem. Jeremiah 44 testifies to a "remnant" who escaped to Egypt in the sixth century, and the Elephantine papyri bear witness to a Judean population in Egypt in the fifth century.

Much in this unit underscores a concern for repopulating the land. In Zech 10:8, the people are projected as growing in numbers: "they will multiply as they (once) multiplied." Similarly, the northern tribes are allotted not only Gilead, a traditional Israelite holding, but also Lebanon—outside of, though bordering on, the land. Just as Zech 8:5 looks forward to a time when Jerusalem's streets will again be full, so too Zech 10 envisions a time in which the land will not be able to hold all its people within its borders.

As several commentators have noted, such a concern may reflect the very real population scarcity of Persian period Yehud. Estimates suggest that the entire province may have held ten thousand inhabitants—perhaps less (Meyers and Meyers 1993, 215-16). In the rural setting of this period and in agricultural communities today, survival depends upon the labor of many hands. (The discussion of rain in 10:1 underscores the agricultural setting of this unit as well.) In Second Zechariah's vision, the small, struggling community would soon be swelled by the influx of returnees.

Theological Analysis

The far-reaching power of Yahweh is a main theme that runs throughout this unit. In the opening verses, Yahweh is the one who causes rain. Since the Enlightenment, "modern" readers are more likely to think of rain as a "natural" occurrence, produced when atmospheric conditions are right. The writer of Second Zechariah, like the writers of all biblical material, does not recognize the distinction between "natural" and "supernatural" powers. Yahweh's parting of the Sea of Reeds is no more of an intervention into the world than Yahweh's sending of rain or drought. These verses remind us of the differences between the ancient world and our own and how foreign the concept of supernatural "miracles" was to the biblical world. For Second Zechariah, the community's dependence on Yahweh to provide rain differs little from its dependence on Yahweh to transform a small, struggling Yehud into a populous nation. Indeed, all things are attributed to Yahweh: not only the people's salvation but also their initial rejection (10:6).

This writer attributes to Yahweh incredible power, but, significantly, in this chapter the power of Yahweh is shared with the people. While in Zech 9 the Divine Warrior marches alone, here in Zech 10 the people are themselves transformed into warriors: "they shall fight, for Yahweh is with them" (10:5). Wandering sheep will be empowered, made strong.

This persistent belief in God's compassion and God's power to overcome seemingly impossible odds rings throughout the book of Zechariah: "Thus says Yahweh of hosts: Even though it seems impossible to the remnant of this people in these days, should it also seem impossible to me, says Yahweh of hosts?" (8:6).

SHEPHERDS OF THE COMMUNITY (11:1-17)

This difficult unit is filled with multiple images. Woodland imagery dominates 11:1-3. Verses 4-17 return to the imagery of shepherd and sheep that appears in chapter 10, but with a more ominous tone.

Literary Analysis

The unit may be outlined as follows:

11:1-3   Announcement of God's punishment in
                 woodland imagery
11:4-14   First announcement of God's punishment in
                 shepherd imagery
11:4-6   Instructions to the prophet
11:7-14   The prophet's fulfillment of the instructions
11:15-17   Second announcement of God's punishment
                 in shepherd imagery

The decision of the NRSV to print the 11:1-3 and 11:17 in poetic line and the rest of the chapter as prose is a good one. The opening verses clearly bear the marks of poetry, especially the extended use of parallelism. Examples are found in 11:2:

> Wail, O cypress, *for the cedar has fallen*
>   *the glorious ones are ruined.*
> Wail, oaks of Bashan,
>   *for the thick forest has gone down.* (AT)

and in 11:3:

> The sound of the *wailing of the shepherds*
>   *because destroyed* are *the majestic ones.*
> The sound of the *roaring of the young lions*
>   *because destroyed* is *the pride of the Jordan.* (AT)

Although 11:17 uses less explicit parallelism, it is more similar in rhythm and style to 11:1-3 than to the narrative which runs from 11:4 to 11:16. Zechariah 11:17 opens with an interjection of mourning, "woe!" which serves the same function as the commands to "wail" in 11:2. The opening poem is linked literally to the narrative that follows the word "shepherds" in 11:3.

Woodland imagery dominates 11:1-2. The destruction of Lebanon, known throughout the Bible for its timber, is described as the destruction of its cedars, cypress, and "glorious ones."

The "oaks of Bashan" are also treated as noteworthy in Ezek 27:6 and Isa 2:13 (which names both Bashan and Lebanon). Bashan and Lebanon likewise are mentioned together in Jer 22:20 and Nah 1:4.

The turn to animal imagery in 11:3 serves several functions. Most obviously, it serves as a bridge between the descriptions of shepherds in chapter 10 and in the prose of chapter 11. Moreover, the language of shepherds and lions evokes other prophetic materials that describe Yahweh's destructive power as terrifying shepherds and devastating trees. In the opening of Amos, for example, Yahweh "roars" and the pastures of the shepherds wither (Amos 1:2; Zech 11:3). Yahweh also "roars" in Jer 25:30; Hos 11:10; Joel 3:16; and Amos 3:8. Also like Amos, Zech 11 depicts the destruction of cities as being devoured by fire (Amos 1:4, 7, 10; see also Zech 9:4).

The effect of these allusions is to set an ominous tone to the beginning of the chapter. The encouraging words that Yahweh offers in chapter 10 are here replaced by threats.

The narrative dominating the majority of the chapter explores the imagery of shepherd and sheep already introduced in Zech 9:16 and Zech 10 and appearing again in 13:7-9. The earlier use of the image was to depict Yahweh as protecting the people, but this unit uses the shepherd imagery in a quite different and often confusing way.

In 11:4-6, the prophetic persona of the piece (literarily, though not necessarily historically, identified as Zechariah) reports Yahweh's instructions. The prophet is to become a shepherd. The sheep he is to oversee are described as "flock of slaughter," ones designated to be killed. A similar usage is that of Jer 12:3, which asks Yahweh to make enemies as sheep destined for slaughter; Pss 44:11; 22; Isa 53:7; and Ezek 34:3 also describe the people as sheep to be slain, although they use a different verb than does Zech 11:4.

The next verse does not appear to blame the buyers of the sheep for slaughtering them; the Hebrew "their buyers slaughter them and are not guilty" suggests the imagery of those who legitimately slaughter sheep. Although sheep today are often considered "cute" and "innocent," they were both food and sacrificial staples in the ancient world; their slaughter was not always considered a tragedy. The "scandal" of 11:4-6 is not that sheep are slaughtered, but that the people are compared to such sheep; the nonaffective, business relationship between shepherds and their flock (11:5) is less a scandal for real shepherds than it is for those who are *compared* to such shepherds. The reason for these instructions to the shepherd is indicated in 11:6: the prophet is to become an unpitying shepherd because Yahweh no longer pities the people. Like other symbolic prophetic actions, such as in the marriage of Hos 1, the action of the prophet represents the action of Yahweh. Zechariah 11:6 ends this initial exploration of the shepherd metaphor with Yahweh's threat: Yahweh will cause total devastation to "all inhabitants of the earth."

Zechariah 11:7-14 reports the prophet's fulfillment of the divine command. He became the shepherd of the sheep earmarked for slaughter and then performed a symbolic action. He took two rods (a less common word than the usual one for shepherds' staffs), named one "Pleasantness" (NRSV: "Favor") and the other "Cords" (NRSV: "Unity"). The connotation of the latter name is intricately related to 11:10 and 14, which explain that the breaking of the rods signifies the breaking of the bonds that unite Yahweh and Israel.

In breaking rods to enact the breaking of God's covenant with the people, the prophet in Zech 11 performs the same type of symbolic actions used by earlier prophets. In Jer 19, the prophet breaks a vessel to symbolize the destruction of Jerusalem, and Jeremiah's competitor Hananiah symbolically enacts the breaking of Babylon's control by breaking a yoke (Jer 28:11). More important, in Ezek 37, the prophet names one stick Judah and the other Israel and then unites them to symbolize Yahweh's promise of restoring both kingdoms. The prophet's actions in Zech 11 stand as the opposite of those in Ezek 37.

On one level, the shepherd in 11:7-14 is the prophet, but several clues suggest that the shepherd also represents Yahweh. Zechariah 11:10, for example, blends the prophetic and divine persona. While the prophet speaks as "I" in 11:7-9, in 11:10 the covenant is described as one that "I made with them." On the level of the narrative, the annulled covenant refers to the promise that the prophet had made to watch the sheep, now rescinded; on the symbolic level, however, the covenant also refers to the Mosaic promises, and hence this "I" also signifies Yahweh. The word used here for "breaking" or "annulling" the covenant is used elsewhere both in the context of the breaking of the covenant between humans and the divine (Lev 26:15, 44; Deut 31:16; Jer 14:21) and also in the context of the breaking of agreements made by humans (Num 30:9, 13; 1 Kgs 15:19).

These clues suggest that in this section, as in 11:4-6 and in Hosea, the actions of the prophet symbolize Yahweh's intentions toward the people. The prophet is acting out God's role as a shepherd who tends, and then abandons, sheep destined for slaughter.

Because he quits in the middle of the job, the shepherd gives others the option of paying him; whether thirty shekels paid to the shepherd is a large or small sum is discussed below, as is where the money is thrown. The breaking of the second staff, "Bonds" or "Unity," breaks the bonds that unite Judah and Israel, in clear opposition to the unity of the kingdoms symbolized in Ezek 37 and envisioned in earlier chapters of Second Zechariah.

Zechariah 11:15-17 turns the shepherd metaphor in a new direction. The prophet's taking on the role of a shepherd is now explained as symbolizing the rise of a new leader who will not care for the sheep. The connection between the first depiction of the shepherd and the second one is highly disputed. Many interpreters, arguing that both depictions express the same point, contend that "shepherds" consistently refers to leaders of the community; that is, they disagree with the claim advanced above that Yahweh is the shepherd of 11:4-14. Redditt, for example, maintains that the shepherds are priests and lay leaders of the postexilic community and that "the prophet twice mimics their behavior" (1993, 685). Indeed, the use of the word "again" in 11:15 suggests that the shepherd in 1:7-14 was unrighteous, an odd description if Yahweh is identified with the shepherd.

For reasons explained above, however, the symbolic actions of the shepherd represent Yahweh's intentions. Not only is this made clear in 11:4-6, but also it is suggested by the fact that the breaking of the second staff nullifies a bond that human leaders would be powerless to affect.

In sum, Zech 11:15-17 is best understood as a second and different use of the shepherd metaphor. First, the prophet takes on the role of a shepherd who abandons his post to symbolize Yahweh's breaking of the covenant with the people; then, the prophet takes on the role of the shepherd to symbolize the kind of leader that will now oversee the community. That is, the second subunit expands the first rather than duplicates it. Because Yahweh has annulled the covenant with the people, he will allow an uncaring shepherd to rule them.

Exegetical Analysis

The NRSV footnotes indicate some, though not all, of the problems that arise in translating this unit. The term translated by the NRSV as "sheep merchants" in 11:7 and 11 is literally "the afflicted (or poor) of the sheep." The phrase is usually emended on the basis of the Septuagint, however, to "Canaanites," often used in Hebrew to refer to merchants (as in Zeph 1:11). Such a change to the Hebrew text requires merely reading the consonants of two words as constituting a single word instead: *lkn* ᶜ*nyy* ("on behalf of the poor") becomes *lkn* ᶜ*nyy* ("for the Canaanites/merchants").

In 11:13, the difference between the Hebrew word for "treasury," which forms the basis for the NRSV translation, and the Hebrew word for "potter," which is found in the MT, is slight. "Potter" is from the root *yṣr*, while "treasury" is from the root *ʾṣr*. The Syriac would support the reading of "treasury," as would later literature that quotes this verse, such as Matt 27. The Septuagint reads "smelting furnace." Although the connection between this unit and Jer 18 (which describes a symbolic action that Jeremiah undertook at the house of the potter) is interesting, that some part of the Temple is being mentioned is indicated by 11:13.

The value of thirty pieces of silver, the shepherd's payment in

11:12-13, is unknown. Based on ancient Near Eastern parallels, Petersen argues that thirty shekels is an insultingly low amount (1995, 97) and that its description as a "lordly sum" (lit., "the glory of preciousness") is sarcastic. Meyers and Meyers, as well as Sweeney, claim the opposite: since thirty shekels is the amount required to redeem a slave in Exod 21:32, it must have been considered a high amount (Meyers and Meyers 1993, 279; Sweeney 2000, 681). The word "shekel" is not explicitly used in the Hebrew; the verb form of *škl* appears in 11:12, though both 11:12 and 11:13 mention "thirty silver." Although we know little about the relative value of currency in the ancient world, the second interpretation is more viable, especially in light of the mention in Neh 10:32 that annual giving to the Temple was only a third of a shekel.

In 11:16, four examples are given of the shepherd's faithlessness. In the NRSV, he does not

(a) care for the perishing
(b) seek the wandering
(c) heal the maimed
(d) nourish the healthy.

The translation of (a) and (c) are fairly straightforward, but the other two are more problematic. The Hebrew of (b) reads "does not seek the youth," though the NRSV has read instead with the Syriac and the Targum (as do Meyers and Meyers 1993, 237). The Hebrew of (d), which the NRSV notes deem "uncertain," literally reads "the one standing he will not nourish" (as in the NASB: "sustain the one standing"). All but (b) are feminine participles.

As Redditt has well summarized (1993, 677-80), scholars have advanced a wide range of explanations for the three shepherds mentioned in 11:8. At different times, the shepherds have been identified as biblical figures, as foreign kingdoms, as Hellenistic rulers, and as local leaders of the people. In turn, the worthless shepherd in 11:17 has been identified with false prophets (Meyers and Meyers 1993, 291), with Persian leaders (Sweeney

2000, 360), and with civic leaders in the postexilic community (Redditt 1993, 685).

Given the lack of information about the shepherds and in keeping with the literary context of the unit, however, the reader's focus better shifted away from determining the identity of the shepherds to the larger message of the unit. As Petersen well argues, Zech 11 claims that Yahweh has abandoned the people; because Yahweh himself is a shepherd who does not pity his sheep he is raising up a shepherd who will not care for the sheep. That is, the lack of effective and benevolent leadership in the community is attributed to God's judgment (Petersen 1993, 100-101).

Meyers and Meyers suggest that Zech 11 does not point to Yehud's future but rather recapitulates its past. Rather than predicting the rise of an uncaring shepherd, the chapter rehearses Judah's history. In the past, Yahweh abandoned the people and broke covenant, leaving the people to unfaithful leaders. In a break with a straightforward chronological sequence, this chapter explains the problem to which earlier chapters in Second Zechariah offer the solution. The breaking of the bonds of Israel and Judah in chapter 11, for example, is envisioned as reversed in chapter 10, which calls for the return of those exiled from the northern kingdom (Meyers and Meyers 1993, 300-302).

Such an understanding resolves many of the problems that interpreters have encountered in understanding Zech 11. Particularly, it accounts for the radical shift between the hope of chapter 10 and the judgment of chapter 11. Despite its appeal, however, this understanding does not account for the note of judgment that continues in Second Zechariah. And, although Meyers and Meyers do point to pieces of twentieth-century literature that share the same disruption of chronological order, they do not explain why Second Zechariah has been edited in this particular way. This enigmatic text, it seems, is not so easily explained.

Theological Analysis

Of all of the many images used in the Hebrew Bible for the deity, that of Yahweh as an uncaring shepherd is one of the harshest. Yahweh is described here as impatient with his sheep (11:8), willing to give them over to the destruction of others and of one another, and as breaking covenant with the people.

Are the sheep to blame for their dire fate? On the one hand, in this unit, only the shepherds and not the sheep receive censure; on the other hand, it claims that the people's reliance upon unfaithful leaders is due to God's abandonment. The overarching theme of the prophets is that Yahweh's punishment is always deserved, again raising the question of what action or attitude of the people has provoked such punishment.

One possible answer is found in the larger literary context of Second Zechariah. Within the context of the book of Zechariah as a whole, the exile is explained as the outcome of the people's refusal to repent.

> Do not be like your ancestors, to whom the former prophets proclaimed, "Thus says Yahweh of hosts, Return from your evil ways and from your evil deeds." But they did not hear or heed me, says Yahweh. Your ancestors, where are they? And the prophets, do they live forever? But my words and my statutes, which I commanded my servants the prophets, did they not overtake your ancestors? So they repented and said, "Yahweh of hosts has dealt with us according to our ways and deeds, just as he planned to do." (1:4-6)

The message of the former prophets is summarized in 7:9-14, which attributes the exile to the people's hardness of heart:

> Thus says Yahweh of hosts: Render true judgments, show kindness and mercy to one another; do not oppress the widow, the orphan, the alien, or the poor; and do not devise evil in your hearts against one another. But they refused to listen, and turned a stubborn shoulder, and stopped their ears in order not to hear. They made their hearts adamant in order not to hear the law and the words that Yahweh of hosts had sent by his spirit through the former prophets. Therefore great wrath came from Yahweh of hosts. Just as, when I called, they would not

hear, so, when they called, I would not hear, says Yahweh of hosts, and I scattered them with a whirlwind among all the nations that they had not known. Thus the land they left was desolate, so that no one went to and fro, and a pleasant land was made desolate.

The strong allusions made to Jeremiah and Ezekiel in the "shepherd material" of Second Zechariah may also suggest that for this writer, the cause of the people's punishment is to be found in the words of the "former prophets," here understood to be a call to repentance.

The allusive, open-ended nature of Second Zechariah may be one reason that it is quoted so often in the New Testament; its images, lacking strong historical grounding, feed the imagination. Zechariah 11:12-13, in which the shepherd throws his wage of thirty shekels of silver into the Temple, is famously quoted in Matt 26 and 27, in which the allusion is attributed to Jeremiah. Interpreters have long debated about whether the writer of Matthew erred in citing sources, though Davies and Allison convincingly argue (following Brown) that the citation is in fact a composite one, combining Zech 11 and Jer 18–19. Matthew's account of Judas's betrayal draws upon the thirty pieces of silver from Zechariah as well as from the discussion of the potter, the purchase of land, and the Valley of Hinnom in Jer 18–19 and 32:6-15 (Davies and Allison 1997, 569).

Reading Zechariah in light of Jeremiah, as the writer of Matthew apparently has, emphasizes particular features of the text. As noted above, the NRSV translation of "treasury" in Zech 9:13 comes from the Hebrew word for "potter," a word also appearing in Jer 19:11. Read together, these prophetic passages provide Matthew with the images of Temple, potter, and judgment—all-important themes in describing Judas's betrayal of Jesus.

Significantly, the way in which Matthew appropriated Zechariah to address events in the Roman period is analogous to the way that Second Zechariah appropriates Jeremiah, Ezekiel, and other prophets to speak to the Persian period. In both cases, the writers found in ancient texts allusion to their own, different situations. In this way, both indicate the elasticity and power that literature holds. At the same time, the multiple ways in which the same text can be applied to later situations calls for a sense of humility on any reading that claims to be definitive, claiming to exhaust the meaning of a text. Just as the words of Jeremiah could mean one thing to the writer of Second Zechariah and another to the writer of Matthew, so too Scripture might speak in additional ways to those of our own and later eras.

THE PROTECTION OF JUDAH AND JERUSALEM (12:1-9)

Opening the final section of the book of Zechariah, 12:1-9 announces God's pending vindication of Jerusalem. All who oppose Jerusalem will be destroyed.

Literary Analysis

Zechariah 12 opens with the label "oracle" *(maśśāʾ)*, which likely applies to the entire final section of the book, and then follows with "word of Yahweh." This opening is similar to those of Zech 9:1 and Mal 1:1, which also begin with both phrases, although in Zech 9:1 the opening is a sentence while in the other two cases it is a verbless label for the collection. Although in Zech 9:1 *maśśāʾ* denotes an oracle *against* a group (as in Nah 1:1 and in many of the oracles in Isa 13–23), this use of *maśśāʾ* marks a polemical oracle *about* Israel. The only difference in the opening of Zech 12 and Malachi is that Malachi adds the name of the prophet.

Zechariah 12–14 is composed of numerous short oracles, many of which begin with the standard prophetic phrase "on that day." Indeed, this phrase appears sixteen times in these chapters, seven times in chapter 14 alone. If one were to follow the practice of standard prophetic scholarship of treating "on that day" as the marker of a new unit, then the chapters would be filled by units of one or two verses. For this reason, outlining the structure of Zech 12–14 is difficult. These chapters often read like a loose collection of sayings, joined only by a formulaic phrase. The themes of the sayings are interrelated, however, often pointing back to previous images or declarations.

The first unit runs through 12:9. The beginning is clear, in that Zech 12:1 marks a new section of the book. Ending the unit at 12:9 is based on no formal marker, but rather on the judgment that 12:10 begins a new theme, albeit one related to the earlier unit.

After its formulaic opening, the unit first establishes Yahweh's power and authority to act. In hymnlike language, Yahweh is described as one who formed heaven, earth, and the human spirit. Interestingly, the participle "one who fashioned [the human spirit]" is yôṣēr, the same word whose meaning was debated in Zech 11:13. In that previous verse, it is often translated as "potter" though usually emended to "treasury." Indeed, Sweeney translates 11:13 as "throw it to your Maker" (2000, 681), reading both occurrences of yôṣēr as referring to Yahweh.

The description of Yahweh as "stretching out the heavens" and creating "the earth" is found twice in Jeremiah (10:12 and 51:15). The latter reference is especially close to Zech 12. Both depict Yahweh's power in the context of outlining the punishment of the nations. In Jer 51, although Babylon was once a golden cup in Yahweh's hand, the Yahweh who controls heaven and earth will now destroy Babylon; and in Zechariah, this same powerful Yahweh will make Jerusalem into a "cup of reeling." Yahweh also fashions the "breath" of humans (NRSV: "spirit"). Although no other passage in the Old Testament places the word "human" in construct with "breath," the passage is similar in vocabulary to Gen 2, in which Yahweh "fashions" (yṣr) the human.

Praise of Yahweh quickly turns to images of Yahweh's protection and exaltation of Jerusalem and Judah. In the course of four verses, four different images of these locales are given. First, Jerusalem will become a "cup of reeling." The prophetic literature often describes a dose of punishment as a "cup" to be drunk (Jer 25:15; 25:28; 49:12; Hab 2:16). The precise form of the noun "reeling" that appears here is not found elsewhere, but a related form appears in similar contexts in Isa 51:17 and 22, in which Yahweh promises to take away from Jerusalem the cup from which she has drunk.

Jerusalem is also called a "stone of a burden" (= "burdensome stone") in 12:3; and in 12:6 the "clans of Judah" are called a "pan of fire" placed on sticks and a "torch of fire" placed on sheaves. These images of danger underscore that those who touch Yahweh's own will be hurt. The military images of horse and rider in 12:4 further stress that no army will take Jerusalem. In a return to the promise made in chapter 10, Jerusalem will again be populated and none will disturb its inhabitants.

Zechariah 12:7-9 explains these benefits in a way that both exalts Davidic leadership and also makes messianic claims secondary to the welfare of the entire region. Although the house of David will be "like God/gods," "like a "messenger of Yahweh before them" (AT), salvation first will come to the "tents of Judah" so "that the glory of the house of David and the glory of the inhabitants of Jerusalem may not be exalted over that of Judah." Indeed, the weakest of the people will be as great as the house of David.

In this unit, which sets Jerusalem/Judah in opposition to the nations, the NRSV translation of 12:2 appears out of place. In this rendering, the cup of reeling is both against the peoples and "it will be against Judah also in the siege against Jerusalem," implying an opposition between Judah and Jerusalem and a superiority of the latter over the former. Other translations likely better capture the sense of the unit as one of protection of both locales and the integrity of Judah. Though not exactly following the Hebrew, the NASB well captures the sense that Judah shares in the protection of Jerusalem: "and when the siege is against Jerusalem, it will also be against Judah." The United Bible Societies Text Project offers two possibilities for translation: (1) "and also Judah will have the duty to participate in the sige *(sic)* of Jerusalem," and (2) "Judah will be in distress in addition to Jerusalem" (United Bible Societies 1980, 420).

The phrase "on that day," ubiquitous in Zech 2–14, appears six times in this unit—at 12:3, 4, 6, 8 (twice), and 9. Repeatedly, the unit paints images of Yahweh's glorious future for Judah and Jerusalem.

Exegetical Analysis

Some scholars have argued that the new heading that begins Zech 12:1 indicates that the book was composed in three parts: they speak of 1–8 as First Zechariah; of 9–11 as Second Zechariah; and 12–14 as Third (or Trito-) Zechariah. Moreover, they trace in Zech 12–14 a more elaborate eschatology than in previous chapters. Such views, however, have failed to convince the majority of interpreters, primarily because *all* of the chapters from 9 to 14 are complex. That is, chapters 9–11 do not have a distinctive enough unifying factor to distinguish them from 12–14.

A second theory claims that Zech 9–11, Zech 12–14, and the book of Malachi were originally three anonymous booklets attached to the end of the Book of the Twelve. In this argument, the booklets had no original unity but were redacted into a larger scheme. Again, this theory has not prevailed, primarily because it fails to take account of the links of vocabulary and theme that distinguish Zechariah from Malachi. Although Zech 9–14 is indeed a montage of themes and images, the material shares with First Zechariah a concern with the well-being of Jerusalem and visions of restoration of the city that are not found in Malachi. The unity of the various pieces of Zechariah suggests that First and Second Zechariah have been more intentionally interwoven than the "three-booklet theory" would suggest.

Indeed, although Zech 12 bears its own distinctive features, it returns to the topic of Jerusalem's restoration explored in Zech 1 and 2. Just as Yahweh was "wall of fire" around Jerusalem to protect it from the nations in 2:5 (Heb. 2:9), so Judah becomes a "pot of fire" and a "torch of fire" against the nations in 12:6. In some ways, the proviso that the house of David will not be exalted over Judah also tempers the vision of the coronation of Branch in Zech 6.

The import of some of the specific vocabulary in this unit is debated. The writer speaks both of Jerusalem and of Judah. The latter is sometimes called the "clans of Judah," at others the "house of Judah," and at yet other times the "tents of Judah." A similar shift in vocabulary is the description of enemies both as "peoples" and as "nations." Are these terms intended to be read as synonyms or as distinctions in nuance?

Although the other variations seem minor and are likely intended as synonyms, the explicit attention given to Judah may be significant in light not only of the concerns of 12:7 but also of the possible tension between Jerusalem and other areas of Yehud in the Persian period. As discussed in the analysis of Zech 7, First Zechariah may bear witness to communities within Yehud that were not comprised of returnees and that did not necessarily accept the primacy of Jerusalem. Although Persian period biblical texts speak almost exclusively of activities centered in Jerusalem, clearly the province was far larger than the urban center of Jerusalem. Carter estimates 20,000 inhabitants of Yehud in the Persian II period (450–332), though some have argued that his numbers are too large (Kessler 2001, 147); no more than 1500 would have lived in Jerusalem (Carter 1999, 201).

Zechariah 12:7, and perhaps the entirety of chapter 12, apparently limits the term "Judah" to areas of Yehud *other than* Jerusalem. "Judah" is also used this way in First Zechariah, in 1:12, 19 (Heb. 2:2); 2:12 (Heb. 2:4); 8:15; and 14:14 and 21. In other cases, "Judah" is paired with "Israel" and thus seems to signify a region that would include Jerusalem (8:13; in Second Zechariah, also 9:13 and 11:14).

In expressing concern with the welfare of non-Jerusalemites, Zech 12:7 may stand in some tension with First Zechariah, which critiques worship at Bethel. The difference between the two passages may be due to the perspectives of their authors, or it may reflect the changed sociopolitical situation of the different time periods of their composition. By the fifth century, Bethel had likely been abandoned or destroyed and thus was no longer in competition with Judah. With Jerusalem less threatened by the worship center at Bethel, the writer of Zech 12 may have felt more magnanimous toward the cities outside Jerusalem.

Jerusalem clearly remains the focus of the writer's attention, however, given that Jerusalem is exalted to the status of the house of David and that nations who threaten Jerusalem will be destroyed. The description in 12:8 of the house of David is complicated by the multiple meanings of several words. The Hebrew word here translated as "God" in the NRSV is *'ĕlōhîm*. A plural form, it is usually translated as a generic label for the deity, though in certain passages it is rendered in its plural form, to denote multiple deities or those with the status of deities (Gen 31; Exod 12:12; Ps 82:1, 6). Hence, here the house of David may be like God or like those with the status of gods. Moreover, as seen in the discussion of the opening chapters of the book of Zechariah, the term *mal'āk* is best understood as "messenger," not "angel." This passage may allude to Exodus (14:19; 23:20; 33:2), in which the messenger of Yahweh leads the people.

In these verses, then, although the non-Jerusalemite areas of Judah are promised salvation by Yahweh, the superiority of the Davidic monarchy and of Jerusalem remain tantamount. The superiority of Jerusalem is also seen in 12:5, in which the clans of Judah attest to Yahweh's presence in Jerusalem.

Theological Analysis

One way in which Second Zechariah is often distinguished from First Zechariah is in terms of the eschatology of the two sections. Most interpreters suggest that while the former envisions God's restoration of Jerusalem as within the human realm, albeit in an idealized fashion, the latter moves closer toward apocalyptic eschatology, in which God can only bring about salvation by transcending human history. For Zech 12, such distinctions are hard to make. The chapter uses the common prophetic phrase "on that day," which bears no eschatological nuances other than "in the future." Moreover, the idyllic future for Jerusalem here described differs little from the vision in Zech 8. Though more metaphorical language is employed here, the exaltation of the house of David, of Jerusalem, and of Judah, all can be realized within human history.

The faint concern here expressed for the cities of Judah beyond Jerusalem tempers slightly the pro-Jerusalem ideology that dominates the book of Zechariah. The writer glimpses the inclusion of others beyond the community of the *golah* ("the exile," those returned from Babylon). The writer also seems to temper strong reliance on a future Davidic ruler. Although "the house of David" remains as a channel for God's promise, the writer's larger concern is with the people and their protection.

Like many prophetic books, Zechariah expresses God's opposition to "the nations." In this chapter, however, those nations remain generic, symbolic of all that stands in opposition to God and God's people. God's power is stressed rather than God's anger against specific nations.

THE PIERCED ONE (12:10-14)

This unit is linked to the preceding one by the use of common vocabulary. Also concerned with the "house of David" and the "inhabitant (singular) of Jerusalem," these verses reveal how the people will come to mourn one who has been pierced.

Literary Analysis

The pierced one is not precisely identified, and the pronouns in Hebrew are often seen to be in contradiction. The phrase in 12:10 literally reads, "When they look upon *me* whom they pierced they will mourn over *him*." If this reading is retained, the "me" would be Yahweh, who speaks earlier in the verse, as indicated in ASV, NASB, KJV, and NIV. To avoid the idea that Yahweh could be pierced, the NRSV alters the verse to read "when they look on the one whom they have pierced." The NJB translation provides a viable alternative: "and they will look to me. They will mourn for the one whom they have pierced." Although this translation ignores the Masoretic indications of pause, it does treat with integrity the consonantal text of the Hebrew. It also recognizes that the phrase "look unto" is often used in the context of paying regard to Yahweh, as in Isa 22:11. That is, the people look to Yahweh and mourn an unidentified one who has been pierced.

The unit ends enigmatically, indicating that each family and gender will mourn separately. The house of David; its wives; the house of Nathan; its wives; the house of Levi; its wives; the Shimeites; their wives; the remaining ones; and their wives—each will mourn separately. Importantly, however, mourning only begins at Yahweh's initiative. Only after Yahweh has poured out a spirit of compassion on the people will they express sorrow for the one they have pierced. The pouring of Yahweh's "spirit" is also described in Ezek 39:29 and in Joel 2:29 and 3:1, though only here is that spirit described as one of "grace" (see, too, Zech 4:7) and "supplication." Yahweh must change the people's hearts before they can mourn.

Exegetical Analysis

The identity of the one who is pierced has intrigued interpreters for centuries. The unit has a "feel" of specificity, leading some to identify this figure with persons from Israel's past, such as Josiah, or with persons in the future, such as Jesus. In the context of the unit, however, the figure appears already to have been pierced: the coming change is the people's mourning. Someone already harmed has not yet been adequately mourned. The term "pierced" also appears in chapter 13 in the context of what will happen to prophets in the future. For this reason, Meyers and Meyers suggest that 12:2 speaks of the violence experienced by true prophets (1993, 339). In the future, the royal family and Jerusalemites will mourn over their failure to heed the prophetic word, as in 7:8-14.

The significance of Hadad-rimmon, named in 12:11, is unclear. The totality of the noun appears nowhere else in the Hebrew Bible, although Rimmon is given both as the name of a person (2 Sam 4:2-9) and of a Syrian god (2 Kgs 5:18). Maier has argued that Hadad-rimmon was a composite name of the Canaanite deity Baal, Hadad being a proper name of the deity and Rimmon a descriptor meaning "thunderer." He further maintains that the mourning described here would have been in times of drought, when Baal the storm god would have been understood as absent. Concern over rainfall would have been especially intense in the fertile agricultural area of Megiddo (Maier 1992, 13). Other theories have seen the mourning here connected with Megiddo as that for Josiah, as described in 2 Chr 35:25. Here, however, as in the case of the pierced one, all interpretations are speculative.

The listing of the mourners by families also raises interpretive questions. Only the significance of the house of David is clear: here, as elsewhere in Zechariah, David represents the royal lineage. The family of Nathan, however, is not so clear, since Nathan was the name of various figures in Israel's past, including a son of David (2 Sam 5:14), a prophet during David's time (2 Sam 2 and 7; 1 Kgs 1), and a man who returned from exile with Ezra (Ezra 8:16). Numerous interpreters have adopted the first option, arguing that David and Nathan together represent royal lines. No other postexilic literature remembers a Nathan as a royal figure, however, leaving this reference obscure as well.

The family of the Levites, and likely also the family of the Shimeites, was priestly. In the Bible, Levite at times refers to all members of the priestly order; at others, it denotes temple functionaries not assigned sacrificial duties. Among the various persons named Shimei in the Bible is a grandson of Levi, the second son of Levi's son Gershon. The precise distinction between Levites and the apparent subgroup of the Levites known as the Shimeites is not explained.

In each of the families, mourning is to be segregated by gender. The "house" is to mourn by itself and its wives by themselves, reminding the reader that women are not assumed to be part of the "house." Meyers and Meyers maintain that this verse reflects the cultic activity of professional women mourners; that the women are singled out for mention indicates that mourning is to be inclusive and elaborate (1993, 346). Such an explanation for this verse is not convincing, primarily because the verses pay so little attention to the women's activities. More significant is the literary connection between this verse and Jer 44:9, which also separately names the crimes of the kings and their wives and the crimes of the people and their wives. In light of the Jeremiah verse, the import of the Zechariah passage may not be that mourning practices were gender segregated in the ancient world, but that the women of these houses were treated as equally responsible for the need for mourning.

Theological Analysis

The enigmas of these verses make determining its theological message difficult. Who is the pierced one whom Yahweh will prepare others to mourn? What is the significance of the attention paid to the house of Nathan and the house of Shimeites? How, without understanding more fully the ancient context of this passage, might modern readers make appropriate and responsible analogies to our own time?

One value of such troublesome texts is to provoke in interpreters a healthy humility. Although preachers and teachers (and commentary writers!) often strive to provide definitive readings of texts, the texts themselves remind us of limitations. Sometimes they invite us into reflection of how little we know about our ancestors in faith, and how precarious it is to claim that we "know" what the Bible says. Heated discussions about the "authority of the Bible" too often overlook that the meaning of the Bible is often itself a mystery.

The disjunction between the writer's insistence on the importance of the event to be mourned and our own ignorance of what that event was also reminds us that what seems "cataclysmic" in one time period is often forgotten by later generations. Those traumas that define our lives (World War II; September 11, 2001; and so on) are important and deserve our attention; we do not know, however, how they will be remembered by those who come after us. This unit affirms that the traumas of an age are important to God, even if they are not remembered forever.

THE END OF IDOLATRY AND PROPHECY (13:1-9)

This unit explains how, "on that day," Yahweh will purify the people. Sins will be cleansed away, prophecy will no longer be necessary, and the remnant of the people will again belong to Yahweh.

Literary Analysis

The opening verse continues the vocabulary of "house of David" and "inhabitants of Jerusalem" employed in the two previous units. These parties, which have been saved from the nations (12:1-9) and given the ability to mourn for those they have pierced (12:10-14), are here cleansed by water, by the obliteration of idols and prophets, and by the refining fire of Yahweh. The purification of the people will occur in three stages:

13:1	A cleansing fountain will be opened
13:2-6	Yahweh will cut off idols and prophets
13:7-9	The shepherd will be struck, and Yahweh will refine a remnant

The first image used for stage one, that of the fountain (13:1), bears eschatological overtones. As in Ps 46:4 and Joel 3:18, Jerusalem is here treated as the center from which the future world will be healed. Although the explicit description of Jerusalem's waters as washing away ritual uncleanness is distinctive here, it is close in perspective to Ezek 47, which stresses that the waters that flow from Jerusalem will return the world to the status of Creation (Ezek 47:9; cf. Gen 1:21).

The thoroughgoing critique of prophets in stage 2 (13:2-6) may be understood in several different ways: as proclaiming the end of prophecy altogether, as critiquing those who function as professional prophets, or as addressed to false prophets—those who erroneously claim to speak for Yahweh. Although the social dimensions of prophecy in the Persian period will be explored further below, the question explored here is how the literary features of 13:2-6 might inform the discussion.

The explanation that the unit refers to false prophets is based on the observation that the prophets are charged with speaking lies (13:3) and deceiving (13:4). The further characterization of the prophets, however, does not suggest that they are false prophets. "Visions" are attributed elsewhere to true prophets (Ezek 7:13; Obad 1; Nah 1:1; Hab 2:2-3) as well as to false prophets (Jer 14:14; 23:16), and the clothing and marks of a prophet in 13:4 and 6 are not alone a cause for criticism, given that figures who most readers would consider "true prophets" also bear the distinctive marks of a prophet (see exegetical analysis below).

In Zech 13:5, the person's reply to the charge of prophesying quotes the response of Amos to Amaziah in Amos 7; when Amos was told to return to his home to prophesy, he proclaimed: "I am no prophet, nor a prophet's son; but I am a herdsman, and a dresser of sycamore trees, and Yahweh took me from following the flock, and Yahweh said to me, 'Go, prophesy to my people Israel'" (Amos 7:14).

Although Amos's response is given credibility by the reader, understood to be a denial that Amos is a professional prophet, the quotation of Amos's words are set here in a more cynical context. Here, those whom the reader already knows to be prophets deny the fact. Similarly, the prophets also deny their "prophetic marks." Rather than admit that their marks or bruises (see below) are signs of their profession, they will lie and claim that their marks come from "the ones who love them." Whether being bruised by intimates at home is meant to be an "innocent" explanation or a sad recognition of the normalcy of domestic violence, those who prophesy are not willing to acknowledge the true origin of the marks on their bodies.

Denying being a prophet and denying the true origin of the prophetic marks are not given as the *reason* for the prophets being called deceitful; rather, syntactically, both serve to prove the larger point that prophets in the future will be ashamed of their visions (Zech 13:4). That is, nothing in the unit indicates that the punishment is to be issued to prophets whose messages are not true. Rather, prophets will be put to death by their own parents for prophesying at all. Such observations suggest that the intent of this unit is to portray a future in which prophecy is abolished.

The repeated formula "on that day" supports such a suggestion. Just as the image of a fountain flowing forth from Jerusalem is one beyond the bounds of normal human experience, so too the end to prophecy will mark the new and glorious future. The writer is not claiming that prophecy has ended in his own time, but rather is affirming something about the new way in which Yahweh will interact with the people in the future.

In this regard, Zech 13 may be using prophetic hyperbole, bold overstatement to underscore a point. In the case of Amos 5, for example, many interpreters explain the prophet's scathing rhetoric against sacrifices not as condemning sacrifices altogether but as criticizing the improper reliance on sacrifices. In the case of Jer 31, few believe that Jeremiah is declaring an end to the Mosaic covenant when the prophet claims that in the future the covenant will be written not on tablets, but on the people's hearts. In the case of Zech 13, the writer may be making a claim, in bold hyperbole, that in the future Yahweh will need no intermediary with the people. Cleansed from sin and ritual impurity (13:1), calling on Yahweh's name (13:9) after the names of the idols have been cut off (13:2), the people will interact with Yahweh directly.

The final subunit (13:7-9) begins with a striking personification. Yahweh speaks directly to a sword and calls it to strike the shepherd so that the sheep are scattered. The connection with the previous unit may be the image of "piercing" employed in 13:3. In 13:3, parents were the ones responsible for stabbing their prophesying children, but here the sword itself is personified as the one to carry out Yahweh's intention.

In the NRSV, these verses are formatted as poetry. They do not have formal poetic style, though often one phrase builds upon the previous one, giving the unit a poetic feel: "Awake, O sword, against my shepherd, against the man who is my associate" (13:7).

The shepherd metaphor is again employed. As in 9:16, 10:3-5, and 11:4-17, the shepherds seem to be leaders of the community, since the flock is described in apparent parallel with "the whole land" in 13:7-8. In earlier chapters, the shepherds appeared to be the religious and civic leaders of Jerusalem. This unit is more ambiguous. If, for example, the entire chapter is read as a continuous thread, then the shepherd may be the prophet who is stabbed in 13:3 and stricken by the sword in 13:7.

After the death of the leader, only a fraction of the people will survive. Two-thirds will perish, and the remaining third will be refined by fire. Only those who still remain will affirm the traditional language of the covenant with Moses: Yahweh will be their God, and they will be Yahweh's people.

The cleansing of the people, which began in 13:1 as positive image, ends in 13:7-9 on a more sober note. The restoration of the people "on that day" will be not merely a washing away of sin but a violent destruction of more than two-thirds of the whole. Only a small remnant will be left to proclaim their bonds with Yahweh.

Exegetical Analysis

As seen in the literary analysis, the precise meaning of much of this unit is debated. Additional factors, such as translational matters, further complicate its interpretation.

In 13:1, the MT does not contain the word "cleanse" as translated in the NRSV. It literally reads "and for the inhabitants of Jerusalem, for sin and for impurity." Most interpreters understand the function of the fountain to be the removal of sin and impurity, and in turn either understand the verb as implied or revocalize the first noun into the verbal form of "cleanse from sin." The pairing of "sin" and "impurity" indicates that both human moral wrongs and states of ritual uncleanness will be removed. Although the word *niddâ* ("impurity") usually refers to impurity related to menstruation, it is likely used here in a broader sense, to include the wide range of behaviors considered to render a person unfit for contact with sacred objects (specific sexual practices, bodily emissions, childbirth, contact with a corpse, and so on; see Lev 12–22).

The discussion of prophecy in 13:2-6 is complex. As argued above, literary analysis supports the interpretation of the unit not as against false prophecy, but rather as claiming that prophecy will cease "on that day." The strong, hyperbolic language is intended to show just how unneeded—and how punishable— prophecy will be in the future. Although literary allusions are often in the eye of the beholder, the description of the prophet's parents as executing them may draw upon the law regarding the "wicked and rebellious son" in Deut 21. There, parents are responsible for bringing to the elders a son who is stubborn and rebellious, a glutton and a drunkard. Even if this provision for child discipline was never actually carried out in ancient Israel, its stridency may have had the effect of a deterrent. The similar claim of Zechariah, which twice stresses that the stabbing is carried out by the father and mother "who bore him," also has a disturbing and perhaps equally deterrent effect.

Distinctive clothing and bodily markings are attributed to prophets elsewhere in the Bible. Second Kings 1:8 describes Elijah as a "hairy man" with a leather belt around his waist; this description usually is understood to refer to Elijah's garments, which may be the "mantle" that Elijah passed to Elisha as the symbolic transfer of his prophetic authority (2 Kgs 2). Scholars such as Lindblom have explained that the primitive clothing of the prophet office was an attempt to exalt Israel's pastoral past over developing urbanism and "higher culture" (Lindblom 1962, 67). The depiction of John the Baptist in Mark 1:6 as clothed in camel hair with a leather strap around his waist likely alludes to this distinctive prophetic dress in order to establish John as a prophet in the model of an ancient prophet.

Prophets are also often recognizable by distinctive marks. In 1 Kgs 20:35-41, a prophet is known when he removes a bandage from his head, suggesting that he bore a recognizably "prophetic" mark on his forehead. The account of boys taunting Elisha in 2 Kgs 2:23 seems also to indicate that one could be identified as a prophet by hairstyle.

The precise marks indicated by Zech 13 are debated. Lacerations on the skin are associated in the Bible with the prophets of other religions (as in 1 Kgs 18:28) and are forbidden for Israelites by the laws of Lev 19:28. Meyers and Meyers have argued that Zech 13:5 refers to "bruises" (1993, 382) and thus would not be prohibited by guidelines in the Pentateuch.

The location of the marks is translated as "the chest" in the NRSV, although the MT literally reads "between the hands." Other translations have the wounds given on the arms, treating "hands" as a general reference to an appendage. That the actual hands might be indicated is suggested by other passages in which distinctive marks are borne on the hand: in Isa 44:5, in which new members of community will have God's name written on their hands, and in Exod 13 and Deut 6, in which the words of Yahweh are to be inscribed on the hands and forehead (figuratively, if not literally). In literary context, the wounds must not have been of a particular pattern, if they could be attributed to the wounds "normally" received at the hands of intimates. That such physical appearances denoting "normal" prophets underscores the argument made above that the prophets criticized here are not necessarily false prophets. In the future, *all* prophecy will cease.

Some interpreters have seen in Zech 13 evidence of the belief that prophecy had already ended. Later, Jewish tradition claimed that "prophecy ended with Malachi" (Tosefta *Sotah* 13:2), and it is possible that the widespread appearance of deutero-prophetic literature in this period was one accommodation to the perception that prophecy had ended; that is, by attaching itself to the name of a prophet known to have lived before Malachi, anonymous literature (such as Second Zechariah and Second and Third Isaiah) could appropriate a venerable pedigree. Petersen's classic study of late prophecy, for example, claims that Zech 13:2-6 is itself deutero-prophetic literature, the goal of which (along with Jer 23:33-40) "was to argue that prophetic performance in the classical mold was a thing of the past, and any attempts at prophetic performance were to be rejected" (Petersen 1977, 38).

What Petersen's argument and the argument that Zech 13 refers to false prophets both fail to take into account, however, is that in Zech 13, the cessation of prophecy is set not in the present, but in the future. In the literary context, not only of the chapter but also the entire collection in Zech 12–14, the changes from current practice will be realized only "on that day," in a future removed from the present. Prophecy itself is not illegitimate, but it will be unnecessary in God's future, cleansed Jerusalem.

The NRSV translation of 13:5 ("the land has been my possession since my youth") relies on an emendation of the Hebrew text. The MT reads "a man caused me to be purchased from my youth." The latter is reflected in the NASB and ASV. It would suggest that the prophet is claiming to be a tiller of the soil and a slave—and thus not free to engage in prophetic activity.

In literary terms alone, it is tempting to read the verses regarding the shepherd as an extension of the proclamation of the future end to prophecy. Although shepherds elsewhere in Zechariah seem to refer to other leaders of the community, Zech 13:7 would not be unique in calling a prophet a shepherd; even Jeremiah, which often calls royal leaders shepherds, also speaks of the prophet's role as that of shepherd (Jer 17:16).

The short description of the shepherd, however, provides little basis for a determination. The word translated by the NRSV as "my associate" in 13:7 provides no further clues. It is relatively rare in the Hebrew Bible, appearing elsewhere only in the book of Leviticus. In Leviticus, it sometimes denotes a relative (18:20) but more often another member of the community (often translated "neighbor").

This entire unit reflects awareness of a wide range of various prophetic traditions and written materials. Already noted are resonances with the books of Ezekiel and Amos and the stories of Elijah. Additional links include those to Ezek 5, whose vision of the future of the people divides them into thirds, and to Hos 2, which ends much as Zech 14 ends. The people no longer call on the name of false gods, but on the name of Yahweh alone (Zech 13:9; Hos 2:16), and Yahweh will answer them (Zech 13:9; Hos 2:21). With the rift healed, Yahweh proclaims "they are my people" and they will proclaim "Yahweh is our God" (Zech 13:9; Hos 2:23).

Theological Analysis

If the claim advanced here is correct (that prophecy will end only in God's perfect future), then this unit does not denigrate prophecy outright. These verses do not suggest that prophecy has already ended or that prophets (professional or nonprofessional) are wrongheaded; rather, like other passages in Second Zechariah, they paint a picture of an ideal world different from the current world. In an ideal world, intermediaries between God and humans are unnecessary.

In a world that is not yet ideal, then, there is still the need for prophets, those whom the Bible depicts less as predicting the future than as speaking the word of God in the midst of human crisis. Zechariah 13 depicts prophets both as those whose identity is evident and also, indirectly, as those whose identity fades behind their message; if indeed the writer of Second Zechariah is anonymous to us, we learn about his hopes and convictions only through the words transmitted to us.

The Christian and Jewish communities have continued to hear God's word in the writings about prophets contained in the Bible. And both have claimed to continue to hear God's word proclaimed through both types of contemporary "prophets"— religious professionals and those more anonymous.

The Bible portrays prophets, at least in part, as those who speak out for justice in the face of community opposition. In an ironic way, a modern prophet might be one who responds to a small detail of this text—that the bruises on the prophet's body can be explained away as "normal" wounds "received in the house of those loved." As long as domestic violence is accepted as "normal," true justice for all people is far away. A modern prophet might include in the vision of God's perfect future an end to such violence.

THE FINAL SUPREMACY OF JERUSALEM (14:1-21)

This final unit of the book of Zechariah not only continues the themes developed in the previous unit but also serves as the fitting culmination of a book that has, throughout, highlighted the importance of Jerusalem and the great plans Yahweh has for the city.

Literary Analysis

The chapter opens with "behold, a day is coming." This is not the same phrase as "on that day" that punctuated chapter 13, though the latter phrase appears in the unit frequently—seven times. "A day is coming" is common to prophetic literature, in which it signifies the Day of Yahweh, a day when Yahweh will come as a Divine Warrior and right the wrongs of the world (for "a day is coming" used in such a way, see Isa 13:9 and Joel 2:1). Hence, the very first phrase signals to the reader that what will follow will be harsh and filled with images of battle.

Determining the structure of the unit is difficult. Although "on that day" is treated elsewhere in the prophets as the marker of a new oracular unit, the frequency of the phrase here complicates the use of this criterion: such a scheme would leave short, choppy units and would fail to explain cases, such as in 14:13, in which "on that day" seems to mark the continuation and not the beginning of a unit.

Theme may provide a more helpful structuring principle:

14:1-2	War against Jerusalem
14:3-5	God defends the city

14:6-11	Miscellaneous promises for Jerusalem
14:12-15	Yahweh's punishment of the nations
14:16-21	Inclusive holiness, for the nations and for Jerusalem

As seen in the outline, the Divine Warrior's coming initially, though briefly, signals destruction for Jerusalem. Yahweh will bring the nations against Jerusalem, and the city will be put under siege. The syntax does not clarify whether Yahweh himself fights against Jerusalem, since the verbs used for the violence done to the city are in the passive voice. The imagery used for that battle, however, is horrific: houses are looted and women raped, and half of the people are taken into exile (more people actually escape than in the previous chapter, in which only one-third escape).

After the brief description of battle *against* Jerusalem, the rest of the chapter tells of Yahweh's fighting *for* Jerusalem. Zechariah 14:4 is perhaps one of the boldest characterizations of Yahweh in the Old Testament, showing Yahweh with feet firmly planted on the Mount of Olives, a vantage point outside Jerusalem. The mountain splits underfoot on its east-west axis, and the two halves move apart, north and south; the valley formed by the shifting mountain halves will be the people's escape route. Here, Yahweh is portrayed not only in strikingly anthropomorphic terms (with feet!), but also as altering the world's topography in the move to reconfigure the status of Jerusalem.

In the series of "on that day" sayings that follow, we learn that

- there will be a cessation of the distinction between day and night and of seasons
- living waters will flow from Jerusalem (see 13:1)
- Yahweh will become king
- land around Jerusalem will be made a plain, and Jerusalem will be the only high point
- Jerusalem will be reinhabited, never again to be destroyed

- those who fight against Jerusalem will suffer plague, and their wealth will be seized
- those of the nations who survive will worship Yahweh and keep the festival of Sukkot
- everything in Jerusalem, even cooking pots and bells on horses, will be holy.

These verses provide rich, striking characterization of various figures. *The earth* will be changed from its original creation; light will cease (see the exegetical comments on 14:6), and water will flow in both the rainy and dry seasons (14:8). *Jerusalem* will become the only high point in the whole land, everything else made a plain so that Jerusalem might be exalted. Jerusalem will become the place where all nations worship, and everything within it will become holy. *Yahweh* will function not only as Warrior, but as King, one who will go to great extremes to protect Jerusalem. *The nations* will be wholly controlled by Yahweh; even their fighting against Jerusalem is at Yahweh's initiation. Those who harm Jerusalem will suffer plague, their bodies rotting. The few of them who survive will be punished if they do not observe Sukkot, honor Yahweh the King, and go up to Jerusalem. Even *animals* are characterized as part of Yahweh's dominion in Zech 14. The animals of the nations will also suffer plague, and the bells on the horses will be holy. Horses are mentioned frequently in the book of Zechariah, perhaps because of their connection with the Persian communication system.

Literarily, the final mention of horses brings the book full circle. In Zech 1, the vision of the prophet was of horses that patrol the earth, and there Yahweh promised, "My cities shall again overflow with prosperity; Yahweh will again comfort Zion and again choose Jerusalem" (1:17). Here, at the close of the book, that promise is shown as soon to be fulfilled. Yahweh is about to transform everything to bring about Jerusalem's exaltation.

Fitting of its subject matter, Zech 14 assaults the senses with images of women raped, of Yahweh straddling a shifting Mount of Olives, of the rotting flesh of the nations. It is a unit whose apparent goal is to shock and thereby, ironically, to comfort. Yahweh's power to transform Jerusalem is without limits.

Exegetical Analysis

Most modern translations agree in translating the act taken against women in 14:2 as rape. In the Hebrew, however, ancient scribes were not so comfortable with such a coarse word and suggested that another, more polite, word be substituted. In an example of a scribal reading instruction called *kethib/qere* (written/read), the Masoretic notes instruct the reader that while "raped" (root, *šgl*) is written, "lain with" *(škb)* should be read.

Another *kethib/qere* is found in 14:6. In the written text *(kethib)*, the last two words seem to be "precious ones will congeal." The Masoretic reading *(qere)*, however, treats the last word as "frost." The reading of "cold and frost" is taken from the Septuagint. Even more important, the Hebrew of the beginning of the verse says "on that day there will not be light," a phrase that is omitted in numerous English translations, including NRSV and NAB. The editors of the BHS suggest that the word "light" *(ʾôr)* should be emended to "cold" *(qôr)* in line with the claim in Gen 8:22 that in the future seasons and day and night will not cease.

This unit employs numerous proper nouns, the significance of which is not clear. The first of these appears in 14:5, in which the valley created by the splitting of the Mount of Olives is said to stretch to Azal. Treated here as a place name, Azal is not known in any other source, and its only identification is based on inference from this passage. Sweeney suggests revocalizing the consonants to read *ʾēṣel*, "side": "the valley of the mountain shall reach to (each) side" (2000, 699).

As for the various locales within the city of Jerusalem listed in 14:10, several are mentioned elsewhere in the Bible. The Benjamin Gate appears also in Jer 20:2; 37:13; and Ezek 48:32; the Corner Gate in 2 Kgs 14:13 and 2 Chr 25:23; 26:9; and the Tower of Hananel in Neh 3:1; 12:39; and Jer 31:38. This last overlap is noteworthy, in that Jer 31:38 reads: "The days are surely coming, says Yahweh, when the city shall be rebuilt for Yahweh from the tower of Hananel to the Corner Gate." As explored below, the similarity between Zech 14 and Jer 31 may indicate a literary relationship between these texts. Determining the precise location of these gates and tower, as well as "the king's wine presses," is difficult. The most logical conclusion is that the place names are intended to underscore the totality and extent of Jerusalem's restoration.

Zechariah 14:10 claims that the land outside of Jerusalem will be made into a plain, so that Jerusalem alone will be exalted. The extent of the plain is from Geba, known in the Bible as the territory of Benjamin; Geba was north of Jerusalem, south of Bethel. The location of Rimmon is less clear, though the text itself claims that it is south of Jerusalem. While the implied distance between Geba and Rimmon would not be huge for the extent of Judah, it is a large area to be leveled for the sole purpose of Jerusalem's exaltation. As in other cases in Zech 14, a literary allusion may also be at work in this verse: in Isa 10:27-29, the Divine Warrior marches forth from Rimmon and "they" (Yahweh's army?) lodge for the night at Geba.

"Canaanites" are mentioned in 14:21, though the noun is translated as "traders" by the NRSV, NAB, and NJB. That "Canaanite" may refer to merchants was explored in the discussion of Zeph 1:11 and Zech 7:7 and 11 (see, too, Isa 23:8; Ezek 16:29; Hos 12:8).

In light of our ongoing discussion about the term "Judah" in the book of Zechariah—whether it is understood to include Jerusalem or to refer to non-Jerusalemite Yehud (see discussions in chs. 7 and 12)—the reference to Judah in 14:14 is noteworthy. Judah is said to fight separately from Jerusalem, although the Hebrew text may be understood as Judah fights either *against* Jerusalem or *in/at* Jerusalem. The latter understanding is more consistent with the book of Zechariah as a whole. Although the book does recognize rivalry between Jerusalem and the rest of Yehud, it also claims that Yehud will recognize the superiority of Jerusalem (7:1-7 and 12:1-6). In this case, despite the rivalry, Judah will fight *for* Jerusalem.

In Zech 14, the festival of Sukkot becomes almost synonymous with worship in Jerusalem. Survivors of the nations are judged only on whether or not they observe Sukkot. Also known as the Feast of Booths or Feast of Tabernacles, Sukkot is one of the three pilgrimage festivals of ancient Israel. Celebrating the fall harvest of grain and wine, the Feast is described in Deut 16:13-15 as one to be observed by all Israel: "Rejoice during your festival, you and your sons and your daughters, your male and female slaves, as well as the Levites, the strangers, the orphans, and the widows resident in your towns" (16:14). In the revisioning of Zech 14, yet others join in observing the festival. All nations worship at Jerusalem.

The mention of Sukkot is significant not only in demonstrating the festival's importance in the Persian period but also in demonstrating the importance of the Temple to this unit. Several interpreters have noted that the Temple is relatively absent from the image of the ideal Jerusalem. The city itself receives far greater attention, and the closing verses could be read to downplay the unique sanctity of the Temple. The Pentateuchal prescriptions for Sukkot, however, presuppose the centrality of the Temple. Although observants dwell in temporary structures ("booths") for seven days, offerings are presented to the Temple ("the place that Yahweh will choose, Deut 16:15). Moreover, 1 Kgs 8 speaks of the dedication of Solomon's Temple as held during "the festival" for seven days in the seventh month, likely referring to "the festival" of Tabernacles—a further indication that in privileging Sukkot, the writer of Zech 14 presupposed a Temple as part of the future Jerusalem.

Zechariah 14 is replete with allusions to other literature, especially prophetic literature. Although several examples have already been cited (Isa 10:27-29; Jer 31:38), Schaefer has explored others at length. Examples include:

Isa 2–4	Elevation of Jerusalem; holiness of Jerusalem
Isa 13	"Holy ones"; no light, flight of people, rape of women
Isa 30:18-33	Multiplication of light; festival
Ezek 38–39	Gathering and judging of the nations
Ezek 47:1-12	Elevation of Jerusalem; water flowing under Temple
Zeph 1	"Merchants"; Jerusalem's punishment followed by nations'; Yahweh as Warrior and King

Other parallels are found in Joel and Isa 24–27, in addition to a long list of passages (Schaefer 1995).

The strongly allusive character of the chapter supports the observations made earlier regarding the literary nature of prophetic activity in the Persian period as well as the likelihood of a written collection of prophetic material by this time. The expansions upon earlier prophetic work also attest to this writer's self-perception that he stood in the line of prophets, interpreting and extending their message in a new day.

The dramatic imagery of Zech 14 and its depiction of a world to be recreated by the Divine Warrior raise the question of whether this literature should be designated "apocalyptic." The term is often used loosely to refer to futuristic visions, though it has no agreed-upon definition. Scholars usually reserve the noun "apocalypse" for a particular style of literature, characterized by features such as the periodization of history, accounts of other-worldly journeys, and, particularly, the belief that the future will be known only by the revelation of divine secrets. Some scholars also speak of "apocalyptic eschatology," arguing that even material without the formal features of an apocalypse may share with them the conviction that God's future salvation will require a radical disjunction with the established course of human history.

Those seeking the origins of later apocalyptic material such as Daniel, Revelation, Enoch, and 3 Baruch have turned to the Hebrew Bible for clues. Although others have claimed that apocalyptic grew out of biblical wisdom traditions or from mantic wisdom, Paul Hanson has argued that apocalyptic grew out of prophecy. He claims that bitter tension between two parties in the Persian period led one group to abandon hope that the world could change and to transform the ancient mythology of the Divine Warrior into a promise of God's radical, apocalyptic intervention in human affairs (see Hanson 1979). According to Hanson, Second Zechariah reflects the apocalyptic hopes of the theocratic faction, disenfranchised by the hierocrats whose voice is preserved in Haggai and Zech 1–8.

It is clear, however, that Second Zechariah does not fit the genre of apocalypse. Unlike in Daniel, there are no divine secrets revealed to a seer, no interpreting messenger, and no animal symbolism. In Zech 14, Yahweh does appear with the "holy ones," which are important to later apocalypses (Dan 8:24), though such language is known from earlier, nonapocalyptic sources as well (Ps 89:6-7; Prov 30:3). Moreover, Zech 14 sounds thoroughly prophetic, using oracular speech forms such as "thus says Yahweh" and "on that day." Indeed, its large number of allusions to earlier prophetic materials and traditions suggests that its writer saw his own claims as continuous with biblical prophecy.

And yet, Zech 14 seems to move beyond the claims of prophecy, at least by one increment. Amos 5, for example, speaks of the Day of Yahweh as darkness, but it does not call for the end of the created order. In other prophetic books, the Divine Warrior marches forth to save Judah and punish the nations, but there is little to compare with the dramatic image of Yahweh straddling two pieces of the Mount of Olives.

Such observations highlight not only the complexity of Second Zechariah but perhaps even more so the instability of the adjectives "prophetic" and "apocalyptic"—as well as the ever-slippery term "eschatological." Importantly, these are modern terms, not those of the biblical writers. These terms are *our* attempts to find words for the different perspectives that we find in texts about how God will bring about change in the present; they reflect *our* attempt to delineate ideological camps in the past (as well as the present), to determine which ideas logically fit together. Second Zechariah frustrates such schemes of categorization and suggests that in the Persian period, prophecy was understood in a much broader way than in contemporary scholarship.

A look at the book of Zechariah as a whole further underscores the difficulty in distinguishing prophecy and apocalyptic. First Zechariah, on the one hand, bears many of the formal literary features of an apocalypse—the interpreting angel and animal and number symbolism—though it does not reflect "apocalyptic eschatology"; its hopes for Jerusalem are focused on the pending and imminent rebuilding of the Temple. On the other hand, Second Zechariah does not share the style of the apocalypse though comes closer to "apocalyptic eschatology" in its radical visions of the future.

Zechariah's bearing upon the *origin* of apocalyptic is thus complex, but what is much more clear is the vast *resources that it could provide* to later apocalyptic writers. Here, in one book, are a vast number of images that could be used in new and important ways. The Passion narratives of the Gospels, for example, are replete with allusions to Second Zechariah: the king riding on a donkey (9:9), the blood of the covenant (9:11), sheep scattered without a shepherd (10:2), thirty pieces of silver thrown into the house of Yahweh (11:12-13), and the purging of traders from the Temple (14:21). In the "little apocalypse" of Mark 13, Jesus has an apocalyptic vision on the Mount of Olives in which people flee (see Zech 14:4-5) from destruction and seasons cease (14:6). Materials from First Zechariah appear in later apocalyptic scenarios as well, most notably the four horses in Zech 1 and 6, which reappear in the book of Revelation. Later readers, likely accepting the unity of the book of Zechariah, found within the collection as a whole many of the elements that could be utilized in forming apocalypses and apocalyptic literature.

Theological Analysis

The value of futuristic visions is variously assessed. Many consider such hopes for the future as fatalistic and quietistic, waiting for divine intervention in human affairs rather than calling for human action. Ironically, the very boldness of God's action can be seen as obviating the need for human initiative. Such visions can function in other ways, however. They can be understood as underscoring the values that writers and their readers attribute to God. Zechariah 14 clearly attributes to Yahweh ultimate power, not only over humans, but also over the created order. Yahweh can subvert the seasons and lights that he himself established; as warrior and king, he rules the earth against all opposition. Such a claim is very good news to those who despair of God's power to intervene on behalf of humans.

Ironically, the very examples given of God's power are the elements of the unit that raise ethical problems for some readers. Yahweh's violent punishment of those who strike Jerusalem—and even of their animals—is ripe for nationalistic and self-important appropriation. When readers are convinced that they are the ones Yahweh will save and their own enemies are the ones Yahweh will punish, then Zech 14 becomes a text supporting our own biases.

The tension in this unit between Yahweh's faithfulness to the covenant people and divine favor to be shared with others, however, provides one avenue of faithful interpretation. This writer, even from a pro-Jerusalem perspective, can imagine a time different enough from his own (and perhaps from our own) in which all of the earth will be holy.

From beginning to end, the book of Zechariah focuses on Jerusalem and on the importance of rebuilding the Temple. It stresses that Yahweh's promise to David has not ended and that God's care of the people will continue, as will the divine call to accountability. In the Persian period, such a message would have spoken powerfully to a small community controlled by a massive Empire. By its preservation in the Jewish and Christian canons, later generations have affirmed that the vision of such a future may provide hope to other communities as well. The vision of a day in which all of the world will be as holy to God as the Temple once was is also worthy of contemporary hopes—and action.

INTRODUCTION:
MALACHI

LITERARY ANALYSIS

In both Jewish and Christian Bibles, the book of Malachi concludes the Prophets. In the three-part organization of the Jewish Bible, it is followed by the Writings; and in Christian canonical order (in which the Prophets appear at the end of the Old Testament in order to emphasize their foreshadowing of Jesus), Malachi is followed by the Gospel of Matthew. The verses marked 4:1-6 in Christian Bibles are 3:19-24 in Hebrew.

Malachi's style is argumentative. Often in rapid-fire dialogue, God and people accuse one another of neglect and disregard of their mutual covenant obligations. The people accuse God of not loving them, not caring about their welfare. God accuses the people, and especially the priests, of showing disrespect and not offering proper sacrifices. As in the case of Haggai, however, the book does not offer direct access to the people's voices or perspectives. In 1:2, for example, the prophet reports what the people say or, rather, infers what they are thinking. Statements such as "What a weariness this is!" (1:13) were not likely verbalized.

The book poses numerous questions, though for a variety of rhetorical effects. At times, questions genuinely request information, as in 2:14 ("Why does he not?") and in 2:17 ("Where is the God of justice?"). Other questions expect the respondent to confirm what the speaker already believes to be true, as in 1:8

("When you offer blind animals in sacrifice, is that not wrong?") and in 3:2 ("Who can endure the day of his coming?"). Questions are also used to contradict what has just been said, as in 1:2 ("How have you loved us?"). Questions are a direct means of accusation, as in 1:6 ("Where is my honor?") and can establish the premise for an accusation to follow, as in 1:2 ("Is not Esau Jacob's brother?") and in 2:10 ("Have we not all one father?").

The driving question of the book, "Where is the God of justice?" (3:17), is answered in 3:1 by the promise of a coming messenger. In the prophetic tradition of announcing a future day of vindication, Malachi envisions a time in which God will restore the priesthood (3:3-4) and separate the righteous from the wicked (4:1-2 [Heb. 3:19-20]).

The book may be outlined as follows:

1:1	Superscription
1:2-5	People and God argue about love
1:6–2:9	Priests and God argue about respect
2:10-16	People and God argue about "profaning the covenant of the fathers"
2:17–3:5	People and God argue about God's justice
3:6-12	People and God argue about scarcity and abundance
3:13–4:3 (Heb. 3:13-21)	People and God argue about the value of serving God
4:4-6 (Heb. 3:22-24)	Closing statements connecting the Law and the Prophets

Most scholars consider the closing statements of the book as editorial additions, included to explain the identity of the messenger described in 3:1 and to link the prophetic message with that of the Pentateuch. The themes of the addition, however, fit well into the book, drawing from Israel's past instruction for the present.

SOCIAL AND HISTORICAL ANALYSIS

The book gives no information about its author. Even the name Malachi, which means "my messenger," may have been borrowed from the figure described in 3:1. Because the book begins the same way as Zech 9:1 and 12:1 do ("An oracle. The word of Yahweh"), Blenkinsopp and others have suggested that the material was an anonymous booklet given independent status in order to make a twelve-book collection of minor prophets (Blenkinsopp 1983, 239-40). Nogalski points to numerous redactions that link Malachi with a larger Book of the Twelve and perhaps with a larger emerging canon (1993b, 204-5). In its final form, however, Malachi reads as a coherent, self-contained book.

Although the book gives no clear chronological markers, it is usually dated to the Persian period, based on the arguments that (1) it presupposes a functioning Temple (1:7, 10); (2) it mentions a "governor," the title given to political leaders of the postexilic community (1:8); (3) it reflects the fall of Edom to the Nabateans (1:2-5); and (4) it refers to the same mixed marriages that concerned Ezra and Nehemiah (2:10-16). This latter point will be challenged in the commentary, but the book's insistence on proper sacrifices and its high regard of Levi as the ideal priest (2:4-6) fit well into the postexilic period, when the Temple took on new importance in the community.

As discussed more fully in the introduction to Haggai, in the postexilic community the priesthood took on much of the importance once attached, in the preexilic period, to the monarchy. Although Malachi acknowledges that the community must answer to a Persian governor (1:8), it holds the priests responsible for oversight not only of sacrifice, but also of instruction. The book calls for no future Davidic king but imagines a time in which the priests will exercise their functions appropriately and fairly.

Paul Hanson (1979; 1986) discerns in Malachi the perspective of a theocratic faction in the postexilic community, one whose more inclusive understanding of community was at odds with that of the hierocrats who controlled the priesthood. Such an understanding is based on the language that Malachi uses for proper priests, "sons of Levi," as well as on the book's polemical style. Though little in Malachi provides clear support for his thesis, Hanson's perspective will be discussed in the commentary to chapter 2.

THEOLOGICAL ANALYSIS

Theological themes usually highlighted in the book of Malachi are (1) its discussion of divorce (2:10-16); (2) its concern with tithes (3:8-12); and (3) its promise of a messenger who will precede the appearance of Yahweh (3:1-4). The latter has been given particular weight in the history of Christian interpretation; its connection with messianic readings of the Old Testament is familiar to many modern persons through its use in Handel's *Messiah*. The discussion of the relative fates of Jacob and Esau in 1:2-5 has also been employed in discussions of predestination, following a particular understanding of Rom 9:13.

Additional theological and ethical concerns are raised by the book's description of the relationship between parents and children or, more precise, the relationship between fathers and sons. Although the NRSV uses gender inclusive language in 3:17 and 4:6 (Heb. 3:24), the nouns in Hebrew are male. Beginning in 1:2 and running throughout the book, fathers are characterized as having total power over their sons, while sons owe their fathers fear and service. Unlike the book of Deuteronomy, in which the primary role of fathers is to instruct their sons, in the book of Malachi, fathers are authoritarian and threatening. By analogy, God is described as the same type of father: as made clear in 1:6, because sons (naturally) honor their fathers and servants (naturally) honor their masters, Yahweh is rightfully offended by Judah's insubordinate behavior.

Pastoral theologian Donald Capps, building upon the work of psychologist Alice Miller, has made a strong and impassioned case that authoritarian parental practices are closely aligned with, and provide the necessary precondition for, child abuse. In particular, the denial of intellectual autonomy to children—the permission to think for themselves—prevents children from recognizing abuse for what it is, from naming the treatment they receive as wrong. Capps, indeed, claims that "a key factor in breaking the vicious cycle of child abuse" is intellectual autonomy for children (1995, 60-64).

By describing God as a father who scolds and shames his son Judah, the book of Malachi perpetuates not only an authoritarian model of parenthood, but also more specifically the ultimate control by the male head of the family. In contrast with Deut 21:18-21, which gives the mother a role in the punishment of her son, Malachi mentions only the power of the father.

Recognizing the ideology that underlies Malachi's argument is important. Precisely because the descriptions of fathers and of God as a father are so familiar in our own culture, we, too, often overlook how differently the roles of "father" have been understood in other times and places. Recognizing Malachi's specific configuration of fatherhood is essential for those who wish to advocate a different model of parenthood—one that honors children's bodies and spirits.

COMMENTARY: MALACHI

SUPERSCRIPTION (1:1)

The introduction to Malachi provides little concrete information about the prophet and his time period. As a prophetic superscription, however, it marks what follows as divine speech.

Literary Analysis

Like other prophetic books, Malachi begins with a superscription describing the prophet and the material to follow. The collection is labeled an "oracle" *(maśśāʾ)*, the same term that introduces collections that begin at Nah 1:1; Hab 1:1; Zech 9:1; 12:1; and the extended diatribes against foreign nations in Isa 13–23. As discussed in the commentary to Nah 1:1, *maśśāʾ* texts tend to draw a sharp distinction between the wicked and the righteous; while the wicked of Nahum is a foreign nation, the wicked of Malachi are within the community itself.

Exegetical Analysis

The superscription offers no historical information. Neither a time setting nor identifying information for the prophet is provided. As noted in the introduction, several commentators have suggested that the book is a collection of anonymous material that took its name from the nameless "my messenger" *(malʾākî)* in 3:1. There is no reason why Malachi may not be a proper name, though without any further identification such as a locale or a father's name, the book remains effectively anonymous.

Theological Analysis

The opening of this last book of the prophetic canon sets it within the theological continuum of the Prophets. Like other prophetic superscriptions, it announces that the divine word is addressed to the community through the vehicle of an individual. In this way, prophetic materials stress both the roles of God and the roles of humans in the process of revelation.

PEOPLE AND GOD ARGUE ABOUT LOVE (1:2-5)

In this unit, God and the people dispute about love. Yahweh points to the destruction of Edom as proof of care for Judah.

Literary Analysis

God begins the discussion with an assertion ("I have loved you"), to which the people respond in doubt ("How have you loved us?"). As proof of the original claim, God points to the current devastation of Edom. Even though Esau (the ancestor of Edom) and Jacob (the ancestor of Israel) are brothers, God has hated Edom but has loved Israel. Love is thus proved by the relative fates of the two brothers, which is described here in physical terms: Edom's devastation is so thorough that God will prevent any future rebuilding. The unit climaxes with the claim that witnessing Edom's perpetual devastation will lead Israel to praise God.

The unit not only introduces the family imagery that will permeate the book but also focuses on the story of two brothers, the rival twins Esau and Jacob, the account of whom appears in Gen 25–27. In the Genesis narrative, Jacob tricks his older brother Esau out of his birthright and their father's blessing; Jacob's favored status comes through his initiative and that of his mother. Although Genesis characterizes Esau as easily deceived and perhaps less intellectually gifted than Jacob, his fate is not described as a punishment for any of his actions. In contrast, Malachi gives no reason why Edom is hated. The only reason given for God's treatment of Edom is that it demonstrates God's care of Israel.

Some commentators have suggested that God's "hate" of Edom should not be interpreted in harsh terms but as meaning "loved less." Pointing to the use of the term "hate" in ancient Near Eastern treaties to describe the one not chosen by the lord, such commentators suggest that God does not "hate," but rather prefers one brother over another. The term does have parallels in the treaty language of the ancient Near East (O'Brien 1990, 64), but its meaning is intended to be raw and shocking, as seen in its usage in 2:16 in which God is described as "hating" particular practices in the community.

Exegetical Analysis

The unit's description of the destruction of Edom in the past tense is often seen as a clue to the dating of the book. If the book treats the devastation of Edom as evidence of God's love for Israel, then for the argument to be persuasive, Edom must have already suffered defeat. Although Coggins maintains that Malachi treats Edom as a typical enemy and not as a specific historical nation (1987, 75), the reader must assent that Edom has been devastated in order for the logic of the unit to succeed.

During much of the twentieth century, Malachi was seen as reflecting the fall of the Edomite state, which was in turn attributed to the Nabatean invasion of Edom in the beginning of the fifth century. The fifth century, then, would provide the date after which Malachi must have been written, since it presupposes that the fall of Edom has already taken place.

The date of Edom's fall and even whether it truly "fell," however, are heavily debated. In fact, the theory of Edom's fall to the Nabateans itself relies upon Malachi as a piece of evidence. The next literary reference after Malachi to the occupation of Edom is by the Greek writer Diodorus Siculus, whose testimony indicates that Edom was inhabited by Nabateans by the year 312. Since the Nabateans were known to have controlled Edom by the fourth century and since Malachi speaks of a fall of Edom, scholars of the late-nineteenth through the mid-twentieth centuries reasoned that the fall of Edom described in Malachi must refer to this otherwise undocumented shift in Edom's population and leadership. Malachi, which they dated on other grounds to the fifth century, was understood to set the date for the beginning of Nabatean control of Edom.

More recent study, however, has questioned this "Nabatean theory." Although the history and archaeology of Edom in the sixth and fifth centuries are highly debated, most agree that settlement of the area did not remain continuous during this period: that is, the Nabateans may not have conquered Edom as much as settled there after Edomite decline. Additionally, it is clear that Edom suffered many declines during its history. A major disruption was in the sixth century when the Babylonian king Nabonidus conducted various campaigns in Edomite territory, perhaps destroying the city of Bosrah. Bartlett has suggested that Mal 1:2-5 refers to the crisis wrought in Edom by the Babylonian armies and not by the Nabateans (1992, 293).

Given the circularity of the argument (using the fall of Edom to date Malachi and Malachi to date the fall of Edom) and the unclear testimony of the archaeological record, a reasonable and sober conclusion is that the book of Malachi recognizes *some* current decline in Edom as evidence of God's care for Judah. Whether this decline is due to a Nabatean invasion, Babylonian campaigns, or another unidentified crisis, Malachi maintains that the fates of Edom and Judah are inversely proportional.

Theological Analysis

The preferential treatment given Jacob in this unit has spurred much discussion. Malachi 1:2-5 is quoted in Rom 9:13 in the context of Paul's discussion of election: just as God chose Jacob over Esau while the two were still in the womb, so, too, God chooses whom God will, irrespective of ancestry and behavior.

Following the lead of Romans, Calvin, in his commentary on Malachi, also connects Mal 1:2-3 with election: "For when many who are descended from Jacob according to the flesh are rejected no less than Esau, it is clear that when God elects individual men his choice is governed by his free favor and pure compassion" (Haroutunian 1948, 293).

Debates within Reformed circles about predestination and its various permutations engage this question about God's justice in choosing some and not others. In 1937, the Presbyterian theologian J. Gresham Machen pointed to Malachi as proof of the Bible's perspective on the issue:

> Even as it is written, "Jacob I loved, but Esau I hated." How could it possibly be said more plainly than in this passage that the predestination of Jacob to salvation and of Esau to rejection was not due to anything that they did or may have been foreseen as doing—even the foreseen faith of one and the foreseen unbelief and disobedience of the other—but to the mysterious choice of God? (1937, 65)

Romans, Calvin, and Machen appropriately recognize that Malachi gives no justification for choosing Jacob over Esau but rather that the book assumes that the choice is God's to make. But the same divine willingness to choose without regard to merit that Calvin attributes to God's sovereignty and beneficence may also be seen as a sign of God's arbitrariness, as Calvin himself acknowledges.

Although both Malachi and these Reformers agree on the sovereignty of God, this unit, when read in its own literary context, is less about God's freedom to choose than about the responsibilities placed on the one chosen. Because Israel is God's favored one, it owes the deity respect.

An additional theological claim is implicit in this unit. It assumes that divine favor may be recognized materially. When Israel asks "How do you love us?" the response is not God's profession of love but rather the contrast between the current states (political or economic) of the two countries. Love is treated here not as a disembodied emotion but as an allegiance that is manifested in action.

PRIESTS AND GOD ARGUE ABOUT RESPECT (1:6–2:9)

This unit continues the parental imagery begun in 1:2-5. Here, however, those accused of disrespect are specified as priests.

Literary Analysis

The unit begins with the statement of a principle intended to be universal and uncontested: A (proper) son honors his father and a (proper) servant honors his master. Subordinates do not vaunt themselves over those who wield power over them. By analogy, then, God, who is father and master, appropriately expects reverence and fear.

Malachi 1:6*d* indicates that the charge of disrespect is leveled against the priests. They have dishonored God by offering sick animals in sacrifice (prohibited in Deut 15:21) and by offering polluted food on the altar of the Temple (prohibited in Lev 22:22 and Deut 17:1). Malachi 1:8 complains that the priests fear God less than they fear their Persian governor.

For their behaviors and attitudes, the priests are threatened with the loss of their profession: God will take away their ability to issue blessings and curses (Num 6:23-27; Deut 10:8), and they will suffer both the indignity and the ritual impurity of having dung spread on their faces (Exod 29:14; Lev 4:11). Removed from the Temple, they will be cast away from God's presence.

The disrespectful behavior of the priests is contrasted not only with that of proper servants and sons, but also with that of Levi, the ideal priest from Israel's past. Just as servants fear their masters (1:6, *yārē'*); NRSV: "respect"), and the nations fear Yahweh's name (1:14, *yārē'*), so, too, Levi feared Yahweh (2:5, *yārē'*), in contrast to the current priests, of whom Yahweh asks, "Where is my fear?" (1:6, *yārē'*).

Although no other passage in the Old Testament mentions a covenant with Levi, similar ideas appear in Deut 33:8-11, in which Levi is described as teacher and priest, and in Num 25:11-13, in which a grant of perpetual priesthood is given to the priest Phineas. Here, the role of the priest extends beyond the oversight

295

of sacrificial worship to instruction: he shares with prophets (and the namesake of the book) the title of "messenger" (2:7, mal'āk).

In terms of style, this unit continues the rhetorical strategy begun in the previous unit of giving voice to the antagonist's thinking. In 1:6 and 1:13, God reports the people's response to having been accused and then explains the fault of their objection: nowhere do the people speak directly. Throughout, the deity's language is harsh and threatening: God is, indeed, portrayed as a dishonored and angry Father.

Exegetical Analysis

The mention of a "governor" in 1:8 is often cited as evidence that the book of Malachi derives from the Persian period, since the books of Nehemiah and Ezra use the same term (peḥâ) to describe the overseers of the postexilic community. It is important to note that the usage of the term (peḥâ) does not itself indicate a Persian provenance, since the word is used in Isaiah and 1 Kings to refer to Assyrian officials. Nonetheless, the term fits the general Persian "feel" of the book of Malachi and, when interpreted in the light of Persian control of Judah, reminds the reader of the pressures on the community. Yehud was in the political position of needing to please Persian overlords; and, although Malachi itself does not challenge Persian control, it does insist that the people's allegiance to Yahweh must take priority.

The profuse description of the covenant with Levi given in 2:4-7 has provoked much discussion. As noted above, no other biblical document mentions such a covenant, though Deut 33:8-11 describes Levi as teacher and priest and Num 25:11-13 speaks of a grant of perpetual priesthood given to the priest Phineas.

At least since the work of Julius Wellhausen, a German biblical scholar of the late-nineteenth century, the Israelite priesthood has been understood to have undergone development over time. In Wellhausen's scheme, outlined in his *Prolegomena to the History of Israel* (1973), access to the priesthood narrowed over time. Even though in the earliest periods of Israel's history all men could serve as priests, priesthood was restricted to the descendants of Levi by the time of the composition of the book of Deuteronomy (which Wellhausen dated to the seventh century), and then only to the sons of Aaron by the time of the Priestly Code (which he dated to the postexilic period). For Wellhausen, Malachi's description of the priests as part of a "covenant with Levi" and as "sons of Levi" (3:3) indicates that Malachi predates the Priestly Code.

In a similar vein, Paul Hanson has argued that during the postexilic period, two groups struggled for control of the priesthood: one that supported the Levites and one that supported the Aaronides. As discussed in the introduction to Haggai, Hanson believes that the Levites were more egalitarian and inclusive, while the Aaronides/Zadokites held a narrow vision for the postexilic community. From Malachi's use of language about Levi, Hanson makes not the developmental argument advanced by Wellhausen but a sociological argument: he sees Malachi as standing firmly with the Levites ("sons of Levi") against the Aaronides (with whom Hanson connects Malachi's references to "the priests" in 1:6 and 2:1). (Hanson's approach is outlined in his 1979 and 1986 volumes.)

The language of Malachi does not bear the weight of either Wellhausen's or Hanson's arguments. Although Malachi does use language that is reminiscent of Deuteronomy, the book itself concentrates its polemic not on the constituency of the priesthood, but rather on the priests' failure to perform their duties. A careful study of the book's language demonstrates that it makes no clear distinction between "priests" and "sons of Levi," since, in 2:7, priests are connected with Levi and praised and, in 3:3, the sons of Levi themselves need purification. (For an extensive discussion of this issue, see O'Brien 1990, especially 26-48 and 101-6.)

Why Malachi uses the language of Levi rather than Aaron is not clear. Although the developmental scheme of Wellhausen and the partisan scheme of Hanson find little corroborating evidence, it is clear that Malachi is using language from Israel's past in criticizing the priests of the present. Given that the book also points to the traditions of Jacob and Esau (1:2-5), Moses (4:4 [Heb.

3:22]), and Elijah (4:5 [Heb. 3:23]), the concern with Levi as a prototype for the proper priest may arise from Malachi's strategy of using religious tradition as a base from which to launch its rhetoric.

What is clear is the important role that the priest holds in Malachi's understanding of the community. The priest is responsible not only for assuring that the sacrificial system functions properly but also for providing instruction. Because the term used for this latter function, *tôrâ,* is most often translated as "teaching," Mal 2:6-7 is often cited as evidence that during the postexilic period, the priests took on the role of teaching. The term, however, can refer to technical priestly rulings, as it does in Hag 2:11.

Theological Analysis

In the history of Christian interpretation, Mal 1:11 at times has been read as an early acceptance of Gentile worship. In literary context, however, the passage serves the larger argument of the unit: since everyone—even the nations—knows Yahweh's greatness, the priests are especially foolish to act disrespectfully.

In its concern with the priesthood and its critique of improper sacrifice, this unit underscores that worship matters to God. In contrast to the popular distinction drawn between "ritual" and "faith," Malachi underscores that the care with which one worships reflects his or her reverence for the divine. As seen in 1:12-13, Malachi's concern ultimately lies with the attitude that informs worship: those who treat it as a "weariness" and disparage the sanctity of the altar in turn pay little attention to what they offer.

The harshness of the language ascribed to God is especially evident in this unit. Yahweh curses those who do not sacrifice properly (1:14) and promises to throw dung in the priests' faces and cast them out (2:3). This language is consistent with Malachi's polemical style and may have the effect of shocking people into realizing the severity of their behavior, but it may also be seen as problematic. The way in which asymmetrical human relationships are treated as natural, even God-given, in

1:6 supports the patriarchal family. Although this language may be offset to some degree by its placing of all things and all human rulers under the sovereignty of God, it nonetheless undergirds the hierarchical distinctions upon which the argument rests.

PEOPLE AND GOD ARGUE ABOUT "PROFANING THE COVENANT OF THE FATHERS" (2:10-16)

This unit returns to accusation of the people as a whole, accusing them of covenant unfaithfulness. The precise nature of their wrongdoing is clear: is God concerned here about divorce and idolatry?

Literary Analysis

Although the previous material has been in the voice of the deity, this unit begins in the voice of the prophet. In rhetorical style, however, it proceeds in the same way as the previous unit, first establishing the premise for the argument and then leveling the accusation. In 2:10, the premise is given in parallel rhetorical questions ("Have we not all one father? Has not one God created us?"), and then the accusation follows in 2:11. Since the community has one Father/God, then its members should not be faithless to one another, profaning the covenant of their "fathers" (NRSV: "ancestors") and "marrying the daughter of a foreign god."

Malachi 2:13-16 elaborates upon the charge made in 2:10-12. In the same pattern of 1:2-5, the prophet (1) asserts a truth, (2) voices the people's doubt of that truth, and (3) defends the truth of the original assertion. The reason God does not accept the people's offering is that they have acted faithlessly against the "wife of one's youth." As outlined below, this unit bears some translational difficulties that complicate its interpretation.

Recurrent vocabulary and themes run throughout the unit. "Covenant" appears in 2:10 and 2:14. "Being faithless" *(bāgad)* not only recurs within the unit (2:10, 11, 14, 15, 16), but also forms an *inclusio* around it.

Exegetical Analysis

The precise nature of the people's faithlessness is given in 2:11, the meaning of which is debated. Most scholars understand this passage as decrying the practice of Judean men divorcing their wives in order to marry foreign women, a situation believed to have prompted the agreement recorded in Ezra 10 for the annulment of intermarriages in the postexilic community. Their understanding is reinforced when Mal 2:16 is translated as "I hate divorce," as it is in the NRSV, and when "the wife of your youth" in 2:14-15 is understood to refer to Judean ex-wives.

Despite this common consensus, however, the issue at stake in 2:11 may be idolatry rather than intermarriage. As I have argued elsewhere (O'Brien 1990, 67-69), the vocabulary used in this unit is also employed in other passages of the Bible, especially in Deuteronomy, to condemn the worship of foreign deities: *bāgad* ("act faithlessly"), *tô'ēbâ* ("abomination"), and *hillēl* ("profane"). Petersen also sees the unit as concerned with idolatry. Employing a minor textual emendation, he reads 2:11*b* as "Judah has profaned the very holiness of Yahweh. He loves Asherah; he has married the daughter of a foreign god" (Petersen 1995, 194). And he offers additional arguments that Mal 2:10-16 is concerned with worship practices in the postexilic community. He shows, for example, that in Deut 4 and 29 and Jer 34, the phrase "covenant of our fathers" refers to the covenant of exclusive allegiance between Israel and Yahweh (Petersen 1995, 197).

Similarly, the issue in 2:13-16 may be one of religious rather than marital unfaithfulness as well. Throughout the prophetic corpus, Yahweh is said to have "married" (*bā'al*, the same verb used in 2:11) the land; following other deities is called "acting faithlessly" (*bāgad*, appearing in 2:10, 11, 14, 15, 16); and "youth" *(nĕ'ûrîm)* is described as a time of closeness between Yahweh and Israel (Jer 2:2; Hos 2:17). Using language similar to Malachi, in Ezek 16:60, Yahweh proclaims, "I will remember my *covenant* with you in the *days of your youth*."

If Malachi is indeed evoking these prophetic models, then it does so with a gender switch: *Yahweh* is *Judah's* covenant wife. O'Brien (1996) and Petersen (1995, 202-6) support such a reading and maintain that the unit as a whole accuses Judah of religious infidelity. Petersen suggests that a later scribe added the charge in 2:15*b*, "let no one be faithless to the wife of his youth," applying the original message against religious unfaithfulness to the issue of marriage. As discussed below, the NRSV translation of 2:16 as "I hate divorce" is disputed: it may be translated as "I hate treachery" and hence does not clearly challenge the reading of the unit as related to idolatry.

Various translational difficulties surface in this unit. In 2:12, the NRSV translation of "any to witness" is based on an emendation of the noun from the MT *ʿr* ("the one wake/aroused") to *ʿd* ("witness"), since *r* and *d* look very similar in Hebrew script. The NJB and RSV offer similar translations, while ASV, NASB, and NKJV attempt to reflect the MT. The NIV reading, "whoever he may be," avoids providing a translation for the troublesome word but suggests that the word "pair" is meant to be inclusive of extremes. All of these translations, however, are challenged by the grammatical construction of the verse, since the three categories of persons named are to be cut off *for* the man, suggesting that they are ones who would be helpful to the accused.

As seen from the numerous translational footnotes to 2:15 in the NRSV, the rendering of the verse is highly disputed. Many words carry multiple meanings, and the syntax linking the individual words may be variously understood. Most translations understand it as affirming that one God created (all of us), that life belongs to God, and that God seeks righteous offspring. If the passage is about intermarriage, as numerous commentators claim, then it may grant value only to the children of Judean wives; if, as suggested above, the unit refers to religious unfaithfulness in the community, then the verse expresses the desire that the Israelite community itself be preserved as righteous offspring.

The opening of 2:16 is usually translated as "I hate divorce" and is in turn used as one basis for the Old Testament understanding of the permanency of marriage. This translation is far from obvious, however. As the NRSV footnote indicates, the verb reads "he hates" in the MT. Even more problematic is that the noun usually translated "divorce" literally means "sending." Van der Woude has argued that "sending" is an abbreviation of the idiomatic expression "to send or stretch out the hand," a phrase that notes a "morally detestable hostile act" (1986, 71). That is, "divorce" is only one understanding of what the Hebrew text says. In the context of the unit as a whole, the issue addressed appears to be one of Israel's unfaithfulness to Yahweh.

The strong language used throughout this unit to condemn Judah's unfaithfulness to Yahweh raises a question about the practices of the postexilic community. Was worship of deities other than Yahweh widespread? Petersen makes the case for the continuing cult of Asherah continued into the Persian period, based on the documents and votive figurines related to her worship in the late Persian and Hellenistic eras (1995, 200-202). Yet, no particular practice need be described here, given that the language for idolatry is used elsewhere in the Bible to refer to a wide range of activities seen as "unfaithful."

Theological Analysis

Although many commentators have understood this unit as one of the Bible's strongest statements against divorce and intermarriage, the argument has been advanced here that its focus is on Judah's unfaithfulness to God. Judah has not honored the covenant of its ancestors and has disregarded its covenant obligations.

When read in such a way, the unit raises several important theological issues. First, it underscores the continuity of prophetic discourse. Although Malachi is often compared negatively to the work of the prophets of the eighth century, it speaks in much the same way as such books as Hosea of the importance of exclusive allegiance of Yahweh. Like Hosea, Malachi characterizes the relationship between God and Israel as a marriage—one of intimacy, in which the wife's loyalty is expected.

And, yet, in its comparison of religious and marital fidelity,

Malachi demonstrates just how slippery the category of gender can be. In 2:11, Judah is described not only as *he* who profaned *(hillēl)* the Temple and *he* who married *(bāʿal)* the daughter of a foreign god, but also as *she* who acted unfaithfully *(bāgĕdâ)*. The Hebrew Bible is notorious for unexplained gender switches, but this use of a feminine form to describe Judah is noteworthy in a book that speaks so frequently about the proper role of sons. If, indeed, 2:14 is describing Judah's unfaithfulness to Yahweh, then that verse also switches the typical gender assignments of the marriage metaphor in the prophets by describing Yahweh as the "covenant wife" of Judah.

It would be an overstatement to claim that Mal 2:10-16 provides a biblical precedent for gender-inclusive language for the deity, but this unit does underscore the metaphorical nature of all language used for God. Just as the deity can be described as "like" a wife, so, too, the language of "father" and "husband" should be seen as comparisons of God's activities to those of humans rather than as essential aspects of God's character. Such a reminder is important in a book such as Malachi, in which God is described in such consistently male language and most often as Father.

PEOPLE AND GOD ARGUE ABOUT GOD'S JUSTICE (2:17–3:5)

Like other units, this one begins with an assertion by the prophet, followed by the protest of the people, which is in turn followed with a defense of the original claim. Here, the prophet accuses the people of wearying God by recognizing no distinction between good and evil and by questioning God's concern with justice.

Literary Analysis

In answer to the question about divine justice (2:17), the unit announces the sending of "my messenger" *(malʾākî)* to prepare for God's appearance. After the priests are purified, Yahweh will quickly punish evildoers. In direct challenge to the people's doubts, the deity will decisively and promptly execute justice.

Various devices express the promptness with which God will judge. Present participles mark 3:1a ("I am sending") and 3:1c ("he is coming"). The Lord will appear "suddenly" in 3:1b, and God promises to be a "swift" witness in 3:5b.

In describing the pending purification of the priests, this unit uses the metaphors of metallurgy and (briefly) of laundering, a metaphor also used in Isa 1:25; Jer 6:29; 9:7 (Heb. 9:6); and Zech 13:9. Here, the messenger/Yahweh is compared to a nonhuman agent of transformation—he is like fire and soap, which cleanse away impurities. After this cleansing, the priests will be returned to their ancient pure state; in this unit, as in 2:4-9, the current priests are compared negatively with their predecessors. A further linkage of the passage with Israel's past is made by the list of evildoers detailed in 3:5. Every item of the list, other than "those who swear deceitfully," appears in the book of Deuteronomy (esp. in chs. 24 and 27), and many of the items also appear in Lev 5, 19, 20, and 25.

Exegetical Analysis

Malachi 3:1 mentions a host of figures: "I," "me," the "Lord" (the title ʾādôn and not the title as substituted for the name of Yahweh, which the NRSV would have printed in all capital letters), "my messenger" (malʾākî), "the messenger of the covenant" (malʾak habběrît), and Yahweh (NRSV: "LORD") of hosts. To whom do these various titles and pronouns refer, and how do those figures relate to one another?

Petersen maintains that "my messenger" (malʾākî) and "the messenger of the covenant" (malʾak habběrît) are the same figure. He understands 3:1-5 to have been expanded through a series of redactions; its basic point is that a messenger first will appear (3:1-4), after which Yahweh will punish wrongdoers (3:5; Petersen 1995, 209-12). Glazier-McDonald, on the contrary, argues that all of the activities other than those outlined in 3:1a-b are attributed to Yahweh. The messenger will prepare the way, but Yahweh alone will purify the priesthood and punish the wicked: Yahweh is the "Lord" and the "messenger of the covenant" (Glazier-McDonald 1987, 132). This disagreement is fueled by the lack of subjects for the verbs in 3:2-4. They are in masculine singular, appropriately translated as "he" in the NRSV. What remains unclear is whether "he" who purifies is Yahweh or the messenger.

A solution to these issues is not simple. Petersen's argument that "the Lord" is Yahweh is supported by the fact that the people are "seeking" him, though it is unclear how the people would find "delight" in either figure. Glazier-McDonald appropriately points to the similarities between this unit and texts that speak of the enthronement of Yahweh as cosmic King (1987, 138). As in Isa 52 and Pss 24, 47, 96, and 97, God's appearance as king is the occasion for the righting of wrongs. Psalm 96 makes the role of the king in establishing justice especially clear: "Yahweh, he is coming, for he is coming to judge the earth. He will judge the world with righteousness, and the peoples with his truth" (Ps 96:13). That is, many of the roles assigned to the messenger are those commonly ascribed to God.

Given the ambiguity of this unit, a reasonable conclusion is that the roles of the messenger and the deity are not sharply delineated in this unit. Indeed, the ambiguity may be intentional, attempting to stress the actions, rather than the agents, involved.

Most interpreters understand the messenger as a prophetic figure, since the superscription treats "my messenger" as the name of the prophet and since elsewhere prophets are described as messengers (Hag 1:13; 2 Chr 26:15-16) and speak in the distinctive style of "messenger speech" ("thus says Yahweh"). In Mal 2:7, however, the priest is also described as a messenger, and the title may refer to any figure commissioned by God for a task (see Exod 23:20).

The complex syntax of 3:1 is often attributed to redaction. Petersen, for example, argues that 3:1*a* and 5 were original, outlining the appearance of a messenger prior to Yahweh's theophany, whereas 3:1*b*-4 are an editor's expansion on the role of the messenger (1995, 209).

The notion of a forerunner sent to prepare the people for theophany is not unique to Malachi. Isaiah 40:3, for example, speaks of a messenger from the divine court who calls others to prepare for Yahweh's appearance. Many of the prophets also function as heralds of God's pending activity. By announcing the pending Day of Yahweh, prophets such as Zephaniah serve as messengers preparing the way for God's appearance. There is no reason why the messenger in Malachi *must* be understood as a prophet, however, given that the book also describes priests as messengers and given that heavenly figures can also be described as heralds (as in Isa 40).

Theological Analysis

In much of Christian tradition, Mal 3:1 has been understood as predicting that a prophet forerunner would precede the arrival of the Messiah. Mark 1:2, which combines Mal 3:1-3 with Isa 40:3, identifies John the Baptist as this messenger and Jesus as the Lord to which he points. By its placement of Mal 3:1-3, the recitative-aria-chorus sequence of Handel's *Messiah* equates the coming messenger of the covenant with Jesus, albeit slightly differently.

Within the context of the book itself, however, the passage does not appear messianic, in that it focuses more on the function of the messenger than on that messenger's identity. The messenger and/or Yahweh will arrive to restore the priesthood to its original purity and to punish wrongdoers—all to prove to the people that they are wrong to question God's justice. The unit stresses that, despite appearances and human doubt, God sees injustice and will act against it; it does not argue that God is just, but rather foresees a time in the near future when God will act justly.

The immediacy of the arrival of the messenger is underscored in the unit. In the context of the book itself, "soon" meant a time in the Persian period, since only the swift execution of justice would answer the people's charges of God's indifference. For later readers, however, "soon" takes on different meanings. In much Christian interpretation, "soon" has been historicized as pointing forward three hundred to four hundred years to the birth of Jesus; for other readers, "soon" belongs yet in the future—in the future of the reader.

PEOPLE AND GOD ARGUE ABOUT SCARCITY AND ABUNDANCE (3:6-12)

This interchange accuses the people of robbing God. God promises that if they offer their full tithe they will receive material reward.

Literary Analysis

The unit employs the same stylistic elements as other units, replete with assertions, questions, and further explanations. The flow of these elements is slightly different, however. The people do not immediately challenge Yahweh's opening assertion, "I do not change." When they first pose a question in 3:7, it is not a refutation, but rather a genuine inquiry: "How shall we return?"

Malachi 3:8 presents a mock dialogue between God and the people. Although the answer to Yahweh's question, "Can anyone rob God?" would seem to be no, it is answered in the affirmative; and the people then ask, again in question form, for explanation. Yahweh explains that they rob by not bringing the full tithe into the Temple storehouse. God promises that if the people rectify their tithing they will be rewarded and the land, apparently now suffering from crop failure, will produce a large yield. It will then be called a land of "delight" (3:12), the third time "delight" has appeared in the book (2:17; 3:1).

Malachi 3:6 is translated causally in the NRSV: Yahweh's changelessness is understood as the reason that the sons of Jacob have not perished. The two phrases may also be translated as simple declarative statements, standing in strict parallelism: "Indeed, I am Yahweh. I do not change. And you are the sons of Jacob. You do not perish." In this latter translation, Judah survives because of its covenant heritage. The people are further fused with their ancestors in 3:7*a*: "from the days of your fathers *you* have turned aside" (AT).

Exegetical Analysis

This unit presupposes that the community is currently experiencing drought and locust devastation. Like the book of Haggai, it underscores the difficulties experienced by the postexilic community and its tenuous existence in the land.

Despite their hardship, the members of the community are encouraged to bring their "full tithes" to the storehouses of the Temple, which will serve as food upon the altar. Not all biblical materials describe the provisions for tithing in the same way. In Deut 12:5-19, tithes are brought to the sanctuary but eaten by the offerant and shared with the Levites; in Num 18:21-32, tithes of agricultural products are given to the Levites who in turn give 10 percent of their tithe as an offering to Yahweh; in Lev 27:30-33, tithes are given directly to Yahweh—apparently, that is, to the sanctuary—and in Neh 10 and 13, tithes are brought to the Temple storehouses and placed under the control of a priest, a scribe, and the Levites. Historians of Israelite religion have attempted to trace the chronological development of tithing practices and to discern where Malachi fits on a developmental scheme. Although the issue is hotly debated, Malachi appears to resonate most closely with the tithing practices in Numbers and Nehemiah, since all three regulate that tithes be brought to the Temple or sanctuary. The phrase "the full tithe," however, is shared only by Mal 3:10 and Deut 26:12.

As discussed earlier, the Temple played an important role in Persian Yehud, serving the interests of Persians as well as the religious life of the community. This passage does not indicate whether the tithes or offerings mentioned were taxed or otherwise shared by the Persians, but the economic burden to support both the indigenous leadership of the Temple and also the Persian overseers would have been heavy upon members of the community. It is little wonder that, especially in a time of agricultural distress, they would have been hard-pressed to meet all of their obligations.

Theological Analysis

This unit raises important theological issues:

The Changelessness of God

In its terse statement, "I am Yahweh. I do not change," Mal 3:6 makes an assertion that later Christian philosophical theology raised to the status of a maxim. Taking their inspiration from Aristotle's description of God as the "unmoved mover," theologians such as Aquinas maintained that in order to be fully divine, God could experience neither limitation nor change.

The philosophical principle of God's impassivity, however, stands in tension with the dominant assumption of the Bible that the deity does indeed change. That God might reconsider an intended course of action is the underlying assumption of the Psalms of lament, as well as of accounts such as that of Abraham negotiating with God over the fate of Sodom (Gen 18). Although Num 23:19 voices a contrary perspective, the prophetic call to repentance likewise presupposes that God's mind might change: "Now therefore amend your ways and your doings, and obey the voice of Yahweh your God, and Yahweh will change his mind about the disaster that he has pronounced against you" (Jer 26:13). "Who knows? God may relent and change his mind; he may turn from his fierce anger, so that we do not perish" (Jonah 3:9). Hope for God's change of heart also fuels Zeph 2:3, as discussed in the commentary on Zeph 2.

As the Jewish theologian Abraham Joshua Heschel argued, the unchanging God of the philosophers is not that of the Bible: in the prophetic books, "not self-sufficiency, but concern and involvement, characterize [God's] relation to the world" (Heschel 1962, 235).

Hence, rather than advancing a theological principle, Mal 3:6 is contextual in nature. Only because God's commitment to the covenant made with Abraham (and passed on through Jacob) is constant do the people avoid perishing.

A God of Abundance

Although the rhetorical style of Malachi invites little sympathy for the accused, the book's mention of economic and agricultural distress suggests that the people's failure to give proper offerings and tithes arises not from stinginess but from the sense of scarcity. In its call to the people to give tithes before the distress ends, this unit makes a counterintuitive promise: God will give them the abundance they currently lack only if they give from the scarce resources they have. Like the book of Haggai, Malachi challenges the people to believe in a theology of abundance— that resources do not need to be hoarded, that God will provide enough for their needs.

If, as suggested above, tithes were not merely Temple offerings, but also part of the Persian taxation system, then God's demand of tithes also serves to support Persian control of the community. As seen also in Mal 1:8, the book never overtly challenges or overtly supports Yehud's current political status, but rather assumes it as a backdrop for its own religious message. Some would consider such an attitude accommodationist, insufficiently active in the political struggles of the day. Others might see in Malachi an argument for remaining faithful to religious obligation in whatever political situation one lives.

PEOPLE AND GOD ARGUE ABOUT THE VALUE OF SERVING GOD (3:13–4:3 [HEB. 3:13-21])

This unit falls into three parts: 3:13-15 develops the accusation that the people have spoken harshly against Yahweh; 3:16-18 is a short historical narrative, reporting the positive reaction of those who feared Yahweh, followed by promises of blessing; and 4:1-3 (Heb. 3:19-21) outlines the differing fates that await the righteous and the wicked on the coming Day of Yahweh. The parts work together to show how God does, indeed, act justly.

Literary Analysis

The accusation that begins the first unit is spoken in a declarative sentence in Yahweh's voice ("You have spoken harshly against me"). It is followed by the response of the people: in two questions and two statements, they question Yahweh's justice and faithfulness, as they did in 2:17. As elsewhere in the book, the words attributed to the people are not likely what the postexilic community actually verbalized; rather, as a powerful rhetorical device, their thoughts are concretized in order to be refuted.

The nature of the second section of the unit is unique in the book—even jarring. Although all of the previous materials have been addressed to the readers as if they constitute the community that the prophet Malachi addressed, this section creates a chronological distance between the reader and those accused by the book by reporting the response of some of those who listened to the prophecy. The righteous are described as those who "feared" (NRSV: "revered") Yahweh, using the same description of proper reverence that appears in 1:6, 14; 2:5; 3:5, 20, and 23.

The phrase "book of remembrance" (3:16) is unique in the Hebrew Bible, though other passages describe God's written testimony. In Exod 32:32 and 33, the sin of the people is described as written in a book from which names can be blotted out; and Isa 4:3 claims that certain ones are "written down" for life. Some interpreters have understood this book as a heavenly ledger that will be consulted to determine a person's state after death (much like Rev 3:5), but the purpose of the book of remembrance in Malachi is to underscore that God indeed distinguishes between the wicked and the righteous, and that, despite the claim in 3:15, the wicked will not escape when they test God.

Those who fear are called God's "special possession," God's *sĕgullâ*. This term is important in the book of Deuteronomy and in other passages related to covenant making. It refers to the special status of a favored vassal, the inferior in a treaty relationship. The father-son language of 3:17 echoes both the parental language used throughout the book and also the language of covenant making, in which the relationship between lord and vassal is often characterized as that between father and son. Malachi 3:17-18 repeats the language and sentiments of 1:6: just as sons properly serve their fathers, so, too, God will spare those who serve. The mention of "serving" also directly refutes the people's protest in 3:14: "It is vain to serve God." Indeed, "serving" appears frequently in the unit, such as in 3:14, 17, and 18.

The third section of the unit continues the proof that, despite the people's complaint in 3:13-15, God does indeed punish the wicked. Employing the language and the image of the "Day of Yahweh," Malachi claims that God will soon intervene to punish wrongdoers. The contrasting fates of the wicked and the righteous are described in various metaphors: the wicked are burned like stubble; those who "fear" God (4:2 [Heb. 3:20]) will leap like calves freed from the stall; and the wicked will be trampled like ashes.

Exegetical Analysis

The recording of a "book of remembrance" in Mal 3:16 highlights the importance of written documents in the ancient world. Much of the writing described in the Hebrew Bible is primarily archival in purpose: it both makes a decision or set of instructions official and serves as a constant reminder—a hedge against forgetfulness. Deuteronomy and the Deuteronomistic History speak frequently of the "book of the law," a document intended to keep people accountable to God's word. In the book of Esther, king Ahauserus is spurred to reward Mordecai after the royal archives are read (Esth 6). In the prophetic books, writing often serves to guarantee that a message will endure into the future: "Go now, write it before them on a tablet, and inscribe it in a book, so that it may be for the time to come as a witness forever" (Isa 30:8).

The book of remembrance in Mal 3:16 is distinctive in that it is not a public document. It is written "before" Yahweh. The preposition *lĕ*- ("to/for"), which precedes "the ones who feared," may indicate that the document is *for the sake* of those who fear Yahweh or *to* those who fear. In either case, the intention of the document seems to be as a reminder to God. Also noteworthy is that the verse does not describe Yahweh himself as writing; rather, the document is written (passive) before Yahweh.

The attention to writing in this passage gives some insight into the function of writing in the ancient world. Although literacy was not widespread but concentrated in the scribal class, written documents nonetheless were understood to carry great weight. Here, like all great kings of the ancient world, Yahweh is given an official document by which to remember the clear and important distinction between the wicked and the righteous.

In its promise that "the day" is coming, 4:1 (Heb. 3:19) draws from the common vocabulary and theology of the "Day of Yahweh." As discussed in the commentary on Zephaniah, this day (also called "that day" or "the day") is envisioned by various prophetic collections as a final settling of accounts, during which the wicked are destroyed and the righteous rewarded. In Zech 14, the wicked are the nations, whereas in Mal 3 and Zeph 1, the wicked are members of the covenant community. In its description of "the day," Mal 4:1 (Heb. 3:19) points back to 3:1-5, which also draws from Day of Yahweh imagery.

The "sun of righteousness" in 4:2 (Heb. 3:20) may be understood in several ways. The NRSV reading of "*the* sun of righteousness" allows the phrase to be understood as a description of God or perhaps of another figure. The JPS translation, "a sun of victory," suggests that it belongs to a description of "the Day" to come.

Various commentators have argued for the former interpretation by calling attention to the connections between 4:2 (Heb. 3:20) and the ancient Near Eastern image of the winged solar disk, an image linked with the Babylonian god Shamash. The sun god is characterized as overseeing justice and as bringing health (Petersen 1995, 225-26). In attributing to Yahweh the attributes of Shamash, Mal 4:2 (Heb. 3:20) succeeds not only in underscoring Yahweh's ultimate power, but also in contrasting two images of heat: while the wicked will burn as in an oven, those who fear Yahweh will experience the healing warmth of the sun.

Theological Analysis

This unit draws a sharp distinction between the wicked and the righteous, even claiming that the distinction is immortalized in a book read by Yahweh. In this way, it reiterates the premise of 1:2-5, in which Jacob and Esau are set on opposite poles. Malachi is indeed a *maśśā᾽*, a text that juxtaposes "us" and "them" (see commentary to Nah 1:1 and Mal 1:1)—even if both groups are within the covenant community itself. In Malachi, Yahweh is clearly a partisan God, one aligned with some over against others. Yahweh is also a God of passionate emotions and dramatic actions.

Liberation theologians find such an image of God compatible with their own understandings. God's justice is made known in the willingness to side with and act on behalf of the poor and oppressed. Only a God who acts decisively against injustice may truly be called a "good" God.

However, in Malachi, God alone discerns between the wicked and the righteous. For some Christian pacificists, the distinction between divine and human justice is crucial: although evil must indeed be punished, punishment is in God's hands alone. The ability to determine who is righteous and who is wicked, as well as the right to punish, is not given to humans but remains a divine prerogative.

The projection of God's righting of wrongs onto a future day of recompense is often labeled an "eschatological" vision. The term is a modern one, commonly understood to refer to "last things" or "ultimate things," though the term itself is rather slippery, referring to a range of diverse ideas. Malachi's description of the "coming day" may properly be called eschatological, in that it speaks of a radical change in events that will take place in the future. But such terminology says little about when or how the book envisions such a change. The sending of the messenger prior to the arrival of Yahweh, outlined in 3:1, is not clearly correlated with the image of the Day in 4:1 (Heb. 3:19), leaving their sequence or other relationship unclear. That is, Malachi has no grand scheme of Yahweh's intervention, but it does underscore that the people's doubts about God's justice are not only misguided but also ultimately dangerous.

CLOSING STATEMENTS CONNECTING THE LAW AND THE PROPHETS (4:4-6 [HEB. 3:22-24])

The two-part conclusion of the book of Malachi invokes two figures from Israel's past: Moses and Elijah. It also returns to the language of fathers and sons that begins the book and ends with a dire warning to the people.

Literary Analysis

The mention of Moses and Elijah draws the reader's attention to Israel's greatest teacher and greatest prophet. Moses, the great lawgiver, is here called "my servant," echoing the language of "serving" (ʿebed) that has appeared through the book and especially in the previous unit. In language typical of the book of Deuteronomy, Moses is connected with "teaching" (tôrâ) and "statutes and ordinances." Elijah the prophet is portrayed as arriving before the coming Day of Yahweh. Because the theme and vocabulary of 4:5 (Heb. 3:23) are very similar to those of 3:1 ("I am sending") and of 4:1 (Heb. 3:19) ("Day of Yahweh" and "the Day"), the passage appears as an attempt to clarify the identity of the messenger described earlier in the book.

Malachi appropriately ends with the language of fathers and sons: just as it opened with a discussion of Yahweh's differing affections for the sons Jacob and Esau and an assertion that "sons honor their fathers" (1:6), so, too, the book ends with an insistence on the reconciliation of fathers and sons. Its final word is one of threat: without such reconciliation, the land will suffer a "ban" (ḥerem), the term used in Deuteronomy and in related literature to describe utter destruction (see, for example, Deut 7:26).

The mention of Moses and Elijah marks at least the third time in the book that figures from Israel's past have been invoked as lessons for the present. The people were reminded of Jacob and Esau in 1:2-5, and the priests were compared with Levi in 2:4-7.

Those who translate 2:15 as "did he not make one?" suggest that "one" refers to Adam, and some have understood the "one father" in 2:10 to be Abraham. Clearly, tradition weighs heavily in the book of Malachi.

Exegetical Analysis

Although most commentators consider these verses to have been added by a later hand, they disagree on two major issues: (1) whether the unit constitutes a single addition or two separate ones; and (2) *to what* the material was added: to the book itself, to a collected Book of the Twelve, to a larger Prophetic corpus, or to a combined Primary History and Prophets.

Regarding the first issue, it is true that the appeal to Moses has a slightly different function than the appeal to Elijah. Malachi 4:4 (Heb. 3:22) has numerous affinities with the book of Deuteronomy and the Deuteronomistic History (calling Moses God's "servant," speaking of "the teaching" *[tôrâ]* of Moses, describing the sacred mountain as Horeb rather than Sinai, and using the vocabulary of "statutes and ordinances") and stresses the role of Moses as lawgiver. The appeal to Elijah, on the contrary, is not Deuteronomic in style but highlights the role of prophet. It appears to be an attempt to explain the identity of the messenger in 3:1.

The two appeals, however, can be seen to be complementary, especially if the material was added not merely to the book of Malachi, but to a forming corpus of the Torah and the Prophets (as suggested by Blenkinsopp 1983, 240) or the Primary History and the Prophets (as suggested by Hill 1998, 365). As a whole, 4:4-6 (Heb. 3:22-24) links the lawgiver and the prophet, suggesting that the two are mutually supportive. In this affirmation of the continuity between torah and prophecy, Malachi supports not only the perspective of Deuteronomy, but also that of later Jewish tradition:

> Yet Yahweh warned Israel and Judah by every prophet and every seer, saying, "Turn from your evil ways and keep my commandments and my statutes, in accordance with all the law that I commanded your ancestors and that I sent to you by my servants the prophets." (2 Kgs 17:13)

R. Isaac said,

> The Prophets drew from Sinai the inspiration of all their future
> utterances. . . . Not only to the Prophets alone does this apply,
> but to all the sages that are destined to arise in after days.
> (Tanhuma Yitro §11, 1231-124b)

Moses and Elijah, both of whom experience God at Horeb
(Exod 3 and 1 Kgs 19), belong together.

If such an understanding of the book's compositional history
is accurate, it bears great import for the history of the development of the biblical canon. It would indicate that the materials
now included in the Hebrew Bible (or at least in the Torah and
the Prophets) were consciously edited to be read together as part
of a single, mutually supporting collection.

Significantly, however, these closing verses also fit well into the
themes of Malachi alone. Levi the ideal priest was one from
whose lips also issued true *tôrâ* (2:6), and the book is replete
with references to the covenant relationship between Yahweh
and Israel. As Hill notes, the postscript to Malachi well serves
"double duty," offering an appropriate conclusion to the book
itself and also connecting it with a larger collection (Hill 1998,
364).

Theological Analysis

The conclusion of Malachi challenges those theological perspectives that draw a sharp distinction between the Law and the
Prophets, or even between Law and Gospel. The prophetic passion for justice, which is shown in the concern for oppressed
workers, orphans, and widows (3:5), is here presented as continuous with Pentateuchal guidelines for observing covenant.
Although some Protestant interpreters, including German biblical scholars at the turn of the nineteenth century, have portrayed
prophets as moral revolutionaries fighting against the "dry legal-
ism" of religion, Malachi testifies both to the life-giving proper-
ties of Torah and to the covenant aspects of prophecy.

Drawing on Mal 4:4 (Heb. 3:22) and on the account of

Elijah's mysterious departure from earth in 2 Kgs 2, later Jewish and Christian interpreters developed numerous understandings of Elijah's role in God's future plans. Linking the Day of Yahweh with the messianic age, Matt 11:2-15 identifies John the Baptist with Elijah the precursor, and Mark 9:11-13 also links John the Baptist with a returning Elijah. Just how prominent the anticipation of Elijah as a messianic precursor was in Judaism of the first century is debated. Although the idea appears in various rabbinic documents, the dating of individual sayings is disputed. In modern Passover seders, however, a chair is left vacant for Elijah, in hopes of his return to set the world aright.

Indeed, the Passover Haggadah well honors the spirit of the book of Malachi in evoking Elijah as the harbinger of restoration and hope:

> The injustice of this world still brings to mind Elijah who in defense of justice, challenged power. . . . For every undecided question, then, of pain and sorrow, of unrewarded worthy and unrequited evil, Elijah would someday provide the answer. There are links between heaven and earth which promise answer and resolution to life's perplexities. Elijah opens for us the realm of mystery and wonder.
>
> Behold, I will send you Elijah the prophet, and he will turn the hearts of the parents to the children and the hearts of the children to the parents before the coming of the great and awesome Day of God!
>
> (Central Conference of American Rabbis 1982, 68-70)

Both the seder and Malachi express the hope, indeed the conviction, that, eventually, God will distinguish between the righteous and the wicked and that there might soon be a day in which people need not ask, "Where is the God of justice?"

BIBLIOGRAPHY

INTRODUCTION

Calkins, Raymond. 1947. *The Modern Message of the Minor Prophets*. New York: Harper & Brothers.

Floyd, Michael H. 2000. *Minor Prophets. Part 2*. Vol. 22 of *The Forms of Old Testament Literature*. Grand Rapids: Eerdmans.

Grayson, A. K. 1992. "Mesopotamia, History of (Assyria)." Vol. 4 of *Anchor Bible Dictionary*. Edited by D. N. Freedman, 732-55. New York: Doubleday.

Nogalski, James. 1993a. *Literary Precursors of the Book of the Twelve*. BZAW 217. Berlin: Walter de Gruyter.

———. 1993b. *Redactional Processes in the Book of the Twelve*. BZAW 218. Berlin: Walter de Gruyter.

Sanderson, Judith. 1992. "Amos." In *The Women's Bible Commentary*. Edited by Carol A. Newsom and Sharon H. Ringe, 205-9. London: SPCK; Louisville: Westminster/John Knox.

NAHUM

Achtemeier, Elizabeth. 1986. *Nahum-Malachi*. Interpretation. Atlanta: John Knox.

Bird, Phyllis. 1989. "'To Play the Harlot': An Inquiry into an Old Testament Metaphor." In *Gender and Difference in Ancient Israel*. Edited by Peggy L. Day, 75-94. Minneapolis: Fortress.

Coggins, Richard J. 1985. *Israel Among the Nations: A Commentary on the Books of Nahum and Obadiah*. International Theological Commentary. Grand Rapids: Eerdmans.

BIBLIOGRAPHY

Craigie, Peter. 1985. *Twelve Prophets*. Vol. 2 of *The Daily Study Bible Series*. Philadelphia: Westminster.

Exum, Cheryl. 1995. "The Ethics of Biblical Violence against Women." In *The Bible in Ethics: The Second Sheffield Colloquium*. Edited by J. W. Rogerson, M. Davies, and M. D. Carroll, 252-71. Sheffield: Sheffield Academic Press.

Floyd, Michael H. 1994. "The Chimeral Acrostic of Nahum 1.2-10." *Journal of Biblical Literature* 113:421-37.

————. 2000. *Minor Prophets. Part 2*. Vol. 22 of *The Forms of Old Testament Literature*. Grand Rapids: Eerdmans.

Grayson, A. K. 1992. "Mesopotamia, History of (Assyria)." Vol. 4 of *Anchor Bible Dictionary*. Edited by D. N. Freedman, 732-55. New York: Doubleday.

Heschel, Abraham. 1962. *The Prophets*. Vol. 1. New York: Harper & Row.

Hiebert, Theodore. 1992. "Warrior, Divine." Vol. 6 of *Anchor Bible Dictionary*. Edited by D. N. Freedman, 876-80. New York: Doubleday.

Kramer, Samuel N. 1940. *Lament over the Destruction of Ur*. Chicago: University of Chicago Press.

Magdalene, F. Rachel. 1995. "Ancient Near Eastern Treaty Curses and the Ultimate Texts of Terror: A Study of the Language of Divine Sexual Abuse in the Prophetic Corpus." In *A Feminist Companion to the Latter Prophets*. Edited by A. Brenner, 326-52. Sheffield: Sheffield Academic Press.

Nogalski, James. 1993. *Redactional Processes in the Book of the Twelve*. BZAW 218. Berlin: Walter de Gruyter.

O'Brien, Julia M. 2002. *Nahum*. Readings. London: Sheffield Academic Press.

Roberts, J. J. M. 1991. *Nahum, Habakkuk, and Zephaniah: A Commentary*. Old Testament Library. Louisville: Westminster/John Knox.

Sanderson, Judith E. 1992. "Nahum." In *The Women's Bible Commentary*. Edited by Carol A. Newsom and Sharon H. Ringe, 217-21. London: SPCK; Louisville: Westminster/John Knox.

Smith, G. A. 1903. "Nahum." In *The Expositor's Bible*. New York: A. C. Armstrong and Son.

Smith, J. M. P. 1911. "Nahum." In *A Critical and Exegetical Commentary on Micah, Zephaniah, Nahum, Habakkuk, Obadiah, and Joel*. Edited by J. M. P. Smith, W. H. Ward, and J. A. Brewer. International Critical Commentary. New York: Charles Scribner's Sons.

Smith, Ralph L. 1984. *Micah-Malachi*. Word Biblical Commentary 32. Waco: Word Books.

Sweeney, Marvin A. 1992. *The Twelve Prophets*. Berit Olam. Collegeville, Minn.: Liturgical Press.

Wessels, Wilhelm. 1998. "Nahum, an Uneasy Expression of Yahweh's Power." *Old Testament Essays* 11/3: 615-28.

HABAKKUK

Carroll, R. 1988. "Inventing the Prophets: Essay in Honour of Professor Jacob Weingreen to be Presented on the Occasion of his Eightieth Birthday." *Irish Biblical Studies* 10:24-36.

Collins, Terrence. 1993. *The Mantle of Elijah: The Redaction Criticism of the Prophetical Books*. The Biblical Seminar. Sheffield: JSOT Press.

Floyd, Michael H. 1993. "Prophecy and Writing in Habakkuk 2, 1-5." *ZAW* 105:462-81.

———. 2000. *Minor Prophets. Part 2*. Vol. 22 of *The Forms of Old Testament Literature*. Grand Rapids: Eerdmans.

Haak, Robert. 1992. *Habakkuk*. Supplements to Vetus Testamentum. Leiden: E. J. Brill.

Hiebert, Theodore. 1986. *God of My Victory: The Ancient Hymn in Habakkuk 3*. Harvard Semitic Monographs 38. Atlanta: Scholars Press.

———. 1992. "Warrior, Divine." Vol. 6 of *Anchor Bible Dictionary*. Edited by D. N. Freedman, 876-80. New York: Doubleday.

———. 1996. "Habakkuk." Vol. 7 of *New Interpreter's Bible*, 623-55. Nashville: Abingdon Press.

Horgan, Maurya P. 1979. *Pesharim. Qumran Interpretations of Biblical Books*. Catholic Biblical Quarterly Monograph Series 8. Washington, D.C.: Catholic Biblical Association.

Mason, Rex. 1994. *Zephaniah, Habakkuk, Joel*. Old Testament Guides. Sheffield: JSOT Press.

Nogalski, James. 1993. *Redactional Processes in the Book of the Twelve*. BZAW 218. Berlin: Walter de Gruyter.

Roberts, J. J. M. 1991. *Nahum, Habakkuk, and Zephaniah: A Commentary*. Old Testament Library. Louisville: Westminster/John Knox.

United Bible Societies. 1980. *Preliminary and Interim Report on the Hebrew Old Testament Text Project.* Vol. 5. New York: United Bible Societies.

ZEPHANIAH

Anderson, Roger W. 1990. "Zephaniah ben Cushi and Cush of Benjamin: Traces of Cushite Presence in Syria-Palestine." In *The Pitcher Is Broken: Memorial Essays for Gösta W. Ahlström.* Edited by Steven W. Holloway and Lowell K. Handy, 45-70. JSOTSup 190. Sheffield: Sheffield Academic Press.

Ball, Ivan Jay, Jr. 1988. *A Rhetorical Study of Zephaniah.* Berkeley: Bibal Press.

Bennett, Robert A. 1996. "Zephaniah." Vol. 7 of *New Interpreter's Bible*, 657-704. Nashville: Abingdon Press.

Berlin, Adele. 1994. *Zephaniah.* The Anchor Bible. New York: Doubleday.

Ben Zvi, Ehud. 1991. *A Historical-Critical Study of the Book of Zephaniah.* BZAW 198. Berlin: Walter de Gruyter.

Calkins, Raymond. 1947. *The Modern Message of the Modern Prophets.* New York: Harper & Brothers.

Christensen, Duane. 1984. "Zephaniah 2:4-15: A Theological Basis for Josiah's Program of Political Expansion." *Catholic Biblical Quarterly* 46:669-82.

Crenshaw, James. 1995. *Joel.* The Anchor Bible. New York: Doubleday.

Crocker, P. T. 1986. "Cush and the Bible." *Buried History* 22:27-38.

Floyd, Michael H. 2000. *Minor Prophets. Part 2.* Vol. 22 of *The Forms of Old Testament Literature.* Grand Rapids: Eerdmans.

Heider, George C. 1992. "Molekh." Vol. 4 of *Anchor Bible Dictionary.* Edited by D. N. Freedman, 895-98. New York: Doubleday.

Hiers, Richard H. 1992. "Day of the Lord." Vol. 2 of *Anchor Bible Dictionary.* Edited by D. N. Freedman, 82-83. New York: Doubleday.

Hillers, Delbert. 1964. *Treaty-Curses and the Old Testament Prophets.* Rome: Pontifical Biblical Institute.

House, Paul R. 1988. *Zephaniah, A Prophetic Drama.* Sheffield, England: Almond Press.

Kerman, Joseph. 1980. *Listen.* 3rd ed. New York: Worth Publishers.

Mason, Rex. 1994. *Zephaniah, Habakkuk, Joel.* Old Testament Guides. Sheffield: JSOT Press.

Nogalski, James. 1993. *Literary Precursors of the Book of the Twelve.* BZAW 217. Berlin: Walter de Gruyter.

Odell, Margaret S. 2000. "Zephaniah." In *HarperCollins Bible Commentary.* Edited by James L. Mays, 671-74. New York: HarperCollins.

Rice, Gene. 1979. "The African Roots of the Prophet Zephaniah." *Journal of Religious Thought* 36:21-31.

Roberts, J. J. M. 1991. *Nahum, Habakkuk, and Zephaniah: A Commentary.* Old Testament Library. Louisville: Westminster/John Knox.

Roche, Michael de. 1980. "Zephaniah 1:2-3: The 'Sweeping' of Creation." *Vetus Testamentum* 30:104-9.

Rodd, Cyril S. 2001. *Glimpses of a Strange Land: Studies in Old Testament Ethics.* Edinburgh: T&T Clark, 2001.

Sweeney, Marvin A. 2000. *The Twelve Prophets.* Berit Olam. Collegeville, Minn.: Liturgical Press.

Szeles, Maria. 1987. *Wrath and Mercy: A Commentary on the Books of Habakkuk and Zephaniah.* Grand Rapids: Eerdmans.

Zalcman, Lawrence. 1986. "Ambiguity and Assonance at Zephaniah 2:4." *Vetus Testamentum* 36:365-71.

HAGGAI

Davies, Philip R., ed. 1991. *Second Temple Studies. 1. Persian Period.* JSOTSup 117. Sheffield: JSOT Press.

Floyd, Michael. 2000. *Minor Prophets. Part 2.* Vol. 22 of *The Forms of Old Testament Literature.* Grand Rapids: Eerdmans.

Hanson, Paul. 1979. *The Dawn of Apocalyptic.* Rev. ed. Philadelphia: Fortress Press.

———. 1986. *The People Called: The Growth of Community in the Bible.* San Francisco: Harper & Row.

Mason, R. A. 1977. "The Purpose of the 'Editorial Framework' of the Book of Haggai." *Vetus Testamentum* 27:413-21.

Meyers, Carol L., and Eric M. Meyers. 1987. *Haggai, Zechariah 1–8.* The Anchor Bible. New York: Doubleday.

Petersen, David. 1984. *Haggai and Zechariah 1–8.* Old Testament Library. Philadelphia: Westminster Press.

———. 1991. "The Temple in Persian Prophetic Texts." In *Second Temple Studies. 1. Persian Period.* Edited by Philip R. Davies, 124-44. JSOTSup 117. Sheffield: JSOT Press.

Redditt, Paul L. 1995. *Haggai, Zechariah, Malachi.* New Century Bible Commentary. Grand Rapids: Eerdmans.

Weinberg, Joel. 1992. *The Citizen-Temple Community.* Translated by Daniel L. Smith-Christopher. JSOTSup 151. Sheffield: JSOT Press.

Zadok, R. 1979. *The Jews in Babylonia During the Chaldean and Achaemenian Period According to the Babylonian Sources.* Haifa: University of Haifa.

ZECHARIAH

Barstad, H. 1996. *The Myth of the Empty Land: A Study in the History and Archaeology of Judah During the "Exilic" Period.* Oslo: Scandinavian University Press.

Blenkinsopp, Joseph. 1998. "The Judean Priesthood During the Neo-Babylonian and Achaemenid Periods: A Hypothetical Reconstruction." *Catholic Biblical Quarterly* 60:25-43.

————. 2002. "The Bible, Archaeology, and Politics: or the Empty Land Revisited." *JSOT* 27:169-87.

Carroll, Robert. 1992. "The Myth of the Empty Land." *Semeia: Ideological Criticism of Biblical Texts* 59:79-93.

Carter, Charles. 1999. *The Emergence of Yehud in the Persian Period.* JSOTSup 294. Sheffield: Sheffield Academic Press.

Davies, W. D., and Dale C. Allison, Jr. 1997. *Matthew.* III. International Critical Commentary. Edinburgh: T&T Clark.

Floyd, Michael. 1996. "The Evil in the Ephah: Reading Zechariah 5:5-11 in its Literary Context." *Catholic Biblical Quarterly* 58:51-68.

Hanson, Paul. 1979. *The Dawn of Apocalyptic.* Rev. ed. Philadelphia: Fortress Press.

Kessler, John. 2001. "Reconstructing Haggai's Jerusalem: Demographic and Sociological Considerations and the Search for an Adequate Methodological Point of Departure." In *Every City Shall Be Forsaken: Urbanism and Prophecy in Ancient Israel and the Near East.* Edited by Lester Grabbe and Robert Haak, 137-58. JSOTSup 330. Sheffield: Sheffield Academic Press.

Lindblom, J. 1962. *Prophecy in Ancient Israel.* Philadelphia: Muhlenberg Press.

Maier, Walter A., III. 1992. "Hadadrimmon." Vol. 3 of *Anchor Bible Dictionary.* Edited by D. N. Freedman, 13. New York: Doubleday.

Meyers, Carol L., and Eric M. Meyers. 1987. *Haggai, Zechariah 1–8.* The Anchor Bible. New York: Doubleday.

———. 1993. *Zechariah 9–14*. The Anchor Bible. New York: Doubleday.

Ollenberger, Ben C. 1996. "The Book of Zechariah: Introduction." Vol. 7 of *New Interpreter's Bible*, 735-45. Nashville: Abingdon Press.

Petersen, David. 1977. *Late Israelite Prophecy: Studies in Deutero-Prophetic Literature and Chronicles*. Society of Biblical Literature Monograph Series 23. Missoula, Mont.: Scholars Press.

———. 1984. *Haggai and Zechariah 1–8*. Old Testament Library. Philadelphia: Westminster Press.

———. 1995. *Zechariah 9–14 and Malachi*. Old Testament Library. Louisville: Westminster John Knox.

Redditt, Paul. 1993. "The Two Shepherds in Zechariah 11:4-17." *Catholic Biblical Quarterly* 55:676-86.

Schaefer, Konrad R. 1995. "Zechariah 14: A Study in Allusion." *Catholic Biblical Quarterly* 57:66-91.

Sweeney, Marvin A. 2000. *The Twelve Prophets*. Berit Olam. Collegeville, Minn.: Liturgical Press.

United Bible Societies. 1980. *Preliminary and Interim Report on the Hebrew Old Testament Text Project*. Vol. 5. New York: United Bible Societies.

VanderKam, James. 1991. "Joshua the High Priest and the Interpretation of Zechariah 3." *Catholic Biblical Quarterly* 53:553-70.

MALACHI

Bartlett, J. R. 1992. "Edom." Vol. 2 of *Anchor Bible Dictionary*. Edited by D. N. Freedman, 287-95. New York: Doubleday.

Blenkinsopp, Joseph. 1983. *A History of Prophecy in Israel: From the Settlement in the Land to the Hellenistic Period*. Philadelphia: Westminster Press.

Capps, Donald. 1995. *The Child's Song: The Religious Abuse of Children*. Louisville: Westminster John Knox.

Central Conference of American Rabbis. 1982. *A Passover Haggadah*. 2nd rev. ed. Harmondsworth, Middlesex, England: Penguin Books.

Coggins, R. J. 1987. *Haggai, Zechariah, Malachi*. Old Testament Guides. Sheffield: JSOT Press.

Glazier-McDonald, Beth. 1987. *Malachi: The Divine Messenger*. Society of Biblical Literature Dissertation Series 98. Atlanta: Scholars Press.

Hanson, Paul. 1979. *The Dawn of Apocalyptic*. Rev. ed. Philadelphia: Fortress Press.

———. 1986. *The People Called: The Growth of Community in the Bible*. San Francisco: Harper & Row.

Haroutunian Joseph, ed. 1958. *Calvin: Commentaries*. Vol. 23 of The Library of Christian Classics. Philadelphia: Westminster.

Heschel, Abraham. 1962. *The Prophets*. Vol. 1. New York: Harper & Row.

Hill, Andrew E. 1998. *Malachi*. The Anchor Bible. New York: Doubleday.

Machen, J. Gresham. 1937. *The Christian View of Man*. London: Banner of Truth Trust.

O'Brien, Julia M. 1996. "Judah as Wife and Husband: Deconstructing Gender in Malachi." *Journal of Biblical Literature* 115:243-52.

———. 1990. *Priest and Levite in Malachi*. Society of Biblical Literature Dissertation Series 121. Atlanta: Scholars Press.

Petersen, David L. 1995. *Zechariah 9–14 and Malachi*. Old Testament Library. Louisville: Westminster/John Knox.

Wellhausen, Julius. 1973. *Prolegomena to the History of Ancient Israel*. Preface by W. Robertson Smith. Gloucester, Mass.: Peter Smith.

Woude, A. S. van der. 1986. "Malachi's Struggle for a Pure Community." In *Tradition and Re-interpretation in Jewish and Early Christian Literature: Essays in Honor of Jürgen C. H. Lebram*. Edited by J. W. van Henten et al., 65-71. Leiden: E. J. Brill.